## Advance Praise F

## *Mindfulness and Insight*

"This book, drawn from the core chapters of Mahāsi Sayadaw's magisterial *Manual of Insight*, offers us the clearest, most direct, most practical instructions in English for the development of insight. Simple but profound, clear but not superficial, the instructions laid down here serve as a trustworthy road map for any serious practitioner who aspires for the goal of the Buddha's teaching."
—Bhikkhu Bodhi, translator and scholar

"Many mindfulness practitioners never encounter the classical renderings of the Buddhist teachings or the precise instructions that make insight meditation a path of liberation. This book on the Mahāsi method of practice is a wonderfully clear and deep guide to what the Buddha called 'the sure heart's release.'"
—Tara Brach, author of *Radical Acceptance* and *True Refuge*

"In this book, the great meditation teacher Mahāsi Sayadaw provides inspiring and brilliantly detailed instruction and guidance for practicing insight meditation. The Mahāsi method is the invaluable foundation of my own mindfulness practice; I am confident this book will be useful for anyone dedicated to the path of insight."
—Gil Fronsdal, insight teacher at Insight Meditation Center in Redwood City, California

"In this valuable extract from the *Manual of Insight* by Mahāsi Sayadaw, one of the great Burmese masters of the twentieth century, Sayadaw describes in detail both the theoretical development of mindfulness and the eminently practical, step-by-step instructions for its practice. *Mindfulness and Insight* is a treasure house of Dhamma."
—Joseph Goldstein, author of *Mindfulness: A Practical Guide to Awakening*

"This book is both a map and method for liberation. Mahāsi Sayadaw exposes the depths of experiential reality, exploding perceived limitations on a meditator's ability to observe mind and body. Clear and coherent, often poetic, this could be the most important book you'll ever read."
—Kate Lila Wheeler, meditation teacher and coordinator of teacher training at Spirit Rock Meditation Center

"For those teaching introductory mindfulness meditation and feeling they've lost touch with the depth of insight meditation, this book is a valuable reminder of the power, promise, and potential of the Dhamma to liberate us from suffering. A sheer pleasure to read."
—Rev. Sumi Loundon Kim, Yale University, author of *Sitting Together*

"In 1976 I was in Rangoon receiving meditation instructions from the Venerable Mahāsi Sayadaw. One of my great discoveries was that if you practiced vipassanā the way the Sayadaw taught it, wisdom would naturally unfold. From his point of view, enlightenment was a possibility for everyone. To practice meditation with Mahāsi Sayadaw's faith was a profound experience."
—Jack Engler, PhD, researcher on the Mahāsi method as an ethnopsychiatric tradition of therapeutic-developmental change

"Mahāsi Sayadaw's teachings are a treasure. They are presented here with authenticity and clarity from one of the greatest meditation masters of all time. When I look to the underpinnings of the current mindfulness movement in the United States and elsewhere, I see Mahāsi Sayadaw's influence. Mahāsi Sayadaw taught a path to insight and freedom that was simple, clear, doable, and direct. I am so delighted these teachings, which so transformed my life, are now available to us all."
—Diana Winston, director of mindfulness education at UCLA's Mindful Awareness Research Center and author of *Fully Present: The Science, Art, and Practice of Mindfulness* and *The Little Book of Being*

# Mindfulness and Insight

## *The Mahāsi Method*

Venerable Mahāsi Sayadaw

*Translated and Edited by the*

Vipassanā Mettā Foundation

Translation Committee

Foreword by Sharon Salzberg

Introduction by Steve Armstrong

Wisdom

Wisdom Publications
199 Elm Street
Somerville, MA 02144 USA
wisdompubs.org



*Library of Congress Cataloging-in-Publication Data*
Names: Sobhana, Mahā caññ' Cha rā to' 'A rhaṅ', 1904–1982, author.
Title: Mindfulness and insight: the Mahasi method / Venerable Mahasi Sayadaw; translated and edited by the Vipassana Metta Foundation Translation Committee.
Other titles: Wịpạthạna shụ nī kyān. Chapter 4–5. English
Description: Somerville, MA: Wisdom Publications, 2019. | Chapters 4 and 5 from the previously published MANUAL OF INSIGHT. | Includes bibliographical references and index. | Translated from Burmese and Pali. |
Identifiers: LCCN 2018023673 (print) | LCCN 2018050885 (ebook) | ISBN 9781614295563 (e-book) | ISBN 9781614295372 (pbk.: alk. paper)
Subjects: LCSH: Vipasyana (Buddhism)
Classification: LCC BQ5630.V5 (ebook) | LCC BQ5630.V5 S65313 2019 (print) | DDC 294.3/4435—dc23
LC record available at https://lccn.loc.gov/2018023673

ISBN 978-1-61429-537-2 ebook ISBN 978-1-61429-556-3

23 22 21 20 19
4 3 2 1

Cover design by Jim Zaccaria. Interior design by Tony Lulek.
Set in TeX Gyre Pagella 9.8/14.5.

Wisdom Publications' books are printed on acid-free paper and meet the guidelines for permanence and durability of the Production Guidelines for Book Longevity of the Council on Library Resources.

This book was produced with environmental mindfulness. For more information, please visit wisdompubs.org/wisdom-environment.

Printed in the United States of America.

# Vipassanā Mettā Foundation Translation Committee

*Project Advisor*
Sayadaw U Paṇḍita (Paṇḍitārāma Shwe Taung Gon Sasana Yeiktha, Yangon, Myanmar)

*Managing Editor*
Steve Armstrong

*Translators*
Hla Myint
Ariya Baumann

*Abhidhamma and Pāḷi Research Consultants*
Sayadaw U Janaka (Chanmyay Yeiktha, Yangon, Myanmar)
Sayadaw U Indaka (Chanmyay Myaing Meditation Center, Yangon, Myanmar)
Sayadaw U Sāgara (Chanmyay Myaing Study Monastery, Hmawbi, Myanmar)
Hla Myint (Myanmar and USA)
Akiñcano (Marc Weber) (Germany)

*Pāḷi Quote Citations, Glossaries*
Ven. Vīrañāṇī

*Abhidhamma Charts*
Steve Armstrong

*Editors*
Ven. Vīrañāṇī
Steve Armstrong
Ariya Baumann
Deborah Ratner Helzer
Kamala Masters

Funding provided by Vipassanā Mettā Foundation

All proceeds from the sale of this book will be used to freely distribute copies to Buddhist monastics, libraries, and meditation centers, and to support opportunities to practice the method outlined in the book.

For further information and to report errors, please visit: www.mahasimanualofinsight.org.

*Namo tassa bhagavato arahato sammāsambuddhassa!*[1]
Without equal is the Omniscient Buddha of nine attributes![2]
Without equal is the Dhamma of six attributes![3]
Without equal is the Saṅgha of nine attributes![4]

When we reflect in this way, the mind becomes particularly clear and delighted. At that moment we observe the mental states of reflection, clarity, and delight as well as the physical phenomena that depend on these mental states as they arise. May virtuous people who practice as instructed in this book attain path, fruition, and nibbāna in this very life. Thus have I composed this manual on the practice of insight meditation.

# Contents

# Foreword

*By Sharon Salzberg*

My colleagues and I brought Mahāsi Sayadaw from Burma to the United States in 1979. He was known as the founder of the lineage in which several of us were practicing—and as a great scholar, a profound teacher, and a visionary. At the time I hadn't realized how much of a visionary he was. Some of the views he distilled from his practice and scholarship—about the degree of concentration needed to develop transforming insight, about the power of the continuity of mindfulness—had large societal and cultural implications. It was because of the work of people like Mahāsi Sayadaw and Ledi Sayadaw, an earlier pioneer, that so many laypeople, so many women, so many who for one reason or another could not ordain into monastic life had the possibility of an authentic practice of liberation returned to them. That possibility had gone into historical decline in many places. When I went to Burma to do intensive practice at Mahāsi Sayadaw's monastery in 1985, it had clearly been renewed there: there were hundreds, and at times thousands, of people from around the world practicing intensively too.

This book is among Mahāsi Sayadaw's best-known works. It describes a journey to freedom, highlighting notable landmarks along the way: seeing our bodies and minds as interrelated; noticing the glorious, renewing, uplifting truth of change, as we see the arisings of sensations and thoughts and emotions; noticing the fleeting nature of absolutely everything we observe, and of we who observe it; seeing that there is nothing at all we can hold on to, with all the attendant fear and dismay that brings; emerging into the great peace of equanimity. From the space of equanimity, the sure heart's release into freedom becomes available.

Please don't read this book as a map against which to judge yourself, but let it open your mind to the innate potential for insight that exists in all of us. We just need to do the work.

# Introduction: The Universal and Timeless Journey of Awakening

*By Steve Armstrong*

## Awakening of Faith

In my midtwenties I was navigating early adulthood without much ambition or direction after completing university studies. I didn't have any genuine interest in meditation, didn't know anyone who meditated, didn't have any inclination toward spiritual teachings, didn't know anything about Buddhism. When a friend shared with me a book of simple drawings illustrating one-liners about mindfulness and suggested I join her for a retreat a short drive from the commune in Maine where we were living, I tagged along imagining it would be something of a holiday.

As it happened, the retreat was anything but a lark! The daily schedule in silence, beginning at 5 A.M., was a grind of tortuously painful sittings (wrapped in blankets to ward off the coastal cold of December), alternating with walking meditations (aimless pacing back and forth, back and forth), and a restless mind detoxing from overconsumption of stimulation of all kinds. The routine was broken only by short meal times and the evening talk about some aspect of mindfulness meditation or the Dhamma, as the Buddha's teachings are called.

Not surprisingly, the teachings went straight to my heart, and though I could not have anticipated the extended effect, a dormant, long-hidden seed sprouted at the very core of my being that has continued to grow. Upon returning to the commune at the end of the retreat, warmly greeted by family and friends, everything appeared familiar, but we were different. We had seen, tasted, and understood our lives from another perspective.

I was most impacted by the teachings where I heard for the first time what I had always known within my heart to be true—a way of being in life that had a purpose and a value beyond career, credit cards, and constant consumption. I first heard there of the mysterious but demanding possibility of a life of awareness, of liberation from mental states that cause suffering. It was the first glimpse, a glimmer of light on the path of mindfulness that I have walked confidently with faith and self-discovery for more that four decades. I now realize that I was inspired then by the possibility of developing the goodness within my own heart—the universal and timeless journey of awakening to the truth of life.

## Contemporary Mindfulness

Mindfulness has now become a popular, secular tool for the skillful navigation of distress in contemporary life. It is widely practiced for managing stressful conditions and physical and emotional pain, the treatment of addictions, and relapse prevention of recurrent depression. It is used to teach students emotional intelligence and how to focus and unleash creativity, and many new applications are emerging regularly across the full spectrum of human activities.

A whole industry of mindfulness meditation has spawned any number of retreat centers, city centers, courses, workshops, and classes. Dozens of mindfulness and meditation apps, hundreds of mindfulness teachers, thousands of mindfulness-based, stress-reduction leaders, and thousands more mindfulness-trained therapists and counselors and proliferating mindfulness teacher-training programs attest to the growing popularity and benefit of mindfulness.

There is a new shelf in the library of books on mindfulness and its various applications in life as well as a whole rack of monthly magazines touting the benefits of mindfulness for those who are interested. In addition, the spiritual proximity and collaboration between the practice of yoga and meditation is flourishing. Mindfulness has become the fascinating subject of neuroscience research, inviting Western science to investigate a refined, subtle understanding of the mind-brain connection and activity, as suggested by deeply practiced Buddhist monks.

We may yet get to confirm the comment attributed to Arnold Toynbee, who when asked what he thought historians would consider the most important development of the twentieth century, reputedly suggested, "The coming of Buddhism to the West may well prove to be the most important event of the twentieth century. Buddhism has transformed every culture it has entered, and Buddhism has been transformed by its entry into that culture."

Mindfulness has arrived. As the renowned meditation teacher Joseph Goldstein acknowledged in his foreword to the *Manual of Insight*, "Although mindfulness in its secular applications has tremendous benefits, it's helpful to remember that the original teachings of the Buddha are about liberation—that is, freeing the mind from those mental states that cause suffering to oneself and others."[8]

It was just this that got planted in my heart on my first Dhamma retreat—the taste of freedom. I didn't then know that I was suffering. I was young, educated, healthy, and active, with seemingly endless possibilities for life. I just didn't have a vision or language for expressing my experience of awareness and the inner sense of having arrived in my life and recognizing it for the first time. Until then, I appeared to myself to be playacting, following a script written elsewhere by others. I now understood my direction in life: liberation from the endless pursuit of aimless indulgence in pleasure. I was inspired to proceed with confidence.

## The Roots of the Tradition: The Asian Elders

Soon after my first retreat, I went on staff at the recently purchased Insight Meditation Society in Barre, Massachusetts. It was there that I got further exposure to the Dhamma and the opportunity to hear and practice mindful meditation with a few experienced students near my age recently returned from years of practice in Asia. That was immensely helpful instruction and guidance—and a heady immersion into an exotic, alternative, spiritually infused lifestyle of the mostly young.

Over the course of those next few years we were exposed to the roots of the Dhamma as the elders of Asian Buddhist traditions from Burma, Thailand, Tibet, Sri Lanka, Vietnam, Korea, Japan, and Cambodia descended on the West, many arriving at IMS to enthusiastic if naïve students. Our exposure to what the Dhamma offered and the many ways of manifesting a Dhammacentric, mindful life expanded exponentially.

The elders of the mindfulness tradition that was practiced at IMS arrived to share their wisdom and encourage us, and in the process expanded our view of what a commitment to Dhamma practice looked like. Mahāsi Sayadaw, the noted Burmese scholar and meditation master who opened a meditation center in Rangoon in 1949 for householders to learn and practice mindfulness, arrived with five other monks, one of whom, Sayadaw U Sīlananada, remained in the Bay Area. Ajahn Chah, the Thai forest meditation master, and his young Western disciple Ajahn Sumedho arrived to share their view of a communal monastic lifestyle to support mindful living. Taungpulu Sayadaw, the Burmese meditation master who spent thirty-three years alone in a cave and reputedly had not lain down or slept for decades, came to offer his teaching, and in the process repositioned our idea of the Buddha's middle path in his direction. Anagarika Munindra, from Bodh Gaya, India, a Pāli scholar and Dhamma student of Mahāsi Sayadaw, offered extensive teachings on extended visits. Dipa Ma, the Bengali housewife with extraordinary accomplishments in both tranquility and insight mindfulness practices, arrived for longer stays and showed us how deep wisdom manifests as gentle love.

His Holiness the Dalai Lama stopped by for a day on his first visit to the United States in 1979 to offer a brief introduction to Tibetan Dhamma teachings. Seung Sahn Soen Sa Nim, the Korean Zen master, came annually to offer students at the three-month retreat a Zen perspective on Dhamma wisdom. Chogyal Namkhai Norbu, the Dzogchen master, also arrived to offer his teaching. Maha Ghosananda from Cambodia arrived during the destruction of monasteries in Cambodia under the Khmer Rouge.

Meeting these elders of the Western mindfulness movement and insight meditation tradition aroused in me the possibility of a lifestyle of mindful awareness and the wisdom of a commitment to awakening and liberation from suffering. Mindfulness practices are foundational to the Buddha's teaching of the noble eightfold path.

Among these elders, it was Mahāsi Sayadaw who was most responsible for the introduction of mindfulness training in short, intensive meditation retreats—specifically for householders, not only for monks and nuns—that served as the model for instruction at mindfulness retreats in the West.

Mahāsi Sayadaw is recognized as one of the most accomplished Buddhist scholars and meditation masters of the twentieth century. Within his native Burma he was respected as an exceptional scholar who wrote over seventy books in the Burmese and Pāḷi languages. During the Sixth Sangha Council in 1956, he was responsible for overseeing the creation of an authoritative edition of the Pāḷi canon, along with its commentaries and subcommentaries. This edition of the canon is still widely used and held in high regard throughout the Theravāda Buddhist world.

In addition to his prolific scholastic achievements, Mahāsi Sayadaw also developed a clear, simple, and easy-to-understand (if not easy-to-master) meditation method for practicing mindfulness for insight based on his personal experience and studies. Having taught the method to his relatives, he found that they were quite successfully able to purify the progress of their insight. With this confirmation, in 1949 he accepted the invitation to teach his method to laypeople as well as monastics, and to guide students in the development of liberating insight at the newly built Mahāsi Meditation Center in Rangoon, Burma. Hundreds of thousands of Burmese and foreign students have since successfully practiced there. After Mahāsi Sayadaw passed away in 1982, Sayadaw U Paṇḍita and other renowned Burmese meditation masters preserved the Mahāsi Sayadaw tradition of teaching, making it available to thousands of Burmese, Western, and non-Burmese Asian Dhamma students.

Mahāsi Sayadaw's meditation method is characterized by clarity and simplicity of instruction, suitable even for those who do not have extensive academic knowledge of the Buddha's teachings, intensive periods of retreat for a limited duration, and a clear method of tracking one's proficiency in mindfulness and the unfolding of liberating insight knowledge. These unique features of the Mahāsi Sayadaw method have led to his recognition as one of the "elders" of what has become the Western mindfulness movement and insight meditation tradition. A number of key figures in the contemporary spread of Buddhist meditation throughout the world hail from the Mahāsi Sayadaw lineage: the first generation of Western *vipassanā* teachers—Sharon Salzberg, Joseph Goldstein, and Jack Kornfield—are students of Mahāsi Sayadaw's disciple Anagarika Munindra and his student Dipa Ma.

These and subsequent generations of Western *vipassanā* teachers who follow the Mahāsi method using an intensive retreat format have established leading centers for training in *vipassanā* meditation, such as the

Insight Meditation Society (MA), Spirit Rock Meditation Center (CA), Tatagatha Meditation Center (CA), Gaia House (England), Meditation Centre Beatenberg (Switzerland), and numerous offshoot centers such as Cambridge Insight Meditation Center (MA), Common Ground Meditation Center (MN), Insight Meditation Center (CA), Seattle Insight Meditation Society, Vipassanā Hawaii (Honolulu), Vipassanā Mettā Foundation (Maui), and many other groups.

The collected recorded teachings, more than forty years' worth, of hundreds of Western Dhamma, mindfulness, and insight teachers were accessed or downloaded from the DharmaSeed.org website more than 450,000 times per month in 2017. Mahāsi Sayadaw's teachings have thus had an undeniable and significant impact on the transmission of the Buddha's Theravāda teachings to the West, grounding them solidly in the practice of mindfulness. The Buddha's teaching points to the development of insight through the practice of mindfulness.

For this abridgement of Mahāsi Sayadaw's *Manual of Insight* we focus on chapters 4 and 5—the development of mindfulness and practical instructions—of which he acknowledged, "Those with little or no knowledge of the Pāḷi scriptures should concentrate on chapters 4 and 5. Even reading and studying only chapter 5 will enable you to practice insight meditation in a straightforward way, and you will be able to realize path knowledge, fruition knowledge, and nibbāna." These take us to our goal of liberation, the end of all suffering.

These two chapters alone offer suitable guidance for our own extraordinary journey of awakening. Nevertheless, the excised chapters of the *Manual of Insight* provide valuable context for Mahāsi Sayadaw's instructions on the development of mindfulness and practice. Therefore a brief overview of Dhamma teachings that identifies and locates mindfulness practice in the service of insight as the means for liberation or realizing the end of suffering is included here.

## The Four Noble Truths

When, under the Bodhi tree, the Bodhisattva realized the end of all suffering, thereby becoming a Buddha, the Awakened One, he articulated his understanding in his first discourse on the four noble truths. This teaching remains the foundation of Buddhist practice wherever Buddhism has taken root as it migrated from India north to the Himalayas, south to Sri Lanka, east to all of Southeast Asia, and now to the West—Europe, Australia, and the American continents. Though the forms, rituals, regalia, and practices differ, having been influenced by indigenous or local customs, the foundation of Dhamma teachings everywhere rests on the four noble truths.

### *First Noble Truth*

The first noble truth acknowledges there are conditions in life we find unsatisfactory. Physical and mental or emotional pain is at times apparent to everyone. Pleasant experiences end, to be replaced by less satisfactory conditions: loss of wealth, job security, friends, as well as status, achievement, reputation, and so on are all too common and painful to experience. We can't say that having abundant wealth, a good job, security, friends, and so on is painful, but we can acknowledge that these things don't last or at least are unstable and beyond our control, and that their unsatisfactory nature is obscured by the pleasantness of experiencing them.

Subtler yet is the nature of existence itself when recognized as an incessant, at times oppressive, burden and obligation everyone bears for themselves. Growing up, securing an education, a career, and material possessions, establishing a stable domestic lifestyle requiring the ongoing daily maintenance of physical, mental, and emotional well-being, of financial, social, professional success, as well as political and civic responsibilities and obligations—all of which are constantly threatened with unsatisfactory possibilities—is burdensome and often felt as oppressive. Each one of us has to do it; we can't have anyone else do it for us. With mutual understanding, we can share the responsibility with others for as long as we maintain the understanding.

Nevertheless, we have to ask, where is all this going? After shouldering these burdens for decades, we die. We don't know what happens at death except that everything we did and acquired stays for others to remember, enjoy, and dispose of. The whole cycle feels somewhat incomplete and unsatisfactory.

These unsatisfactory conditions—physical and emotional pain, the instability and insecurity of changeable conditions, and the oppressive burden of daily maintenance of life—are not apparent nor easy to acknowledge, let alone accept as an adult fact of life. That is why the Dhamma suggests that this first fact of life has to be uncovered, revealed, and investigated by mindful awareness.

### *Second Noble Truth*

The second truth reveals that the cause of all unsatisfactory conditions is craving, clinging, wanting, and not wanting. We want pleasant physical, mental, emotional, financial, and social experiences. We spend our lives pursuing, securing, and indulging in them, hoping to avoid unpleasant experiences. We are beset with challenges and obstacles at every turn. We oscillate between hope and chagrin as we perceive the conditions ahead.

Even now as we are enjoying the fruits of our labor, we are keeping an eye on the future and making plans for more pleasantness ahead. When the future arrives, it may be pleasant or not. If pleasant, it doesn't satisfy us as much as we expected or hoped for. It has a degree of unsatisfactoriness contained within it. Pleasure doesn't last and we'll soon be looking again for another experience to try to satisfy our desire for pleasure, security, stability, fulfillment, purpose, meaning, recognition, abundant wealth, friends, knowledge, and so on. It never ends, this desire for more pleasant experiences and less unpleasantness.

This is the second adult fact of life: desire is never satisfied, and when satisfied momentarily, it isn't as satisfying as we hoped it would be. Even with that, it doesn't last! It is the understanding through mindful awareness that recognizes this fact and arrives at the wisdom of letting go of desire.

## *Third Noble Truth*

Is it even imaginable that the unsatisfactoriness of pain, instability, insecurity, and oppressiveness can come to an end? This was the third realization of the Buddha—that the end of suffering is possible. The third noble truth is frequently acknowledged in a way that makes it seem unlikely, far off, only for a few extraordinary meditators—a rare, exotic, and esoteric state that is all but inaccessible. Nibbāna! What does that even mean? Whatever we think it means, it is sure to be otherwise.

The third noble truth points to the possibility of ending our personal, interpersonal, and existential suffering. Finding the cause for our dissatisfaction in desire, wanting, and not wanting, the Buddha saw that the roots of desire are in not seeing things as they truly are and not understanding things correctly. It is mindfulness that sees things as they are and wisdom that understands them correctly. "Correctly" here means understanding in such a way as to relieve suffering and not cause more suffering. The Buddha acknowledged that this was possible by training the heart and mind. This is the task for each one of us to confirm for ourselves.

## *Fourth Noble Truth*

The fourth noble truth is the path to be developed for realizing the end of suffering for ourselves. The noble eightfold path is essentially three trainings. The first is the training in non-harming by refraining from killing, stealing, harmful sexual activity, speaking falsely, and intoxication leading to heedlessness.

When we act out our delusions, desires, and aversions in ways that cause harm to ourselves or another being, the suffering is immediate and obvious. It is through mindfulness training that we notice the intention before speaking or acting, which gives us pause to consider whether this action aligns with our sensitive heart or closes our heart to ourselves or another being. When we value our human relationships in this way, we purify our speech and behavior of the "transgressive torments" that manifest and are motivated by greed, aversion, and delusion that would cause harm.

In this way, we avoid by restraint the suffering of painful and hurtful interpersonal relationships as well as the regret, remorse, guilt, and shame we might feel within and the social opprobrium, punishment, and retribution we might receive from others. Even this much reduction in suffering would be substantial. When we look over the daily news, we see that it is a catalogue of human misery caused by just such lack of restraint. We can do better in our own lives by mindful awareness of the intention to speak and act, and the result is the happiness of more internal and external harmony.

However, even if we are careful not to act out in ways that cause harm to self or others, we might be internally obsessed and inflamed with what we would like to do or say under the influence of desire, aversion, and confusion. This inner suffering might not be obvious to others in a way that causes them harm, but we suffer with anxiety, depression, fear, blaming, obsession, compulsion, and so on, while scheming and strategizing on how to get rid of our internal suffering.

This is the place for the second training of the noble eightfold path—the practice of mindfulness for managing distressing conditions, which with practice can bring substantial and often immediate relief. Just by becoming aware of the narrative of our suffering, what we are feeling emotionally, how it feels in the body, and identifying the nature of our mental state offers a reprieve from the obsessive, indulgent, tormenting suffering of the heart and mind. There is a huge difference between being caught in anger ("I'm so angry!"), being aware of the narrative of self-righteous anger ("He did this to me!"), and being aware that anger has arisen and it feels like this. Momentary mindfulness purifies the mind for that moment of the "obsessive torments" that manifest as rampant thoughts of aversion, desire, or delusion.

With sustained interest in mindful awareness of inner suffering, we enjoy relief from the mind's compulsive indulgence in painful habits. The mind is momentarily pure of obsessive torments. This often manifests as calmness, spaciousness, and stability with a certain degree of clarity. This seclusion from obsessive painful mental states is a great relief and a kind of happiness we can't buy or get from others, but only from developing our own mind.

Still, we know how unpredictable life is and we never know just when some event is going to trigger an internal obsession or emotional outburst that compels us to speak and act out in a way that causes harm. We just cannot control external conditions to insulate ourselves from adventitious unpleasant conditions. We also are not so continuously mindful that we can catch every stimulus that might condition a mental or physical reaction. For this fact of life, the Buddha offered a subtler and more powerful training, the development of insight that purifies our understanding of "latent torments."

Latent torments are the deeply embedded mistaken beliefs and unexamined assumptions that cause us to believe that resorting to the dysfunctional strategies of desire, aversion, and delusion will be effective in securing our happiness. Insight into these beliefs and assumptions gradually allows us to understand their nature and how they cause us to suffer. When seen in this way, wisdom develops. It is wisdom that removes the now-seen assumptions and the mistaken beliefs. With that, the proliferation of desires, aversions, and delusions are cut off at the root within the heart and mind long before they arise in the mind obsessively and get acted out.

These three trainings of the noble eightfold path—living in harmony, seclusion of mind through mindfulness, and the development of insight wisdom—are the work of mindful awareness applied in these three ways. In every case, mindfulness is necessary and the result is less suffering.

## The Three Trainings of the Noble Eightfold Path

### *Purifying Speech and Behavior: Living in Harmony*

The first training of the noble eightfold path comprises the three factors of right speech, right action, and right livelihood to purify the mind of anger, desire, and delusion so that we do not speak or act in ways that cause harm to others. Generally this involves undertaking the five precepts to refrain from killing, stealing, sexual activity that causes harm, lying, and intoxication. Mahāsi Sayadaw acknowledges:

> The five precepts are universal and exist whether or not the Buddha's teaching exists. They apply equally to all human societies regardless of time or place. To break the five precepts necessarily constitutes an offense, while observing them necessarily creates merit. That is simply the way it is. It is not something that was decided by the Buddha.

We all know just how challenging it is to train our speech and behavior in this way, and we also know how painful it is to be on the receiving end of others not keeping the precepts. Past indiscretions can torment the mind and cause a lot of guilt, regret, remorse, and self-condemnation, and can challenge our ability to establish continuity of mindful awareness, as Mahāsi Sayadaw says:

> Over the course of that time of practice, . . . people will tend to reflect on their morality, and if they find deficiencies in it, their hearts will not be at peace. They tend to have a lot of remorse when remembering a past violation, even if their morality is pure at the moment. If they cannot do away with their remorse, worry and anxiety might break their insight meditation.

However, the aspiration to awaken is powerful, and when one sincerely intends to practice mindful awareness, the power of intention with applied effort can support the development of awareness, as Mahāsi Sayadaw encourages:

> One should exert self-control: think, talk, and act only in wholesome ways; let only wholesomeness come in through one's six sense doors; take extra care to arouse only wholesomeness; bear patiently with whatever may happen; and make great effort not to entertain unwholesome thoughts. With this kind of self-control, one rarely thinks of anything unwholesome.

Mahāsi Sayadaw also offers support by confirming:

> For the most part moral violations by laypeople do not cause obstacles to enlightenment. . . . One can attain concentration, insight knowledge, path, and fruition the moment one's perfections (*pāramīs*) are well-enough developed.

He counsels:

> Protect your morality with great care, just as you would protect your very life. You should not be negligent about your behavior, thinking that you can correct it later. You might die at any time. Morality is especially important for those who are practicing meditation.

And he acknowledges the benefit to our insight practice in this way:

> When such people reflect that their morality has been pure for a long time, or at least for the time that they have been practicing meditation, they will surely feel delight, joy, happiness, calm, and tranquility. As a result, their concentration and insight knowledge will improve.

In this way, the first training of the eightfold path—purifying speech and behavior—involves mindful awareness of the intention to speak and act. Actually, one must be aware of one's mind throughout the entire day, since we speak and act nearly continuously except when sleeping. If we could take this first training to heart, practicing diligently, our minds would be very familiar and settled when we undertake the second and third trainings of the eightfold path.

### *Purifying the Mind: Seclusion from Obsession*

The second training of the noble eightfold path comprises the three factors of right energy, right mindfulness, and right concentration. The "right" in these factors refers to the fact that they do not cause suffering or that they lead one toward less suffering or the end of suffering.

This training is the development of an ongoing continuity of mindfulness to the point of the mind being momentarily free from any hindrance, obstruction, or adventitious thought for an enduring period of time—that is, the mind is purified. Subjectively the mind feels calm, clear, continuous, stable, bright, and secluded but not dissociated from sensory contact with the world.

This state is generally recognized as being a serene, tranquil relief from the usual chatter of the mind. In the Pāli language of the Buddha's teaching it is called *samādhi*, often translated as "concentration," which refers to collectedness, continuity, and stability of mind. It is often experienced as the mind being quiet after a period of strenuous meditative effort and it is a great relief and a very welcome "spiritual goodie," as one of my teachers called it.

The Buddha taught an array of mindful meditations. When meditative effort results in a continuity of remembering to recognize the meditative object moment to moment, the mind becomes momentarily pure. Hence purity of mind is a function of the continuity of mindfulness.

As one contemplates in an ongoing way the meditative object in order to block hindering thoughts, the mind gradually becomes settled and tranquil. When the meditative object is a conceptual idea, thought, or object—for example, the recognition of breathing in and out (conceptual only), a sight (visualization), sound (mantra), or mental state (love, compassion, and so on)—the mind's attention is repeatedly directed toward that object. With some continuity, the mind becomes more closely connected and attuned in a sustained way to the object and less available to stray thoughts. This seclusion is *samādhi*, which offers immediate relief from internal and external stressful conditions.

In insight meditation (mindfulness of momentarily changing physical and mental objects), the felt sense of the present-moment experience of the body or mind is the object to be noted. As taught by Mahāsi Sayadaw, the rising and falling of the abdomen is used as a primary object to direct attention toward. In the beginning of practice one can only conceptually imagine the experience of the movement in the abdomen, as explained below:

> Although a meditator practices observing at the beginning of his or her practice, one cannot discern mental and physical

> phenomena. His or her comprehension is still quite ordinary: he or she sees the object in a conceptual way.

Initially, as the meditator directs the attention to the abdomen, often a conceptual image of the form or shape of the anatomy appears or the idea of the location of the abdomen is what is seen. With continued attention, one will "see" the manner or mode of the abdomen—for example, flat, distended, deflated, bloated, and so on. Only with persistent observation will one become aware of or "see" the essential, unique quality, characteristic, or nature of the experience (*sabhāvalakkhaṇā*)—for example, tension, movement, pressure, pulling, and so on. The first two ways of knowing are conceptual and cannot lead to genuine insight. They may be sufficient for tranquility or calmness, and with some continuity possibly hindrance-free *samādhi* only.

In addition, initially the act of mindfulness and the object being observed are not concurrent. The object often appears and has ended before the awareness sees it. Mindfulness is slow or late getting to the object. With persevering interest and attention to the object, the arising of the object and the mindfulness of it will begin to occur simultaneously or concurrently. Only then is mindfulness sufficient to gain insight into the unique nature of the experience and eventually the universal characteristics.

Conceptual observation and nonconcurrent awareness are the entry point of practicing insight meditation for everyone. But once they are established and the experience of insightful mindfulness is concurrent with objects, practice can proceed.

Every moment's experience is different. So even though the attention is directed or called toward an ongoing sequence of changing objects or experiences, the mind is free of hindering thoughts moment by moment. As Mahāsi Sayadaw explains:

> When . . . the process of (insight) meditation continues with uninterrupted purity, thoughts or other hindrances do not interfere in the process. At such times each and every noting produces a strong and clear concentration on the physical or mental phenomenon that is the object of meditation. This is

> momentary concentration aroused by moment-to-moment observation . . . (which) develops naturally in the course of insight meditation practice . . . (and) is enough to bring about the mental purification required for path knowledge and fruition knowledge (enlightenment).

The challenges to establishing sufficient continuity of mindfulness to gain deeper insight are the familiar hindrances of attachment, aversion, sloth and torpor, restlessness, and doubt, along with other adventitious interfering thoughts. These arise when one is unable to observe momentary experiences as they occur. The effort to overcome and understand these hindrances is the essential work of mindful insight meditation. This involves a multistepped approach dealing skillfully with the habitual tendency of the mind to resort to these dysfunctional strategies to try to secure our happiness, security, and well-being.

*Working with the hindrances*

1. The first step is to recognize these mental states manifesting as thoughts and feelings when they occur. This is not so easy, in part because we are so habituated to acting them out that we often do not recognize them but instead just assume and justify that this is the way we are. Even when we know these are unskillful mental states that cause us to suffer we still find it challenging to identify them when they occur. More often we are caught in the narrative about them rather than recognizing them.

   > Sensual desire often takes the form of thinking about sense objects, which is a distraction. There may also occur a mild desire connected with the practice itself.

   By making a continuous effort to recognize the primary object of the rising and falling of the abdomen, we eventually will begin to recognize what our present-moment experience is when it is not our intended object. Attending to the relatively benign, mundane, ordinary experience of the rising and falling of the abdomen when breathing, gradually some continuity of mindfulness grows. With that, when another experience calls our attention away from the primary object, the mind trained in mindfulness, remembering to recognize the present moment, does indeed recognize it.

> You will realize that unwise attention is what arouses sensual desire and the other hindrances, and wise attention is what dispels them.

2. With this, we frequently experience a momentary reaction of chagrin, disappointment, or self-condemnation at the failure of our efforts. This also needs to be recognized and accepted. After all, mindfulness is noticing the present moment! In recognizing a deeply conditioned habit of mind we are actually succeeding at mindfulness, in spite of our aversion to recognizing it. A skillful way of responding to this recognition is to just relax and accept, "This is the way it is for me, for now."

   Everyone wants to be a good meditator, but we all get plenty of negative feedback about how we are doing. The personal-history review that mindfulness seems to undertake exposes the considerable experience of similar suffering to recognize and accept. It is as if we uncover the deep experiential roots of our personality, bringing them to awareness with the light of mindfulness.

   I remember the time I first saw an unconscious habit of mind that I had never seen before. I had been practicing as a monk at the Mahāsi Meditation Center in Yangon for some time and the momentum of mindfulness was quite continuous. Nevertheless, I began to notice a periodic collapse of energy and confidence. Upon looking closer, I noticed a subvocal assumption of "Oh poor me, I can't do this practice!" followed by a rationalizing belief, "I'm too old!" or "I'm too stupid!" or "My misspent youth in the commune damaged my mind!" and so on.

   When I recognized the underlying unpleasant feeling the

thought was less domineering and believable. I suffered when caught in a self-pitying thought. When I was able to recognize the momentary and unpleasant mental feeling, I was actually practicing quite well.

I made it a point then to always quickly note such feelings, and the indulging in self-pitying thoughts stopped arising. This is how we stop suffering: by coming out from the story of our suffering into awareness of the reality of our momentary experience.

3. With that recognition and relaxed acceptance, we can then exercise some restraint in not acting out the tormenting mental state, choosing instead to be patient and bear with it or to replace it with an antidote. Loving-kindness is an antidote to many kinds of aversion. Forgiveness is an antidote to blaming. Borrowing confidence from others' stories of their challenges helps to momentarily overcome one's own doubt. There are many ways to skillfully address an overwhelming, habitual, reactive state of mind other than pushing it away out of aversion or indulging it by acting it out.

> Doubt about the fact that insight wholesomeness consists of simply observing the presently arising mental and physical phenomena is skeptical doubt. This doubt is so subtle that it is rarely detected but is instead mistaken for investigation. This doubt masquerades as analytical knowledge. A doubtful meditator who falls prey to wavering and procrastination cannot continue on with practice. Be careful not to mistake doubt for analytical knowledge.

4. It is helpful then to reframe our understanding to remember that this experience is the very place to establish mindful awareness. The habitual nature of these states indicates that we have indulged in this way of thinking often. So often, in fact, that when it occurs again, we may exclaim, "I'm always

impatient!" "I'm always depressed!" in effect, eternalizing a momentary experience when it is just for this moment we are feeling that way. Making a point of noticing when you are not impatient or depressed can be a relief!

However, once we feel like we are always this way, it is just a short, slippery slope to believing "I am an impatient person" or "I am a depressed person." Uprooting such solid identities from the mind is the work of *vipassanā* insight by noticing the underlying assumptions and beliefs that support the identity.

> Contemplation of sunlight, moonlight, starlight, and light that arises in (the perceptual field of the mind during) meditation is called "observing light." In the context of insight practice, (when one is) contemplating mental and physical phenomena in such a way that they are vividly known . . . sleepiness, dullness, and laziness disappear.

5. It is mindfulness that reveals the actual nature of the mental state by plunging into it and tasting its unique flavor—that is, how it is experienced—rather than being carried away by our thoughts or story about the experience. When mindfulness remembers to recognize the present-moment experience it comes face to face with it, enters it, and observes it from inside. This is the unique characteristic of mindfulness.

> A restless state of mind that wanders away from an object while observing it is a mental state called restlessness. It flies away from the object. Due to restlessness the mind cannot remain very long with an object but often wanders elsewhere . . . and because of this restlessness the noting mind is . . . overshooting the object that should be noted. . . . Momentary concentration that focuses on mental or physical objects from moment to moment is called nondistraction, a mental state that is the opposite of restlessness. Whatever mental defilements may

occur, one should be resolute and persistent in noting them without any interruption.

6. With that immediate, direct contact with the present-moment experience of the difficult mental state it is no longer a hindrance to practice but becomes instead a mental object of mindfulness that is being known in the present moment. Mindfulness like this sees, and wisdom realizes the following in a way that cannot be learned otherwise:

    - This experience is not satisfactory!
    - I did not invite this experience, nor can I get rid of it. It has arisen due to its own causes and conditions.
    - This experience is fleeting, not permanent.

    These three realizations are naturally arising, insightful understandings, the result of mindful awareness of any and all experience. Knowledge of these three characteristics of all experience—unsatisfactoriness (*dukkha*), conditionality (*anattā*), and impermanence (*anicca*)—liberates the mind from wrong views that cause suffering.

    > If . . . one observes mental and physical phenomena the moment they occur, one will realize that there is nothing to them but mind and body, which are conditioned, impermanent, unsatisfactory, and not-self. As a result, one will be free from attachment. . . . Thus the wholesome action of insight liberates one from . . . the cycle of suffering.

*Wrong views that cause suffering*

What, we might ask, are the wrong views that cause suffering? The answer is not exotic, esoteric, opaque, religious, abstruse, philosophical, or remote. It is just challenging to observe, accept, and abide with.

The first observation is to recognize and acknowledge that we enjoy pleasant sensory experiences, such as pleasant sights, sounds, smells, tastes, touch sensations, thoughts, and feelings. We don't enjoy unpleasant sensory experiences. Behaviorally, we are constantly pursuing more pleasure and avoiding unpleasant and painful experiences by scheming and strategizing, planning, and advocating for ourselves. Our whole lives are geared to this pursuit of pleasure with careers, relationships, families, possessions, and so on. Is this true for you?

The next observation is that we cannot control what we experience; we are not omnipotent and able to make things happen the way we want. Adventitious conditions outside of our immediate control impact us all the time, often derailing or obstructing our plans and strategies. When this happens we often feel sad, angry, depleted, defeated, and depressed, and may blame others or harm ourselves with emotionally reactive behavior to avoid the pain of disappointment by indulging in intoxicants or other obsessive, compulsive, or addictive behaviors. Is this true for you?

The third observation is to acknowledge that even when we do get what we want, whether it is material possessions, knowledge, recognition, relationships, achievements, abundance of any good thing, and so on, it somehow doesn't make us feel as happy as we thought it would. In addition, we don't feel satisfied for very long. We also fear the loss of what we have acquired and have to take measures to insure our continued, ongoing enjoyment of it, necessitating worry, anxiety, more planning, expense, insecurity, vulnerability, struggle, and fear. Is this your experience too?

If so, the questions to ask ourselves, then, are: Why am I doing this? What makes me think it is possible to get what I want? Why am I not yet satisfied with all that I have achieved and acquired? Do I believe it is possible to be satisfied in an enduring way? Will I ever have enough? If so, what would it take?

Somewhere beneath all this busyness, acquisition, and struggle are some deeply held beliefs and assumptions that compel us to act in this unfulfilling way.

- We deeply believe that pleasant experiences will make us happy.

- We feel that we ought to be able to make our body pleasing and our mind happy.
- We assume that if we get what we want, then we'll be happy.
- When unhappy, we have a subtle feeling that this is the way it will always be.
- When happy with some experience, we also expect it to continue to make us happy.
- We assume or hope for things to last forever—for example, good eyesight, clear mental faculties, easeful mobility, long-lasting relationships, and so on.
- At bottom, we feel that suffering is wrong or suffering shouldn't be happening or that we are failures because we suffer.

When we review these assumptions and beliefs, we can see how false they are, but we still feel and act them out as if they were true. These false beliefs are so deeply embedded in the heart and mind that they are ordinarily inaccessible to our awareness when we most need to see them for what they are—false. Instead we act them out in the darkness of delusion and suffer as a result.

Mindfulness of momentary experiences exposes these beliefs and assumptions at the very time that they are actively conditioning our suffering. Mindfulness sees and feels the dissonance between what we believe and the reality we experience. With faith and confidence in the right views of the Dhamma accompanying our efforts to be mindfully aware, the mind can stabilize and see deeply into the causes of suffering while wisdom realizes and understands their impermanent, unsatisfactory, and impersonal natures. Each time we are able to observe willingly with awareness and understanding and without struggling to get rid of the suffering, the habit of these wrong views, assumptions, and beliefs is weakened and the strength of awareness and wisdom grows, becoming more accessible with experience. In time, these opaque assumptions and beliefs will no longer assert their reactive, domineering effect. Instead, wisdom will be available to guide a compassionate response to current conditions. Gradually the dysfunctional strategies of greed, anger, and confusion will no longer dominate our mind, and awareness with insightful wisdom will guide our way.

### *Beginning insight*

Mahāsi Sayadaw identifies this process of mindfulness of the unique nature of all wholesome and unwholesome momentary mental and physical experiences (Step #5) as necessary and sufficient to unify and purify the mind and as the foundation on which true *vipassanā* knowledge arises. (Step #6)

> The basic level of insight with momentary concentration begins with knowledge that discerns mental and physical phenomena. At this level of concentration, thoughts and hindrances cannot interfere with one's practice. As a result, the mind is free of hindrances and so realizes the specific characteristics of mental and physical phenomena, which in turn gives rise to the knowledge that discerns mental and physical phenomena. . . . It is impossible to be aware of the true nature of mental and physical phenomena without this basic level of concentration. This momentary concentration constitutes a purification of mind that aids the development of insight knowledge, such as the knowledge that discerns mental and physical phenomena.

He then makes a subtle discernment regarding the strength of this kind of momentary concentration and what is known as absorption concentration as experienced in *jhāna*, and he delimits their respective purposes. Tranquility concentration brings one closer to *sukha*—happy comfort of body and mind—while momentary insight concentration beings one closer to *dukkha*—pain, instability, and oppressive vulnerability.

> Momentary concentration can grow as strong as if the mind were concentrated on a single object. Although it moves between different objects, the preceding and succeeding mind-moments are equally concentrated on one object after another. When

> this happens, the strength of the momentary concentration is comparable to that of absorption in tranquility meditation. The difference is that the object of absorption in tranquility is always the same and thus cannot help one to clearly see mental and physical phenomena, their impermanence, and so on. The object of insight concentration constantly changes, which helps one to clearly see mental and physical phenomena, their impermanence, and so on as the insight knowledge matures. This is the only difference between the objects for the two kinds of concentration—for example, observation of the conceptual form of the breath produces tranquility, while attention to its touch and movement produces insight. The mind can grow equally concentrated with either type of object.

Thus this first fledgling realization of the three universal characteristics is known as the first *vipassanā jhāna*. While there is no absorption into any object, the development of the five *jhānic* factors—connecting, sustaining, joy, *sukha*, and one-pointedness—is equivalent to what is necessary to access the first absorption *jhāna*. But here the object of mindful awareness is insight knowledge, which has now become a self-verified, empirical wisdom.

With this, Mahāsi Sayadaw offers the rationale for the *Manual of Insight* when he acknowledges:

> Those who take the vehicle of insight to enlightenment need not develop tranquility in advance in order to purify the mind, but they may begin with pure insight. The momentary concentration that arises when their insight practice grows strong enough then serves as mental purification. The principal emphasis of this book is to explain precisely this point: how those who take the vehicle of insight to enlightenment practice—that is, how to develop pure insight without a foundation of tranquility concentration.

## *Purifying Understanding: Liberating Insight*

The third training of the noble eightfold path comprises two factors: right view and right thought.

When we view a news clip, we see and hear 10 to 20 seconds of action and we know for ourselves what occurred. Then news commentators come on to offer views and analyses that reflect their beliefs about what we all saw—they give their "spin" on how to understand the event and what it means. At the end of 30 minutes of commentary, we don't know what to believe about what we saw. We too may have our views and opinions about the event, but the question arises: What perspective are we taking or what spin are we caught in or what lens are we viewing the action through? And where, we might ask, did we get our view from in the first place?

Sayadaw U Paṇḍita, the successor to Mahāsi Sayadaw at the Meditation Center in Yangon, used to say, "We live under multiple layers of delusion." He then would acknowledge that the task of removing these layers of delusion is the work of mindfulness insight meditation.

The first layer of delusion is revealed by noticing how often we are lost in an interior dream, fantasy, or story when we are trying to be aware of the present moment. Isn't it amazing! It doesn't take long when practicing mindful awareness to realize that much of our time is spent on autopilot, not really aware of what is happening. Neither are we aware of the narrative we spin about what is happening to us. Even with sincere interest and effort, clearly remembering to mindfully recognize conventional reality with any continuity is a challenge. What we assume and believe about our experiences is equally opaque.

Our beliefs and assumptions about ourselves and our lives are deeply conditioned by parents or other primary caregivers and then bolstered by extended family members, peers, teachers, and religious, educational, economic, political, civic, and social pundits from whom we learn how things are from their point of view. Implicit in this conditioning is the belief that this is what we need to know and do in order to belong among them—to be happy, liked, and successful. We acquire a consensual view of reality, a conventional mutual understanding with medical, judicial, political, psychotherapeutic, and extralegal mechanisms for handling major, harmful, and intractable differences of views and opinions.

We only have to look at the daily news to realize that these mutual understandings are implicit at best and often nominal in practice, resulting in a tremendous amount of suffering when the implied consent is not forthcoming. Clearly some other way of understanding our suffering is necessary if we, individually or collectively, are interested in freeing ourselves from suffering and the causes of suffering.

This is what the Buddha achieved and shared with us: the way of understanding suffering, the cause of suffering, the potential for the end of suffering, and the path to the end of suffering. The four noble truths are the right views—meaning the way of understanding that minimizes suffering and/or leads to its ending. Embedded within these four right views are additional skillful views to support our journey of awakening to the truth.

We can recognize the four noble truths and the other right views as a roadmap to liberation. But it is just a map and we each must take the journey for ourselves. For this we need to hear what the right views are. While there are extensive discourses and commentaries on right views, once they are heard or read, we must develop wise attention to confirm for ourselves whether these views hold true. This is where insight meditation comes to bear. For it is insight that reveals the truth underlying the conventional view of reality. Revealing what is real, true and ultimate reality is the work of insight.

When the Buddha was asked by a group known as the Kalamas how they could determine which spiritual teachers were offering the correct method or the truth, he instructed them:

> Don't go by reports, by legends, by traditions, by scripture, by logical conjecture, by inference, by analogies, by agreement through pondering views, by probability, or by the thought "This contemplative is our teacher."
>
> When you know for yourselves that "these qualities are skillful, these qualities are blameless, these qualities are praised by the wise, these qualities when adopted and carried out lead to

> welfare and to happiness," then you should enter and remain in them.[9]

We too are faced with the similar challenge of determining whether what we have heard or believe is true. If called to discover for ourselves what is true for us, and we hear of the Dhamma, then with faith and the aspiration to awaken we can take up the practice of mindfulness. By attending to our present-moment physical and mental experience, our personal history will come into view. This often fascinating archeology of the heart reveals layer upon layer of conditioning. Dhamma instructions and teachings offer a way of understanding the challenges of life and the extensive pain and suffering we have endured because of that conditioning. The first noble truth becomes glaringly obvious.

Mindfulness is always accompanied by a quality of straightness of mind that prevents self-deception. It is our internal integrity-compliance monitor. With this as an ally, we slowly begin to discover the deep empirical reality beneath the narratives we employ to create, protect, and defend the sense of "my self"—of "me" and "mine." The familial stories of class, religion, wealth, and education that we've inherited along with our genetic and epigenetic potentialities are just the tip of the iceberg of additional layers of conditioned, frozen beliefs and assumptions around our gender, sex, ethnicity, and species that condition how we act in the world.

Mindfulness of serial present-moment experiences unravels the narrative tapestry of "me" and how I became who "I am." When seen in this way, frame by frame, memories and fantasies eventually reveal underlying assumptions and beliefs formerly opaque to ordinary awareness. Seeing these deep roots of conditioning as the basis of our relative reality often provokes a tremendous personal reaction of distress, disbelief, and disillusionment, and only gradually can stability of mind be restored and maintained. Each reactive tendency or dysfunctional strategy for dealing with pain also has to be seen—that is, disassembled pixel by pixel by mindful awareness of them. It takes courageous, persevering interest to plunge into the physical and mental phenomena beneath the narrative in the mind to the empirical reality of moment-to-moment experience.

With the increasing momentum of mindfulness, the collected stability of the mind is able to see more deeply into the unique characteristics of each momentary experience, tasting the actual flavors of life's experiences. As Sayadaw U Pandita has acknowledged, "Life without mindfulness is like food without salt!" Insipid.

As the veils of consensual, conventional reality begin to part, Dhamma teachings of right view are available to offer another way of understanding. But it is only through the direct experience of mindful awareness that we can confirm for ourselves that the Dhamma offers a skillful way of understanding what we now see are the adult facts of life. One attribute of the Dhamma is *ehipassiko*, roughly meaning "to see for yourself whether the Dhamma is true, useful, wise."

Initially, through the activity of mindful awareness—that is, remembering to recognize, observe, and taste present-moment experiences—empirical wisdom realizes an extensive catalogue of known events consisting of a self-confirmed, empirical knowledge of what is real. As Mahāsi Sayadaw acknowledges, "Only what we experience personally is ultimate reality."

When mindfulness pierces the veil of conceptual reality to recognize the unique flavor of each moment and puts aside the conditioned, conventional view of them, we begin to see the truth of our experience through the Dhamma eyes of right view. We also begin to access the universal characteristics of all phenomena. We realize that all of our experiences are impermanent—fleeting, unstable, and therefore unsatisfactory—and impersonal, arising due to causes and conditions we cannot control.

> When first beginning practice, one can accurately focus one's mind on objects only when one notes them by labeling them one by one. Eventually, though, one learns to experience the ultimately real phenomena that lie beyond names or concepts. In this way, the perception of the solidity and continuity of phenomena vanishes and one is able to understand the three universal characteristics.

The wisdom of these realizations is entry into true *vipassanā* insight. Mahāsi Sayadaw acknowledges as much when he confirms:

> In order to develop true insight knowledge, starting with knowledge that discerns body and mind, one should observe ultimate mental and physical phenomena and not conceptual objects.
>
> As ultimate reality emerges, concepts submerge.

Insight mindfulness observes the single, most obvious, distinct, present mental or physical phenomena of one's own experience in each moment.

> One should not seek external objects for insight meditation, because doing so often causes a restless mind. Restlessness, in turn, results in a slower development of concentration and insight knowledge. . . . Because those who engage in reflection and thinking based on their general knowledge do not acquire empirical insight, neither do they develop concentration and insight knowledge.
>
> Insight can only be accomplished when one understands mind and body internally . . . as they really are, whereas academic knowledge accomplishes nothing. Any objects perceived through reflection and speculation are concepts and not ultimate reality, because they do not really exist either internally or externally.

In the first chapter of this book, Mahāsi Sayadaw identifies the four factors that offer the only way of empirically knowing any experience. These are its characteristic or salient qualities, its manifestation or the way it presents itself, its function as a task or goal achievement, and its proximate cause or the condition(s) it depends on.

> We can only experience an ultimately real phenomenon in terms of these four factors. If we perceive an object in any other way, the object we perceive is not a genuine, ultimately real phenomenon but a concept of something, such as its manner,

> identity, image, solid form, and so on. We can experience a phenomenon as it really is if we observe it the moment it takes place.

Only in this way can mindful insight remember to confront and directly observe the present-moment physical or mental experience—by connecting with and sustaining attention on it, thereby enabling us to deeply touch into it and clearly recognize its distinctive, unique nature without being swept away by thoughts about it.

## Five Spiritual Faculties

The five spiritual faculties guide the appearance and maturing of insight knowledge from initial understanding of the mind and body up to full-liberated awakening. The activities of these five qualities of mind appear sequentially through a cause-effect relationship, mature gradually, develop cyclically, and result in the progressive unfolding of liberating insight knowledge. As Mahāsi Sayadaw reveals:

> When an insight meditation practitioner's faith, effort, mindfulness, concentration, and wisdom have become strong and balanced, the process of meditation continues with uninterrupted purity. Thoughts or other hindrances do not interfere in the process.

Whatever we think or believe that faith, effort, mindfulness, concentration, or wisdom are, they are only real for us when one of the four factors of each faculty is experienced directly, being empirically known by mindfulness—that is, when it is tasted for ourselves.

For example, while we might ordinarily think of faith as an inspired thought, a matter of belief, a religious command, a spiritual feeling, an intuitive hope, or some assurance from ancient times, if we take the Buddha's admonition to the Kalamas not to accept anything based on hearsay, logic, tradition, and so on, but to investigate through direct observation to know for ourselves, then it is only through mindful awareness of the experience of faith that we will know it.

As mindfulness revealed on my first retreat, faith is a direct personal experience of its proximate cause, manifestation, function, and characteristic, not a belief I read in a book, nor something I heard in a talk, nor knowledge I had acquired even without knowing it was faith I was experiencing. I wasn't looking for faith in particular, I wasn't seeking to confirm whether I was experiencing faith's manifestation, function, and so on. I was just aware of the following elements of my present-moment experience: clarity (faith's manifestation), direction in life (faith's function), confidence (faith's characteristic), inspiration in undertaking a lifestyle shift (faith's function and proximate cause), and so on, so that when faith arose, it was felt experientially without the conceptual knowledge of what it was. If I had previously heard the right views of the nature of faith, I might have recognized its appearance, but those conceptual right views were not available to me at that time. This is the way of authentic insightful knowing through mindfulness.

*Saddha*—faith or confidence—can be empirically known in one of these four ways. It arises when there is something to place confidence in—for example, the Dhamma, one's inherent goodness, a teacher, and so on, which is its proximate cause. It manifests through steadfastness and unwavering resolve and the unambiguous clarity of recognition of the present momentary experience. This clarity serves as one's spiritual compass pointing in the direction of goodness in the heart. With this spiritual compass, one confidently aspires to trust setting forth on the journey of awakening.

The awareness of faith conditions the arising of effort. Even though the Bodhisatta had mature *pāramī*, faith also needed the spark of clearly seeing and understanding the adult facts of life of an elderly being, a sick being, and a corpse to ignite the spiritual urgent arising of effort. Our own personal spark, that keenly felt sense of urgency—"Now is the time!"—is the proximate cause for exerting effort. Once aroused, effort manifests as strength of mind that does not wither or collapse in the face of pain, difficulties, and challenges. Effort functions to support the concurrent mental factors of attention, intention, connecting, sustaining, and so on in the activity of mindful awareness. Effort is characterized as marshaling and supporting these concurrent mental factors in the activity of awareness.

When empirical knowledge of effort arises, some element of the present-moment experience (the sense object) appears to the mind through one of the sense doors. With prior right view of awareness, mindfulness functions to remember, confront, and observe the sense object. With this manifestation of mindfulness, the unique quality of the object is intimately pierced and touched or tasted from inside. Clearly recognizing (perception) the unique flavor of the object is the proximate cause of mindfulness, which is characterized as preventing the mind from being carried away on a stream of thoughts about the object.

Continuity of empirical mindfulness manifests as *samādhi*, momentary one-pointedness, purification, or stability of mind. When striking a balance between tranquility and alertness, the comfort of body and the happiness of mind are the proximate cause for *samādhi*. A purified mind does not wander and is not distracted by hindering thoughts; this characteristic is due to the unification and stability of the dispersed elements of the mind. *Samādhi* manifests as peace of mind.

When any factor of *samādhi* is empirically known, wisdom arises through wise attention illuminating the object. Wisdom pierces the conceptual veil of the object by observing the intrinsic nature of mental and physical phenomena the moment they arise in terms of their general and specific characteristics. *Paññа* manifests as nonbewilderment, that is, as nondelusion.

As self-verified wisdom grows, so does one's faith in the practice, in one's teacher, in the Dhamma, and in one's ability to practice effectively. With that increased faith, more wise and continuous effort arises and so forth. In this way, the strength of the five faculties increases gradually, cyclically, and progressively through the stages of insight to the realization of enlightenment.

The relationships between the four factors (characteristic, function, manifestation, and proximate cause) of the five spiritual faculties (faith, energy, mindfulness, one-pointedness, and wisdom), along with the additional mental faculties of attention and perception integral to mindful wisdom, are shown in Appendix 1.

> You could realize path, fruition, and nibbāna at any time, once the mental faculties of faith, energy, mindfulness, concentration, and wisdom fall in harmony.

## The Spectrum of Wisdom

According to the Buddha's teaching, the practice of insight meditation enables one to realize the ultimate nature of mind and body, to see their common characteristics of impermanence, suffering, and not-self, and to realize the four noble truths.

The spectrum of wisdom manifesting through insight practice arises from the direct observation of serially arising, present-moment physical and mental experience as object. We begin with a conventional, consensual, conditioned belief of each experience and gradually come to understand the skillful way of not suffering with any experience. This is the path of purification of understanding leading to liberation from mental states that cause suffering.

While there are many ways to articulate the emergent wisdom of practice—that is, many different lenses from which to view the understanding—Mahāsi Sayadaw describes in thorough detail the progress of insight knowledge through the lens of a growing realization and acceptance of the three universal characteristics: all conditioned experiences are impermanent, are incapable of providing stable satisfaction, and are impersonal, not amenable to personal control.

These characteristics are found in everything we experience when we look closely. Not seeing them reveals that we are out of touch and therefore out of sync with the way things are. Being out of sync causes friction, which is experienced as suffering. By coming to realize these characteristics, in each moment we move into alignment and stop struggling, stop suffering, and enjoy the realization of peace.

As there are many details of this unfolding knowledge to be discovered, Mahāsi Sayadaw cautions that obtaining a detailed understanding of the progression of insight knowledge beforehand may impede one's practice of insight.

> Those who know or have heard about the stages of insight knowledge may encounter even more fluctuations. This is why it is better not to learn how the insight knowledges progress in advance.

Out of respect for Mahāsi Sayadaw's understanding, and in order to not add obstacles to your practice, I will limit my discussion to a general overview of insight topics. In this way, I hope you will be inspired to embark on the journey of awakening to discover for yourself all that your perfections (*pāramīs*) support acquiring.[10]

> It is not possible to know in advance whether your *pāramīs* are mature enough to reach a particular level of (enlightenment). . . . You cannot yet decide that your *pāramīs* are not mature. Besides, your current practice itself naturally helps your *pāramīs* to mature, so you should not evaluate whether or not your *pāramīs* are mature.

## The Purification of Understanding

Why are the universal characteristics so important to discover?

Undertaking the precepts to purify behavior arrests the acting out of unconscious dysfunctional strategies of attachment, aversion, and confusion that would cause harm to others. This is an immediate and obvious benefit that supports harmonious relationships with others and less interpersonal suffering. But even when we are exercising restraint we may still be tormented by obsessive thoughts fueled by greed, aversion, and delusion.

These obsessive, tormenting thoughts can be prevented by continual mindful awareness. In the event they do get a chance to arise, mindfulness arrests their proliferation and there is a chance to observe the thoughts with interest to learn about their nature. While an obsessive thought of desire, irritation, or confusion is an unwholesome state of mind, awareness of it is a skillful, wholesome state of mind.

The continuity of mindfulness gives rise to *samādhi*, the seclusion of mind from the obsessive torments, resulting in an internal tranquility and stability. This too is an obvious and beneficial result in that it prevents compulsive and obsessive thinking that can easily lead to unskillful, addictive behaviors.

Nevertheless, even with purification of behavior and purification of mind, situations arise when we get triggered into obsessive thinking or harmful behavior. This is possible because of wrong understanding. We get hooked by misunderstanding the situation we find ourselves in. When we speak of the insights into the three universal characteristics, we are pointing to three unexamined assumptions that are latent within our minds that, when activated, cause suffering.

### *Seeing the Characteristic of Impermanence*

While we know conceptually that all things are impermanent, we do not live from that understanding and instead often act as if we assume it is possible and even probable that present conditions will endure. Authentic insight into the impermanence of conditioned things occurs when mindfulness sees the momentariness of the unique characteristics of events, as Mahāsi Sayadaw acknowledges.

> Contemplation of impermanence refers to seeing conditioned phenomena arise and pass away while observing their unique characteristics.
>
> If one is only aware of impermanence itself, without observing the unique characteristics . . . , then genuine knowledge derived from contemplation of impermanence cannot develop. This is because the impermanence that one is aware of is merely conceptual.
>
> We begin to develop contemplation of impermanence from the moment that insight becomes clear enough to break up the continuity of phenomena.

Merely by seeing the momentary breaking up of conditioned experience frame by frame into the pixels of phenomena enables an understanding that what existed a moment ago no longer exists. It is a completely new phenomenon.

Every morning when we look in the mirror we see something very familiar and assume it is a reflection of the same person. But because we don't pay wise attention to what we see, we don't recognize that things have changed—unless there is a dramatic difference in appearance that we could acknowledge, but even then we'd still think it is the same person. If we saw a fast-forward film of a series of mug shots taken in the same location every day of our lives, we'd see the gradual change, as if we had morphed from infancy to childhood to youth to adult to middle age to senior (if you've gotten that far), but actually nothing ever morphs. Instead a whole new arising occurs in each moment.

It is as if we experience a death in each moment, since nothing is the same really, moment to moment. The concept of "me" remains the same, but the actual mental-physical experience is different. Conventionally speaking, we need to recognize the continuity of individuals and our relationships with them. That works well until it doesn't—when someone dies or the nature of the relationship changes. The concept or our understanding of the relationship assumes a permanency in the mind, but the reality of experience no longer exists. That dissonance causes suffering.

> We only live in each present moment of consciousness. Past moments no longer exist anywhere. They never return. They are gone forever, just like the dead consciousness of one who has died. This is why the cessation of each moment of consciousness is said to be a being's death.

*Vipassanā* has been likened to learning how to grieve effectively, mourning the loss of everything that occurs. Although we acknowledge the external event is no longer present, we can feel that loss. What we also feel is the loss of our identity conditioned by our attachment to a person or event. That loss leaves a huge emptiness that insight practice learns to recognize without immediately rushing to fill it with another identity to attach to.

> The purpose of insight meditation is to observe mental and physical phenomena as they truly are, from moment to moment, and to uproot the attachment that lies dormant in them.

> The purpose of insight is to eliminate the field of latent defilements.

The latent tendency to perceive permanence where there is none is abandoned by insight into the characteristic of impermanence. This must be seen, not just once but many times, in order to effectively uproot the underlying tendency to assume permanence, stability, and continuity.

But the question must be asked, which defiled perception of permanence must be abandoned?

> Past defilements have already disappeared and no longer exist, so one does not need to abandon previous defilements. Future defilements will come into existence at some point, but they have not yet arisen at the moment of observation, so one does not need to abandon future defilements either. Whenever one is observing impermanence in the present moment, only wholesome insight awareness exists and there are no defilements to be abandoned, so one doesn't need to abandon present defilements, either. When the mental and physical phenomena that arise at the six sense doors are not rightly observed and understood to be impermanent, while these mental and physical phenomena are being perceived to be permanent, conditions are actually right for defilements to be able to arise. So you should understand that defilements that could arise when conditions are right are the defilements that must be abandoned. These defilements, which cannot be described as actually existing in the past, present, or future, are called "latent defilements."

By developing the insight perception of impermanence, wisdom abandons the latent defilements that lie dormant in the mind, causing the potential to suffer in the future.

> To "lie dormant" does not mean that they exist hiding somewhere but that they provide an opportunity for the mental defilements to arise when conditions are right, because either insight knowledge or path knowledge has yet to abandon the defilements.

Because potential suffering no longer exists once latent defilements are abandoned, there will be no chance for obsessive reflection that could lead to unskillful behavior that harms self and others and causes suffering. This is the end of suffering that is possible through insight knowledge of impermanence, a characteristic of all conditioned experience. This knowledge purifies the mind of misunderstanding.

### *Seeing the Characteristic of Unsatisfactoriness*

There is a tendency to believe that a pleasant experience is satisfying. When we experience pleasant phenomena we tend to attach to it and hold on to it for future enjoyment too. Yet unsatisfactoriness (*dukkha*) has three aspects: physical and mental pain, the changeability of pleasant experience, and the condition of arising and passing away. When we do not see these aspects of something, we attach to it, either with indulgence in pleasant experience or with aversion toward unpleasant experience.

Seeing pain as pain is not insightful, it's obvious. However, seeing the other two aspects of *dukkha* is less obvious. Pleasant phenomena aren't painful, but they don't last—that's unsatisfactory! Yet we don't always act with that knowledge. Instead we assume that what is pleasant now will always be pleasant or will be pleasant any time we want to indulge in it. Your favorite meal is pleasant once a week or so. But if you had to eat it every day, you would soon find it boring or disgusting. There are many initially pleasant experiences in life that are like that. When we do not see the *dukkha* characteristic within pleasant experiences, we are forever chasing after them.

We can look on unfortunate people who are controlled by addictive behaviors that destroy everything they most value—their health, lives, careers, relationships—and we understand, there but by the power of mindful awareness go I. Whether we act out addictive behaviors or not, we all are familiar with obsessive thinking and compulsive physical habits, both of which may cause immediate harm, possibly long-term danger, and certainly internal dissonance from the lack of integrity to care for ourselves skillfully. That is suffering.

It is said that the characteristic of *dukkha* is hidden by constantly shifting postures.

> If one adjusts the posture as soon as one experiences any kind of unpleasant feeling due to remaining in one position for a long time, then even the occurrence of mental and physical pain doesn't appear, let alone the impermanence of mental or physical pleasure or the condition of being subject to arising and passing away, because they are concealed by changing the posture.

Nevertheless, steady, continuous mindfulness of momentary mental and physical phenomena sees their unique characteristics and, when mature, also sees the universal characteristic of unsatisfactoriness.

> The knowledge that understands presently observed objects to be unsatisfactory is called "empirical contemplation of unsatisfactoriness."

Similar to the insight knowledge of impermanence, the insight wisdom of unsatisfactoriness abandons the latent defilements that lay dormant in the mind and would cause the potential to suffer in the future. This knowledge purifies the mind of misunderstanding.

### *Seeing the Characteristic of Impersonality*

The assumption that we are autonomous beings able to control the experience of our own bodies and minds is deeply rooted in delusion. Since we are not aware of this assumption, we believe that we exist in the body, the body is mine, I own my own body, and so on, and along with that comes my suffering about my body and my mind when they are not compliant with my wishes.

From a relational, consensual perspective this is a necessary and useful belief. Where beings are not able to exercise effective, autonomous self-agency because of enslavement, prohibitions, political or social disempowerment, or shaming to submit to external authority, there is tremendous obvious suffering. That is extremely unskillful behavior for perpetrators and is unfathomably painful for victims. It is occurring rampantly as we read this.

There is every reason to respond vigorously with truth-telling, political and economic action, compassionate confrontation, and personal decisions not to support or turn a blind eye to such suffering. In addition, it is necessary for each of us to look deeply into our own lives to see how we might be benefitting from such exploitation and take steps to minimize that and to remedy the harm done. That would be compassionate wisdom in action.

That's not what we are referencing when we identify the impersonal nature of mental-physical phenomena. Instead, we are acknowledging that we can't control the mind. All kinds of thoughts and feelings come to the mind that we would rather not have to endure; so too with physical experiences of the body, from growing up, to aging, to being vulnerable to disease, and ultimately to death—these experiences all arise due to their own causes and conditions that are not under our control. We have no self-agency.

In addition, because of the continuity of physical and mental experience, we do not see the individual phenomena that only in the composite appear to be a solid "me" either in the body or the mind. When we hold on to an idea of "my self" as some solid, enduring thing, we lay the ground for suffering whenever that sense of self is not affirmed by external conditions, which, as I have discovered, happens frequently.

I'd like to share a personal experience of how a sense of entitlement resulted in a painful identity, which when seen with awareness resulted in a liberating understanding of impermanence, unsatisfactoriness, and the evanescence of identity.

Some time ago, owing to a change of schedule, I was going to miss my appointment unless I could fly stand-by on an earlier flight from the West Coast to the East Coast. I called the airline and was reassured that there were plenty of open seats available on the red-eye flight I needed to take. When I arrived at the ticket counter to get a stand-by boarding pass, I was told that it was unlikely there would be any room, as an earlier flight traveling the same route had been canceled and its passengers transferred to this flight.

I was anxious to get to my appointment, so I reminded the ticket agent that I was a high-mileage frequent flyer with the airline and had an appointment early the next day, so if there was even one seat, I'd like to get it.

What pandemonium at the gate! When I eventually got to the counter I again mentioned to the gate attendant that I was a high-mileage frequent flyer and was told to stand over to the side with the others waiting for a chance to fly stand-by.

As the ticketed passengers were nearly boarded, we three stand-by hopefuls were ushered into the end of the line. I again reminded the flight attendant that if there was even just one seat available, I'd like it, as I was a high-mileage frequent flyer with the airline.

At the door of the plane no one thought there would be any available seats, but as it turned out one middle seat way in the back was found, and I eagerly raised my hand for the selection and was ushered forward to the door. As I was allowed on, I was relieved and excited that I had gotten selected. I got to my seat, cramped as it was, and settled in as best as I could, when I noticed that they had found a second empty seat for one of the remaining stand-by passengers and the door closed and we were about to push back from the gate.

One last announcement for a destination check: "This plane is going to Boston; if you are not intending to go there let us know." To my surprise and the flight attendants' amazement, one fellow in a first-class seat realized he was on the wrong flight, got up, and asked to leave the plane. The door was reopened and he departed, but before closing the door, the flight attendant invited the remaining stand-by passenger onto the plane and ushered him to the empty first-class seat!

"WHAT!" my hand went up to the call button. "Hey! I'm the high-mileage frequent flyer. Shouldn't I get that seat?" As the plane was pushing back from the gate I was told: "Stay seated. You're on the plane. We're leaving. You have a seat."

I felt I was entitled to that seat, after all the miles I had flown on the airline, and on and on reeled my mind with self-righteous indignation, fuming with the way I was being treated as it angrily composed the letter I was going to write to the airline upon arrival in Boston. For the first half hour after takeoff I was beside myself until I realized, "Hey, I'm on the plane. Going to get to Boston on time for my appointment. What's the problem? If I keep up this anger for the next five hours, I'm going to be a wreck for my appointment in the morning." That got me to settle down and let it go, grateful to be on the flight.

I arrived on time. Made my appointment. Was happy to have made it. Still a high-mileage frequent flyer. So what was the problem, really? The only problem was I didn't get any confirmation from the airline of my status as a frequent flyer. Other than that, I still got my miles. Still had my status with the occasional perks. The only thing that changed was I stopped suffering when I let go of my story of who I was and my expectations of how I should be treated and my anger. Everything else remained the same!

How often do we hold on to a narrative in our mind about something that is causing us suffering, when to stop suffering only requires that we become aware of deeply seated beliefs and assumptions that cause the suffering. With that awareness, and noticing how we are feeling and what we are doing, we can choose to stop suffering by letting go of the story—we just need to notice the option and make the choice. Our unseen assumptions and beliefs condition the suffering, and unless we see them, we will be caught by them and suffer. Mindful insight gives us the option to become aware of what is actually happening as momentary mental and physical experience, as well as the assumptions underlying our story of what's happening. It's only a story! Believing it causes suffering; seeing and understanding it relieves the suffering.

This is the wisdom that mindfulness reveals: The experience of *dukkha* is painful. The understanding of *dukkha* is liberating!

> There is no self that can do whatever it wants, but only natural phenomena that arise according to conditions.

It is the training of the mind through Dhamma knowledge, skillful reflection, and development of mind that manifests such wisdom. But even here we cannot take personal ownership of the mind or the wisdom. These are naturally occurring mental phenomena, and to identify with them as me, mine, or who I am is the subtlest attachment to be recognized and let go of.

> If you think that you are practicing, or that the practice is yours, then the practice is not free from personal identification and cannot be considered to be removing an erroneous view of personality.
>
> If you are proud of your practice, thinking, "I am able to practice well, I have learned to practice properly," then your practice cannot be considered removing conceit.
>
> If you are attached to your practice, thinking that you observe well, that your practice is going well, or that your noting is good, then your practice is not yet considered to be removing attachment, because it cannot remove attachment.

Even identification with the knowing capacity of the mind is attachment and not seeing the impermanent nature of knowing itself.

> At times the number of different objects to note may shrink to one or two, or all of them may even disappear. However, at this time the knowing consciousness is still present. In this very clear, open space of the sky there remains only one very clear blissful consciousness, which is very clear beyond comparison and very blissful. But this consciousness is not going to stay permanent. Its fractionation into segments as knowing and passing away, knowing and passing away, is evident. It has to be noted as "knowing, knowing." Yogis tend to take delight in this clear, blissful consciousness. This is known as "dhamma raga." Under these circumstances, advancement toward higher knowledge becomes impossible. Such delightfulness will therefore have to be noted [as also impermanent].

What remains? When all conditioned phenomena of experience—including challenging torments, "spiritual goodies" such as tranquility, joy, bliss, balance, insight, and wisdom, along with the knowing capacity of the mind itself—are realized to be impermanent, unsatisfactory, and impersonal, what is left? Only the release of the unconditioned—*nibbāna*—and the cessation of conditioned phenomena, which has the nature of peacefulness.

> One realizes the truth of suffering by fully understanding it, realizes the truth of the cause of suffering by abandoning it, realizes the truth of the cessation of suffering by experiencing it, and realizes the truth of the path to the cessation of suffering by developing it.

Insight into the three universal characteristics of impermanence, unsatisfactoriness, and impersonality purifies our understanding and frees the mind from immediate and future suffering. More than the benefit of harmonious relationships and freedom from remorse offered by mindful behavior, and more than the tranquility that comes from the mindful management of stressful conditions, is the liberation from mental states that cause suffering via mindful insight of the three characteristics, which purifies our understanding. This liberation is the greatest benefit of mindfulness practice.

## Conclusion

Mahāsi Sayadaw explains how mindfulness for insight liberates the mind.

> If one does not observe mental and physical phenomena every time they arise at the six sense doors, one cannot realize that there is nothing to them but mind and body, which are conditioned, impermanent, unsatisfactory, and not-self. As a result, one will develop an attachment to the objects that one fails to observe. If, on the other hand, one observes mental and physical phenomena the moment they occur, one will realize that there is nothing to them but mind and body, which are conditioned, impermanent, unsatisfactory, and not-self. As a result, one will be free from attachment to objects that one is able to observe. Thus the wholesome action of insight liberates one from attachment and thus is considered renunciation. This renunciation, in turn, liberates noble ones from the cycle of suffering (*saṃsāra*) by developing insight step by step until nibbāna is attained. And so the wholesome act of insight is called

> "the great liberation of noble ones" because of its liberating effect.

It is only appropriate to let the Buddha have the last word.

> The purpose of my teaching of the holy life of the Dhamma
> is not for gaining merit,
> nor good deeds,
> nor rapture,
> nor concentration,
> but for the sure heart's release.
> This and this alone is the reason for the teachings of the Buddha. (MN 29)

# Preface

*By Mahāsi Sayadaw*

According to the Buddha's teaching, the practice of insight meditation (*vipassanā*) enables one to realize the ultimate nature of mind and body, to see their common characteristics of impermanence (*anicca*), suffering (*dukkha*), and not-self (*anattā*), and to realize the four noble truths.

To reject the practice of insight meditation is to reject the teaching of the Buddha, to undermine others' faith and confidence in the practice, and to abandon the prospect of attaining the path and fruition. The following verse from the *Dhammapada* shows how big an offense this is:

> The unwise who rely on evil views
> to malign the teachings of the noble arahants
> who live the Dharma
> produce fruit that destroys themselves,
> like the *kathaka* reed that dies upon bearing fruit.[5]

Access to the Dhamma is a precious opportunity. We are fortunate to be alive at this point in history when we have the teachings of the Buddha. The teachings are a precious gift for all of us to realize the path, fruition, and nibbanā that are the most valuable dhammas. But this opportunity does not last forever and will pass. The span of our lives ends before long. We can die at any time. And while we are still alive, we may lose the ability to practice if we become weak or sick, if conditions are too dangerous, or if other problems or difficulties arise.

We should not waste our time! Is it not better to practice now so that we will not find ourselves helpless on our deathbeds without any reliable spiritual achievement to support us? The Buddha reminded us constantly that we have to practice effectively beforehand as long as there is time.

Today the effort must be made;
tomorrow Death may come, who knows?
No bargain with mortality
can keep him and his hordes away.[6]

Regret is useless. If we do not practice although we have the opportunity, we will feel regret when we are sick, old, and weak, lying on our deathbeds, or reborn in the lower realms. Before it is too late, keep in mind the Buddha's admonitions:

Meditate, bhikkhus, do not delay or else you will regret it
later.
This is our instruction to you.[7]

Are you able to appreciate the attributes of the Dhamma from personal experience: Do you know that it has been well explained by the Buddha? That it can be empirically experienced here and now? That it gives immediate results? That it invites one to come and see, to realize the truth for oneself? Go to a teacher and practice systematically under his or her guidance according to the instructions in this book, which offers the essential and effective theory and practical instructions for mindfulness in the service of the development of insight. It is insight that liberates the mind from mental states that cause suffering. Your experience will be satisfactory and you will realize special insights. You will realize for yourself that the Dhamma is endowed with the aforementioned attributes.

# The Development of Mindfulness

I will begin by explaining the way in which to meditate and the way of correct seeing and understanding based on the Pāḷi texts, commentaries, and subcommentaries.

A person who takes the vehicle of insight observes presently arisen consciousness of seeing, hearing, smelling, tasting, touching, or thinking, the physical bases of these kinds of consciousness, physical phenomena arisen due to these kinds of consciousness, or physical phenomena arisen due to the objects of these kinds of consciousness. According to the Pāḷi texts, commentaries, and subcommentaries, "seeing" refers to the entire mental process of seeing, not to each individual mental moment of it.

## Checking Meditation against the Pāḷi Texts

### *Five Kinds of Phenomena*

One should note seeing as "seeing" at the very moment of seeing. The same applies for hearing and so on. When one notes "seeing," one experiences any of the following five kinds of phenomena: (1) eye sensitivity (*cakkhuppasāda*), (2) form base (*rūpāyatana*), (3) eye consciousness (*cakkhuviññāṇa*), (4) the mental contact (*phassa*) between eye and object, and (5) feelings (*vedanā*) that are pleasant, unpleasant, or neither unpleasant nor pleasant.

For example, when the clarity of a meditator's eyesight becomes obvious to him, the meditator is mainly experiencing eye sensitivity. When the visible form that has been seen draws one's attention, one is mainly aware of the visual object. If one notices the mental state of seeing, then one is realizing eye consciousness. If the contact between one's eye and the visual object is clear, then one is experiencing mental contact. If one finds the object to be pleasant, unpleasant, or neither unpleasant nor pleasant, then one is mainly aware of feeling.

You may ask, "If this is so, then rather than noting seeing as 'seeing,' shouldn't one note it as 'eye sensitivity,' 'the visual object,' 'eye consciousness,' 'mental contact,' or 'feeling,' according to what one clearly experiences, so that the labels will be in harmony with what they indicate?"

This sounds very reasonable. In practice, however, it would keep the meditator so busy thinking about exactly which object they were experiencing in a moment of seeing that there would be many gaps between notings. In other words, one would not be able to focus on present objects. In addition, one would fail to note the thinking and analyzing, so one's mindfulness, concentration, and insight knowledge would not be able to mature in a timely manner. Therefore you should not note while simultaneously trying to find a word that perfectly matches the label with the experience. Instead, you should simply note seeing as "seeing" every time you see. In this way, you will avoid such difficulties.

The term "seeing" should be understood to refer to all of the phenomena involved in the mental process of seeing. For this reason, it is called a concept that refers to what ultimately exists (*vijjamānapaññatti*). It is also called a concept that refers to ultimately real phenomena (*tajjāpaññatti*). So words such as "earth" (*pathavī*), "mental contact" (*phassa*), and so on are all concepts that refer to ultimately real phenomena. Still, the question may be raised, "Won't my attention be drawn to the concept of the word being used instead of connecting with the ultimately real phenomena that it indicates?"

This is true in the immature stages of meditation. When first beginning practice, one can accurately focus one's mind on objects only when one notes them by labeling them one by one. Eventually, though, one learns to experience the ultimately real phenomena that lie beyond names or concepts. In this way, the perception of the solidity and continuity of phenomena (*santatighana*) vanishes and one is able to understand the three universal characteristics. This is confirmed by the following passage from the *Mahāṭīkā*:

> Should one observe ultimately real phenomena in terms of concepts that refer to ultimately real phenomena?[11] Yes, in the

> beginning of the practice one should. However, when one's practice is mature, one's mind will reach the ultimately real phenomena beyond the concepts that refer to them.[12]

This passage refers specifically to meditation on the Buddha's attributes, but it can serve as good guidance in the case of insight meditation as well. During certain stages, such as the insight knowledge of arising and passing away, phenomena arise so rapidly that it is not possible to label them individually, and one must simply be aware of their characteristics. This will be explained in the next chapter. However, one will realize it for oneself when one attains those knowledges. So one shouldn't waste one's time deciding what to note. One just notes "seeing" every time one sees. Then one experiences objects in terms of their characteristics, functions, manifestations, or proximate causes. Then one understands these phenomena as they really are.

*Four aspects of phenomena*

Some may wonder whether it is possible to experience phenomena accurately without an education in theory. It is possible if we mindfully observe mental and physical phenomena the moment they occur. Ultimately real phenomena are made up of nothing but the particular aspects of their (1) characteristics (*lakkhaṇā*), (2) function (*rasā*), (3) manifestation (*paccupaṭṭhānā*), and (4) proximate cause (*padaṭṭhānā*).

So if we directly experience an ultimately real phenomenon, we understand it in terms of one of those four factors—in other words, we can only experience an ultimately real phenomenon in terms of these four factors. If we perceive an object in any other way, the object we perceive is not a genuine, ultimately real phenomenon but a concept of something, such as its manner, identity, image, solid form, and so on.

We can experience a phenomenon as it really is if we observe it the moment it takes place. This type of experience is neither imagination nor reasoning, but awareness of a phenomenon in terms of its characteristic and so on. If we observe a lightning bolt the moment it strikes, for example, we will certainly be aware of its unique characteristic (brightness), its function (to remove darkness), its manifestation (whether it is straight, branched, or arcing), or its proximate cause (a cloud and so on). It is impossible, on the other hand, to perceive the lightning bolt as it really is if we imagine or analyze it after it has disappeared. Likewise, if we observe phenomena the moment they occur, we can understand the characteristics and such of these truly arising mental and physical phenomena just as they really are, even without any theoretical knowledge of them.

We cannot understand the characteristics and such of these truly arising mental and physical phenomena as they really are by merely thinking or reflecting on them, without noting them as they arise in the present moment, even if we have theoretical knowledge of them. For example, if you note an unpleasant feeling, you can understand its characteristic (unpleasantness), its function (stress), its manifestation (discomfort), or its proximate cause (contact between the mind and an unpleasant object), as it really is with personal experience.

Actually, the proximate cause of an object is distinct from the observed object itself. So during the early stages of meditation[13] you should not pay attention to it. This is why the *Abhidhammatthavibhāvinī* subcommentary only says that one should be mindful of an object in terms of its characteristic, function, and manifestation, and that this understanding is considered purification of view (*diṭṭhivisuddhi*). The *Mahāṭīkā*[14] explains that the proximate cause is not mentioned because it is a separate phenomenon. In the case of meditation on the four fundamental elements, for example, when one observes any of the four primary material elements, it is not necessary to pay attention to the remaining elements that are its proximate causes. Otherwise one would be observing objects different from that which one intended to note.

In the same way, in the case of knowledge that discerns mental and physical phenomena, we need only be aware of present mental and physical phenomena the moment they occur; we needn't yet be concerned with their causes. If we were to observe objects in terms of their proximate causes, then when observing a primary material element, we would first need to be aware of the other three elements. When observing eye sensitivity, we would first need to observe the primary material elements that are its proximate causes. The moment a feeling became obvious, we would first need to note the mental contact that was its proximate cause. Or the moment contact became obvious, we would first need to observe the object.

Thus when one object is most obvious, we would have to be aware of a different one. In other words, we would have to note the first object later. This might make it seem like we could gain knowledge that discerns conditionality (*paccayapariggahañāṇa*) by skipping knowledge that discerns mental and physical phenomena. It is significant that the *Visuddhimagga* and Abhidhamma subcommentaries[15] do not include observation of proximate causes in their instructions for the first level of knowledge. The reason that the *Abhidhammattha Saṅgaha* includes proximate causes is because the proximate cause becomes obvious and can be observed at later stages of purification of view when one is about to attain knowledge that discerns conditionality.

A person can realize only one of the four aspects of characteristic, function, manifestation, and proximate cause at a time. When noting a mental or physical phenomenon in a given moment, only one of these four aspects is obvious, so a person can observe only one of them at a time. Since two, three, or four aspects are not obvious at the same time, a person cannot be aware of all of them at once. Fortunately, it is not necessary to be aware of an object from all aspects at the same time in order to accomplish one's aim. Indeed, understanding an object from a single aspect serves the purpose. As the *Mahāṭīkā* says:

> Why are both characteristic and function mentioned here [in the case of the four primary material elements]? Because they are intended for meditators of different dispositions. When meditating on a primary material element, one person may experience it in terms of its characteristic and another in terms of its function.[16]

If a person observes one of the four primary material elements solely in terms of its characteristic or solely in terms of its function, it fully serves the purpose. One cannot simultaneously observe both its characteristic and its function. The reason why the commentary explains both its characteristic and its function is because people have different dispositions and inclinations. Let me elaborate. When observing one of the four primary material elements, the specific characteristic is obvious for some people, and therefore they can observe and realize only the specific characteristic; for others its function is obvious and therefore they can observe and realize only the function.

## Contemplation of the Body

### *The Case of Seeing*

When noting "seeing," a person can experience any one of the five factors of seeing from any of its four aspects. I will explain each of these cases in order.

#### *Eye sensitivity*

When we experience our eye as clear or sufficiently clear that a visual object appears to it, the eye sensitivity is understood in terms of its unique characteristic (*sabhāvalakkhaṇā*).

When we experience eye sensitivity carrying our attention to an object or allowing us to see an object, the eye sensitivity is understood in terms of its function.

When we experience the eye sensitivity as the basis for seeing or the starting point of seeing, it is understood in terms of its manifestation.

When we are aware of the solid, bodily eye, the eye sensitivity is understood from the aspect of its being a proximate cause.

#### *The visual object*

When we accurately understand a visual object, we know that it appears to the eye (its characteristic), that it is seen (its function), that it is an object of sight (its manifestation), and that it is based on the four primary material elements (its proximate cause). This explanation accords with the Pāḷi texts' explanation that the phrase "understands the eye, understands forms"[17] means that "the eye sensitivity and visible form are understood in terms of characteristic and function."[18]

*Eye consciousness*

When we accurately understand eye consciousness, we know that it occurs in the eye or sees visible forms (its characteristic), that it takes only visible form as its object or that it simply sees (its function), that it is directed toward the visible form (its manifestation), and that it occurs because of attention, the conjunction of functioning eye with visual objects, or good or bad kamma (its proximate cause).

*Mental contact between eye and object*

When we accurately understand visual contact, we know that it contacts a visual object (its characteristic), that it encounters visual objects (its function), that it is a meeting of the eye, a visual object, and sight (its manifestation), and that visual objects give rise to it (its proximate cause).

*Feelings that are pleasant, unpleasant, or neither unpleasant nor pleasant*

When we accurately understand a pleasant feeling, we know that it is pleasant (its characteristic), that it feels pleasant (its function), that it arouses pleasure in the mind (its manifestation), and that it is caused by contact with a pleasant or desirable object or by a peaceful mind (its proximate cause).

When we accurately understand an unpleasant feeling, we know that it is unpleasant (its characteristic), that it feels unpleasant (its function), that it arouses displeasure in the mind (its manifestation), and that it is caused by contact with an unpleasant or undesirable object (its proximate cause). When we accurately understand a neither-unpleasant-nor-pleasant feeling, we know that it is neither unpleasant nor pleasant (its characteristic), that it feels neither amusing nor boring (its function), that it is tranquil (its manifestation), and that a balance between pleasure and displeasure causes it (its proximate cause).

Note that eye consciousness itself is associated only with neutral feeling. According to canonical discourses that deal with insight, however, we should observe all six senses in terms of these three types of feeling. The reason for this is that the complete mental processes for the six senses include units of mentality that are directly associated with pleasant or unpleasant feelings, as well—namely, investigation (*santīraṇa*), impulsion (*javana*), and registration (*tadārammaṇa*). This will become obvious below when we deal with the *Abhiññeyya Sutta* and the *Pariññeyya Sutta*.

I will elaborate in order to broaden our understanding. The subcommentaries say:

> An unwholesome resultant feeling that is neither unpleasant nor pleasant (*upekkhā*) can be considered an unpleasant feeling since it is disagreeable; a wholesome one can be considered a pleasant feeling since it is agreeable.[19]

Based on the use of the words "agreeable" and "disagreeable" in the above passage, it is reasonable to assume that if an object is neither agreeable nor disagreeable, the feeling involved should be regarded as neither unpleasant nor pleasant. Although sense consciousness itself is associated with neither unpleasant nor pleasant feelings, we are likely to feel pleasure when encountering a pleasant sight, a sweet sound, a fragrant odor, or a delicious flavor. When we experience the fragrant smell of flowers or perfume, or consume tasty food and drink, the feeling of pleasure is obvious. On the other hand, we feel displeasure when we encounter unpleasant sights, sounds, odors, or flavors, such as the smell of something rotting or burning, the taste of bitter medicine, and so on. Body consciousness is of two kinds as well: pleasant and unpleasant. It would seem that when an object is neither unpleasant nor pleasant, it should be possible to feel not only pleasant or unpleasant feelings but also feelings that are neither unpleasant nor pleasant. Such neither unpleasant nor pleasant feelings, however, should be considered a lesser form of pleasure.

As mentioned above, eye sensitivity, visible form, eye consciousness, mental contact between the eye and the object, and feelings that are pleasant, unpleasant, or neither unpleasant nor pleasant are the five factors that constitute sight. At the moment of seeing, we note "seeing, seeing" and, as explained before, come to know its characteristic, function, or manifestation according to our disposition and inclination. At the mature stages of purification of view, we may also be able to know its proximate cause. With this purpose in mind, the Saṃyutta Nikāya[20] and *Paṭisambhidāmagga* say:

> Bhikkhus, the eye should be fully understood, forms should be fully understood, eye consciousness should be fully understood, mental contact between eye and form should be fully understood, and whatever feeling arises with mental contact—whether pleasant or painful or neither painful nor pleasant—should be fully understood.[21]

*Learning and logical thought*

Knowledge gained through learning and logical thought is not insight. Mental and physical phenomena are understood as they really are by being aware of them in terms of their characteristics and so on the moment they occur. This understanding or insight knowledge is superior to learning and logical thought. It is superior even to knowledge derived from tranquility meditation (*samathabhāvanāmaya*). The textual reference on this point is:

> "Wisdom of full understanding" (*abhiññāpaññā*) is a knowledge that understands ultimately real phenomena by noting them in terms of their characteristic and so on.[22]

In the ultimate sense, this is knowledge that discerns mental and physical phenomena and knowledge that discerns conditionality.

> Full understanding (*abhiññātā*) is an understanding of [ultimately real phenomena] derived from knowledge [that discerns mental and physical phenomena and conditionality] and is superior to knowledge derived from learning, logical thought, and even to some derived from tranquility meditation.[23]

This passage makes it clear that learning and logical thought do not even belong to the realm of basic knowledge, let alone to that of higher insight knowledges.

The *Abhiññeyya Sutta*[24] says that one must fully understand the eye, one must fully understand visible form, and so on, in this way generally exposing different points one after the other in due order. If a person were to note one object five different ways, many other objects would pass by unobserved. In any event, one's mind cannot note quickly enough to notice all five factors in every instance of sight. Such an approach would also contradict the *Paṭisambhidāmagga*, a text in the Pāḷi canon, which says that a person who has reached the stage of insight knowledge of dissolution can be aware of both the disappearance of an object and of their awareness of its disappearance itself. So a person should observe only one object for each instance of sight. The purpose of noting and understanding is fulfilled when one observes and understands one distinct phenomenon among these five.

The *Pariññeyya Sutta*[25] explains how it is fulfilled. At the mature stages of the first two knowledges, whenever one notes "seeing," one comes to know that the seeing did not exist before and that it has now appeared. Thereby one also understands the appearance of these five phenomena. One further understands the disappearance of these phenomena, seeing them vanish after they have arisen—using sharp mindfulness one sees them instantly disappear. When one begins to see arising and disappearance, one understands the characteristic of impermanence (*aniccalakkhaṇā*). Because phenomena are not exempt from arising and disappearance, they are unsatisfactory—this is understanding the characteristic of unsatisfactoriness (*dukkhalakkhaṇā*). And because they arise and disappear even though one doesn't wish them to, there is no self that has any control over them—this is understanding the characteristic of not-self (*anattālakkhaṇā*). Thus one fully understands the general characteristics of impermanence and such of all five of these phenomena that are present in each moment of sight.

The *Abhiññeyya Sutta* and *Pariññeyya Sutta* both explain all six of the sense doors in the very same way. According to the *Pariññeyya Sutta*, when a person understands the general characteristics of impermanence and such by observing one distinct phenomenon among the five phenomena, one fulfills the aim of fully understanding these phenomena at the moment of seeing them. When one accomplishes this understanding, the phenomena cannot give rise to defilements.

### *The arising and nonarising of mental defilements*

When a defilement arises in connection with sight, it arises at the moment of seeing based on a distinct object that one sees. When there is no distinct object and it is not known, the defilement does not arise. Affection or hate for a certain person only arises because one has previously met or seen that person. It may also happen due to hearing about that person from somebody else. Let's assume that you have neither met this person nor heard about him; you don't even know that this person exists on the planet. Because this person is not distinct to your mind and you do not know him, it is impossible for affection or hate to arise in your mind with respect to him. The same follows for a form that you have not seen in the past or present, and have never imagined. Such a visible form is like a woman or man that lives in a village, town, country, celestial realm, or universe that you have never visited before. Because there is no such visible form obviously present in your mind, greed, hatred, and other defilements cannot arise with respect to it. This is why, at the request of a monk named Māluṅkyaputta, the Buddha gave meditation instructions by raising questions as follows:

> "What do you think, Māluṅkyaputta? Do you have any desire, lust, or affection for those forms cognizable by the eye that you have not seen and never saw before, that you do not see and would not think might be seen?"
>
> "No venerable sir."[26]

With this first question, the Buddha explicitly states that visible objects that are not apparent cannot arouse mental defilements. In other words, it isn't necessary to make any effort to prevent mental defilements from arising with respect to such objects. On the other hand, this implies that mental defilements can arise from distinct objects that one can actually see. So if one can use insight meditation to prevent affection or hatred from arising, then defilements cannot arise even with apparent visible objects, just as is the case with visible objects that are not apparent. The point is that one should observe the objects one sees so that the defilements are abandoned by means of insight meditation, just like the objects that one does not see. Such implied meanings are called *neyyatthanaya* (the implicit method), *avuttasiddhinaya* (the method established without being said), or *atthāpannanaya* (the deductive method) in Pāḷi.

What makes us love or hate someone when we see him? In an ultimate sense, it is the visual phenomenon, the visible form delineated by the skin. Based on this visible form we think about the person and come to regard the whole of his body as what we like or dislike. If we didn't see the external visible form of the person, we wouldn't think of the whole of his body as what we like or dislike. Since, consequently, attachment would not arise when the person is seen, it naturally follows that defilements do not arise and therefore would not need to be abandoned. On the other hand, an object that we become attached to the moment we see it can arouse mental defilements any time we think about it. Therefore we must observe the objects that we see so that they do not lead to love or hate, just as objects we don't see do not lead to love or hate.

The Buddha gives the same question and answer with respect to the other senses of hearing, smelling, tasting, touching, and thinking.

> "Here, Māluṅkyaputta, regarding things seen, heard, sensed, and cognized by you, in the seen there will be merely the seen, in the heard there will be merely the heard, in the sensed there will be merely the sensed, in the cognized there will be merely the cognized.
>
> "When, Māluṅkyaputta, regarding things seen, heard, sensed, and cognized by you, in the seen there will be merely the seen, in the heard there will be merely the heard, in the sensed there will be merely the sensed, in the cognized there will be merely the cognized, then, Māluṅkyaputta, you will not be 'by that.' When, Māluṅkyaputta, you are not 'by that,' then you will not be 'therein.' When, Māluṅkyaputta, you are not 'therein,' then you will be neither here nor beyond nor in between the two. This itself is the end of suffering."[27]

In the *Udāna-aṭṭhakathā*,[28] the phrase "When you are not 'therein'" is said to mean that one is neither in the six internal sense bases (eye, ear, nose, tongue, body, and mind) nor in the six external sense bases (visible forms, sounds, odors, tastes, touch, and thoughts), nor in the six kinds of consciousness that are between the two of them. When one is not in the six internal sense bases, the six external sense bases, or the six kinds of consciousness, it is the end of suffering.

The explanation of this verse is as follows: When you see a visual object, just let seeing be seeing, do not let mental defilements intrude by thinking about the form that has been seen. You should observe the visible form that you see so that the defilements have no chance to arise. Being mindful of the visible form, you will know its true nature. You will understand it as having the nature of just being seen, disappearing after it has arisen, and disappearing even while being noted. Thus you will realize that it is impermanent, unsatisfactory, and not-self. Even though you see this visible form, it is the same as an object that you do not see, so you don't mentally grasp it as something to be loved or hated, or as solid matter. Even if you happen to think of it, you will not reflect on it with delusion. You will remember it as impermanent, unsatisfactory, and not-self, just as you found it to be when you first noted it. Thus defilements of love or hate will be unable to arise based on thoughts connected with that visible form.

In other words, every time you see, you must observe so that no defilements can arise. When hearing a sound, smelling an odor, experiencing a taste, touching any kind of tangible object, or thinking a thought, you must observe so that ensuing thoughts and defilements have no chance to arise. You just let hearing be hearing, and likewise with the rest. As you just let seeing be seeing, hearing be hearing, and so on, and uninterruptedly continue to note, you gradually develop the moral conduct, concentration, and understanding that are developed hand in hand with the practice of insight meditation. Finally, this leads to moral conduct, concentration, and wisdom associated with path knowledge.

The *Udāna-aṭṭhakathā* elaborates still further on this verse.[29] When you continuously note a visible form as "seeing," for example, seeing is just seeing. When noting a visible form, the nature of "just seeing" is obvious, as is the nature of impermanence, unsatisfactoriness, and not-self, but it is not obvious that the visible form is something to be loved or hated or a so-called person. These objects are seen like objects that are not apparent. They do not become objects based on which defilements arise, and given that you have no attachment to these objects, defilements cannot arise. This is why the Pāḷi texts, commentaries, and subcommentaries say that such objects do not leave behind dormant defilements (*ārammanānusayakilesā*). Insight meditation temporarily removes defilements and so is described as "temporary seclusion" (*tadaṅgaviveka*), "nonattachment" (*virāga*), "cessation" (*nirodha*), and "release" (*vossagga*). An insight practitioner is considered "a person who is temporarily liberated from defilements" (*tadaṅganibbuta*), as stated in the Saṃyutta Nikāya. One is not carried away by defilements connected with seeing and so on; one is not attached to the object one sees, nor is one averse to it; and one also does not entertain thoughts of taking things to be permanent, satisfying, and self.

Because such persons can abandon the perception of permanence and so on, their understanding is called "full understanding by abandoning" (*pahānapariññā*). Understanding the disappearance of the visible form that is seen is "insight full understanding by abandoning" (*vipassanāpahānapariññā*). Understanding the complete cessation of all conditioned phenomena that include the visible form that is seen together with the noting mind is "path full understanding by abandoning" (*maggapahānapariññā*). That is immediately followed by fruition (*phala*). Both path knowledge and fruition knowledge take nibbāna as their only object. At that point, "you will not be therein" with sense objects. That is, you will no longer have attachment (*taṇhā*), pride (*māna*), or wrong view (*diṭṭhi*).[30]

The commentary on the passage above explains that path and fruition refer to the arahant path (*arahattamagga*) and the fruit of arahantship (*arahattaphala*). We cannot say of a fully enlightened being, an arahant, that he is here in this life or world because he does not have any attachment. Likewise, we cannot say that he is "there" (in the next life or another world), as he will not be reborn after death. Therefore not being "here or there" (in this world or the world beyond) means the complete cessation of the cycle of unsatisfactoriness, as there is no more attachment and no more arising of any new mental and physical phenomena. This is called "nibbāna without residue" (*anupādisesanibbāna*).

Some scholars interpret this line in this way: At the moment of path and fruition, the six internal sense bases (eye, ear, nose, tongue, body, and mind) do not appear to the mind and therefore one cannot observe them. The six external mundane sense objects (visible form, sound, smell, taste, touch, and mental objects) do not appear to the mind and therefore one cannot observe them. The six kinds of consciousness (seeing, hearing, smelling, tasting, touching, and thinking consciousness) do not appear to the mind and therefore one cannot observe them. Path knowledge and fruition knowledge arise by taking the cessation of the sense bases, sense object, and consciousness as their object. Realizing the nature of cessation with the attainment of path and fruition is called nibbāna, the end of unsatisfactoriness.

The Venerable Māluṅkyaputta responded to the Buddha by interpreting the Buddha's brief discourse in his own words as follows:

> Having seen a form with mindfulness muddled,
> attending to the pleasing sign,
> one experiences it with infatuated mind
> and remains tightly holding to it.
>
> Many feelings flourish within,
> originating from the visible form,
> covetousness and annoyance as well,
> by which the mind becomes disturbed.
> For one who accumulates suffering thus,
> nibbāna is said to be far away.[31]

This verse explains that one cannot attain nibbāna if one lacks mindfulness at the time of seeing. The phrase "attending to the pleasing sign" indicates that unwise attention leads to desire. The phrase "with mindfulness muddled" means that one fails to be mindful of visible forms as they really are: impermanent, unsatisfactory, and not-self. The phrase "one experiences it with infatuated mind" implies also that one hates it if it is undesirable and ignores it in delusion if it is neutral.

> When fully mindful, one sees a form,
> one is not inflamed by lust for forms,
> one experiences it with dispassionate mind
> and does not remain holding it tightly.

> One fares mindfully in such a way
> that even as one sees the form,
> and while one undergoes a feeling,
> [suffering] is exhausted and not built up.
> For one dismantling suffering thus,
> nibbāna is said to be close by.[32]

This verse explains that one can attain nibbāna if one possesses mindfulness at the time of seeing. The Buddha presented the same instructions for the remaining senses of hearing, smelling, tasting, touching, and thinking. Then the Buddha confirmed Māluṅkyaputta's interpretation of the instructions by saying: "Well spoken, Māluṅkyaputta!" The Buddha then told Māluṅkyaputta that the meaning of the brief instructions for insight meditation should be retained in detail. Thereafter, the Buddha repeated the above verses again. The Venerable Māluṅkyaputta practiced insight meditation according to this summary and before long he became one of the arahants.

The *Māluṅkyaputta Sutta* conveys three main points: Phenomena that are not apparent and not perceived through one of the six kinds of consciousness naturally do not arouse defilements, so one should not try to note them. Phenomena that are apparent and perceived through one of the six kinds of consciousness and that are not being noted do arouse defilements, so one should note them—defilements that arise when one is not mindful are abandoned by noting them. And if one is mindful of an apparent phenomenon, defilements do not arise from phenomena that are either apparent or not apparent, so when one notes one apparent phenomenon, then the purpose of noting and understanding is fulfilled for all phenomena.

Thus if one understands the arising and passing away and sees the impermanent nature and such of one phenomenon by noting it each time one sees it, then the aim of understanding the five factors involved at the moment of seeing is fulfilled.

The complete discourse can be found in the Saḷāyatanasaṃyutta.[33]

*Defilements*

Although one tries to constantly note seeing as "seeing," defilements will often intrude when insight knowledge is still immature. However, you should not feel disappointed. You should not give up. You can overcome defilements by noting them over and over again, just as a person handwashing clothes gets them completely clean by repeatedly beating and squeezing them. The difference is that a person can easily see how clean the clothes are getting, but a meditator has no way of knowing how many defilements he is eradicating every day. Only when we reach path knowledge and fruition knowledge can we know how many defilements we have eradicated. To illustrate this point, the Buddha gave the example of a carpenter who doesn't notice the wooden handle of his axe being worn down by use until the impression of his fingers appears on it after months or years. This discourse can be found in the Khandhavagga of the Saṃyutta Nikāya.[34] In the same way, a meditator cannot know exactly how many defilements she has overcome until path knowledge and fruition knowledge have been attained.

However, as insight matures, defilements arise less and less often and disappear once they are noted. They no longer persist. Instead the noting mind flows continuously most of the time. Later one's insight knowledge becomes so powerful that it prevents unwholesome impulsion from arising. Instead wholesome impulsion arises during the mental process of seeing, even with regard to a visual object that is likely to arouse attachment. At that point, the mental process of seeing may even stop with determining (*votthapana*), the mind moment that determines an object prior to impulsion. Then one clearly sees that defilements are extinguished during the practice of insight meditation. According to the commentary on the Saḷāyatanasaṃyutta of the Saṃyutta Nikāya:

> The statement "bhikkhus, . . . slow might be the arising of his mindfulness"[35] means that mindfulness is slow to progress. But once it develops, some defilements are suppressed; they can no longer persist. For example, if attachment enters through the eye door, one notices this defilement occurring in the second mental process. In this way, one causes wholesome impulsions

> to arise in the third mental process. It is not surprising that a meditator can suppress defilements by the third mental process. One can even replace unwholesome impulsions in the mental process of seeing with wholesome impulsions after seeing-related mind moments, from the life continuum (*bhavaṅga*) and adverting (*āvajjana*) up to determining (*votthapana*),[36] even when the visual object is desirable and conducive to attachment. This is the benefit an intensive meditator can get from insight practice, which becomes strong and develops the mind.[37]

This passage shows that a meditator at intermediate levels of insight knowledge may have defilements at the moment of seeing, but she can transform them into wholesome states by the third mental process. The sentence "It is not surprising . . ." shows that no defilements arise in a meditator at higher levels of insight knowledge; instead pure observation continuously flows. This passage also implies that the subsequent mental process can perceive the mental process of sight.

*Sense experience without impulsion*

The following section is included to show that the mental process of seeing may even stop at determining.

> For a mature (strong) meditator, if there is unwise attention when an object enters through the eye door or any other door, her mind will fall into life continuum without arousing any defilements after subsisting for two or three determining mind moments. This is how it is for a meditator at the peak of practice.
>
> For another type of meditator in this situation, a mental process accompanied by defilement arises. At the end of that mental process he realizes that the mind is accompanied by defilement and so starts to note it. Then, during the second mental process, the mind is free from the defilement.
>
> For yet another type of meditator, only at the end of the second mental process does she realize that the mind is accom-

> panied by defilement and so starts to note it. Then, during the third mental process, the mind is free from the defilement.[38]

The three types of meditators described here are a first-class meditator (one at the highest level of mature insight meditation), a second-class meditator (one at an intermediate level of mature insight meditation), and a third-class meditator (one at the lower level of mature insight meditation). Regarding the second and third types of meditators, the translation of the original Pāḷi passage is clear enough and no additional explanation is needed. For the first type of meditator, owing to repeated insight practice, even if the mind moment that adverts to a sense object arises with unwise attention, it will not be strong enough to take the object clearly. This is also the case for the subsequent mind moments of the five physical sense consciousnesses (*pañcaviññāṇa*), that which receives (*sampaṭicchana*) the sense object, and that which investigates the sense object. As a result, the determining mind moment that is also called the mind-door-adverting consciousness (*manodvārāvajjana*) is not able to determine the sense object clearly. It occurs two or three times, repeatedly considering the sense object that is referred to in this verse as "after subsisting for" (*āsevanaṃ labhitvā*). However, because the sense object cannot be determined after two or three times, the mental units of impulsion do not arise and life continuum arises.

This type of mental process is called "a mental process that ends with determining" (*votthapanavāravīthi*). It can occur not only in the case of sense objects but also for mental objects. Objects are not experienced clearly in this kind of mental process. One experiences only a general sense of seeing, hearing, or thinking. After emerging from the life continuum (*bhavaṅga*), there arises at the mind door an insight-based mental process that notes the not very distinct seeing. For such a meditator, wholesome and unwholesome mental processes do not occur at all by way of the five sense doors. Mental processes of insight impulsion arise only at the mind door.

*Sixfold equanimity*

This type of mental process can be experienced very clearly at the level of the insight knowledge of equanimity toward phenomena (*saṅkhārupekkhāñāṇa*), where equanimity prevails and one remains balanced. One verifies this point with one's own experience at that level and one is said to possess sixfold equanimity (*chaḷaṅgupekkhā*) like an arahant. As the Pañcaṅguttara Tikaṇḍhakīvagga of the *Manorathapūraṇī* says:

> It is good for a bhikkhu from time to time to dwell equanimous, mindful, and clearly comprehending, having turned away from both the repulsive and the unrepulsive.[39]

The commentary explains this as follows:

> This part refers to sixfold equanimity, which is comparable to an arahant's mental state. However, it is not really the equanimity of an arahant. In this discourse, the Buddha refers only to insight. An accomplished meditator (who has attained knowledge of arising and passing away) can have this kind of equanimity.[40]

Another commentary, on the *Mahāhatthipadopama Sutta*,[41] says:

> Here, *upekkhā* refers to sixfold equanimity. This is the type of equanimity possessed by an arahant that gives one a balanced attitude toward both pleasant and unpleasant objects. However, a monk may take his success at insight practice for arahantship, since he experiences this type of equanimity through the strength of his intensive practice. Thus insight itself can be called sixfold equanimity.[42]

The following story of the Venerable Potthila deals with this kind of mental process. Using the simile of catching a reptile, a remarkable young novice instructed Venerable Potthila to practice insight until impulsion was eliminated at the five sense doors.

*The Story of Venerable Potthila*

In the time of the Buddha, there lived a monk by the name of Potthila. He had learned and taught the complete canonical texts during the lives of six past buddhas, including Buddha Vipassī. He did the same in the time of our Buddha. However, he did not practice meditation. Thus the Buddha deliberately called him Empty Potthila (*Tuccha Potthila*)[43] whenever he met him.

As a result, a feeling of spiritual urgency arose in Venerable Potthila. So he thought: "I have learned the entire canonical text together with the commentaries by heart and I am teaching it to five hundred monks. Yet the Buddha calls me 'Empty Potthila.' This must be because I have no spiritual attainment like the *jhānas* or path and fruition."

He then left for a place 120 yojanas[44] away, with the aim of practicing meditation. In that forest monastery he met thirty arahants and humbly asked the eldest monk to give him guidance on how to practice meditation. However, the eldest monk, wishing to suppress Venerable Potthila's pride in his canonical knowledge, sent him to the second most senior monk. That monk, in turn, sent him to the third most senior monk, and so on. In the end, Venerable Potthila was compelled to meet with the youngest arahant of the group, who was a seven-year-old novice.

By then Venerable Potthila was not showing any more pride in his canonical knowledge. Instead he paid respects to the novice with his hands folded together and humbly requested that the young arahant give him guidance in meditation. How admirable! A senior monk is not allowed to bow down to a junior one, but he may fold his hands together in respect (*añjalīkamma*) when requesting guidance, pardon, and so on. It is really admirable that such a highly learned, senior monk was able to show such humble respect for the Dhamma rather than arrogantly thinking, "I will practice as I have learned rather than accepting guidance from anybody."

But the novice rejected his request, saying, "Venerable sir, I am still young and not very knowledgeable. I am the one who should learn from you." Yet Venerable Potthila persisted in his request.

"Well, if you follow my instructions meticulously," said the novice, "I will teach you how to practice meditation."

Venerable Potthila promised, "Even if you ask me to walk into the fire, I will do exactly as you say." In order to test his sincerity, the novice then asked him to get into a nearby pond. Without a second thought, the senior monk immediately began walking into the pond.

However, just as the edge of his robe got wet, the novice called him back and taught him to practice as follows: "Venerable sir, suppose there were an anthill with six openings and a lizard inside. If you wanted to catch the lizard, you would have to close off five of the openings first and then wait at the sixth one. In the same way out of the six sense doors, you must work only at the mind door, leaving the other five sense doors closed."

Here, "leaving the other five sense doors closed" means not to allow the sensory mental process to reach kammic impulsion. It does not mean to literally close one's eyes, ears, and so on. This would be impossible, as there is no way to "close" the tongue or the body. But even if it were possible to do so, it would not serve any purpose. That is why the Buddha said in the *Indriyabhāvanā Sutta*:

> If that is so, Uttara, then a blind man or a deaf man will have developed mental faculties, according to what the brahmin Pārāsariya says. For a blind man does not see forms with the eye and a deaf man does not hear sounds with the ear.[45]

Moreover, the Buddha teaches us to be mindful of the senses by experiencing them, not by avoiding them. This is consistent with many canonical texts, such as the following:

> Here, having seen a form with the eye, a bhikkhu is neither joyful nor saddened but dwells equanimous, mindful, and clearly comprehending.[46]

The Buddha never taught to protect oneself by preventing sense experiences from occurring. So we can conclude that "to close the sense doors" means to not allow the sensory mental processes to continue through to impulsion. The phrase "to work only at the mind door" means to develop insight just by working at the mind door. The point here is to practice until one develops sixfold equanimity.

Since Venerable Potthila was a highly learned monk, he fully understood the young arahant's meaning, as if a light had been turned on in the darkness. While the senior monk was practicing as instructed, the Buddha emitted rays of light and encouraged him with the following guidance:

> Wisdom arises from [spiritual] practice;
> Without practice, it decays.
> Knowing this two-way path for gain and loss,
> Conduct yourself so that wisdom grows.[47]

The *Dhammapada-aṭṭhakathā* says that at the end of this verse, Venerable Potthila became fully enlightened, an arahant. This is how to develop insight to the level of sixfold equanimity: by noting seeing as "seeing" the moment it occurs, and so on for the rest of the senses.

*More evidence*

From the evidence already provided, it is clear that the aim of understanding is fulfilled by understanding one phenomena at the moment a mental process arises. However, I will provide here some additional references from the commentaries and subcommentaries to more strongly substantiate the above-mentioned points.

> Having realized physical phenomena very well, three aspects of mental phenomena—mental contact, feeling, and consciousness—appear.[48]

If a person is able to note physical objects very well, then each time he notes a physical object, the noting mind as a mental phenomenon appears on its own. While one is taking a physical phenomenon as one's object, the mental phenomena at the five sense doors like the body consciousness, the eye consciousness, and so on appear on their own. They do not, however, appear all together as a group: when mental contact is distinct, it appears; when feeling is distinct, it appears; when consciousness is distinct, it appears.

Either mental contact, feeling, or consciousness will become apparent to a beginning meditator. For example, when you are experiencing hardness or softness (the earth element), you note it as "touching, touching," "hard, hard," or "soft, soft." For some, the mental contact that strikes against hardness or softness is distinct. For some, the feeling that experiences hardness or softness is distinct. For some, the consciousness that merely cognizes hardness or softness is distinct.

Thus when mental contact is distinct, one can only empirically observe the true nature of mental contact. However, mental contact never arises alone. Besides mental contact, mental factors like feeling, perception, volition, as well as consciousness also arise. It is not possible for mental contact to be split apart. Therefore, when mental contact, being the distinct phenomenon, is understood, then the feeling, perception, other mental factors, and consciousness that arise together with it are said to be apparent and are also said to be understood. But this doesn't mean that they aren't understood if they aren't apparent.

Imagine that five ropes are tied together and four of them are immersed in water. You can see only one rope. If you pull this rope, you not only pull this single rope but all five ropes that are tied together. In this example, the rope that you can see is like the mental contact that is apparent. The ropes that are immersed in water are like the feeling, perception, and so on that are not apparent. Pulling the rope that you see and thereby pulling the ropes immersed in water is like noting and understanding the apparent mental contact and thereby including the nonapparent feeling and so on. When feeling or consciousness is apparent, it can be understood in the same way. As the *Mahāṭīkā* says:

> The commentary explicitly mentions the realization of mental contact (*phassa*) as mental contact. However, when mental contact is realized, the other mental phenomena are also

> apparent—that is, feeling (*vedanā*) as feeling, perception (*saññā*) as perception, volition (*cetanā*) as volition, and cognition (*viññāṇa*) as cognition.[49]

In this subcommentary, it is shown that when mental contact is apparent, one can observe it in terms of its unique characteristics. However, when mental contact is apparent, the other accompanying phenomena of feeling, perception, volition, and consciousness are also apparent. This means that being apparent fulfills their purpose.

The commentaries to the *Sakkapañha Sutta*[50] and the *Satipaṭṭhāna Sutta*,[51] as well as the Satipaṭṭhānavibhaṅga of the *Vibhaṅga-aṭṭhakathā*, an Abhidhamma commentary, say:

> When mental contact is apparent to a person, not only is this mental contact apparent but also feeling that feels, perception that perceives, volition that wills, and consciousness that cognizes. Therefore, it is said that all five phenomena are noted.[52]

You should understand the meaning of the two passages from the commentaries cited above as follows: For that person mental contact is distinct, and so one observes mental contact only in terms of its unique characteristic and so on. However, it is said that she observes the five "contact-led" phenomena (*phassapañcamaka*) because mental contact never arises alone. It always occurs together with feeling, perception, volition, and consciousness.

You should not interpret the passages as follows: When mental contact is distinct to a person, she observes the five contact-led phenomena by reflecting about them based on her knowledge learned or heard from others, because she knows that mental contact never occurs alone but is always accompanied by feeling and so on. Nowhere do the Pāḷi texts, commentaries, or subcommentaries explain that one should observe by means of reflection based on knowledge learned or heard from others. They always explain that the noting must only be done with empirical knowledge.

For example, the moon is apparent to people only by way of its visible form. People can only see that visible form. Its smell, taste, and touch are not apparent. However, we can say that they see and understand the moon by way of seeing its visible form. Likewise, when mental contact is apparent and observed, we can say that other accompanying phenomena are also apparent. I have already explained this point several times before, but here is more textual support for it:

> Eye consciousness is associated with three aggregates: feeling, perception, and mental formations. These aggregates can be experienced along with eye consciousness. Thus they are called mental phenomena that can be perceived along with eye consciousness (*cakkhuviññānaviññātabbā*).[53]
>
> If mental contact is understood in three ways—namely, with full understanding of the known, full understanding by investigation, and full understanding by abandoning—three kinds of feeling are also understood, since they are rooted in contact or associated with contact.[54]

Here the Pāḷi terms are understood as follows: "Full understanding of the known" (*ñātapariññā*) refers to insight knowledge that discerns mental and physical phenomena and insight knowledge that discerns conditionality.[55] "Full understanding by investigation" (*tīraṇapariññā*) refers to insight knowledge by comprehension and insight knowledge of arising and passing away.[56] "Full understanding by abandoning" (*pahānapariññā*) refers to the remaining insight knowledges up to path knowledge.[57]

> When a particular type of consciousness is understood, the associated phenomena, whether mental or physical, are also understood, since they are rooted in or come along with that consciousness.[58]

It is clear from these passages that if one understands any constituent of an obvious object, the aim of understanding not only the five contact-led phenomena but all other phenomena involved in that single mental process is fulfilled. Moreover, given the term "come along with" (*sahuppannattā*), it is reasonable to assume that if one observes and understands any part of an obvious object, whether mental or physical, the aim of understanding all associated mental and physical phenomena is fulfilled.

The following passages are from the *Bahudhātuka Sutta*[59] in the Pāḷi canon and its commentary:

> "There are, Ānanda, these six elements: the earth element, the water element, the fire element, the air element, the space element, and the consciousness element. When he knows and sees these six elements, a bhikkhu can be called skilled in the elements."[60]
>
> Here, "knows and sees" refers to path (*magga*) and insight (*vipassanā*).[61] The terms "the earth element, the water element" show that we are not a being but only elements. Moreover, other elements should be added to these six so that there is a total enumeration of eighteen elements. When this enumeration is made, one should break down the consciousness element into its six varieties—that is, the eye-consciousness element and so on. When the eye-consciousness element is noted, the noting of the eye that is its base and the physical matter that is its object is also fulfilled. It is the same for the other kinds of consciousness elements. When the mind-consciousness element is noted, the noting of the two other elements, the mind element and mind-object element, is also fulfilled. The Buddha mentioned these six elements in the discourse because he wanted the bhikkhu's practice for liberation to lead him all the way to the goal.[62]

To explain the quote above: A monk can be called "skilled in the elements" when he sees and understands them by means of insight knowledge and path knowledge. One who understands the six elements can fully understand the tangible element and the mind-consciousness element.

In the mental-object element, only the water element and the space element can be understood. The remaining elements of the mental-object element and the eye element, the ear element, the nose element, the tongue element, the body element, the visible form element, the sound element, the smell element, and the taste element cannot be understood. So doubts can arise with regard to the statement that one can understand the eighteen elements. In order to dispel these doubts, the Majjhima Nikāya commentary states, "Moreover, other elements (*tāpi purimāhi*) . . . ," which it explains as follows: There are six kinds of consciousness elements—the eye-consciousness element, ear-consciousness element, nose-consciousness element, tongue-consciousness element, body-consciousness element, and mind-consciousness element.

If one understands the eye-consciousness element (seeing), then understanding the eye element (the physical basis of the eye) and the visible form element (the form that is seen) is fulfilled. If one understands the ear-consciousness element (hearing), then understanding the ear element (the physical basis of the ear) and the sound element (the sound that is heard) is fulfilled. If one understands the nose-consciousness element (smelling), then understanding the nose element (the physical basis of the nose) and the smell element (the smell that is smelled) is fulfilled. If one understands the tongue-consciousness element (tasting), then understanding the tongue element (the physical basis of the tongue) and the taste element (the taste that is tasted) is fulfilled. If one understands the body-consciousness element (touching), then understanding the body element (the physical basis of the body) and the tangible element (the touch that is felt) is fulfilled. The Pāḷi texts directly mention this tangible element. At the moment of touching, one can empirically observe and understand hardness, softness, heat, warmth, cold, stiffness, and suppleness. If one understands the mind-consciousness element (thinking), then understanding the mind element (comprised of receiving [*sampaṭicchana*] and five-sense-door-adverting [*pañcadvārāvajjana*] consciousnesses) and the mental-object element (the thought that is thought) is fulfilled. Thus as the aim of understanding the remaining elements is fulfilled, although one essentially understands only the six elements, all eighteen elements are understood.

In conclusion, it is clear from this Pāḷi text and its commentary that by understanding one of the consciousness elements one fulfills understanding of its physical basis and its mental or physical object as well. Therefore, based on the phrase "come along with," if one observes and understands any distinct mental or physical phenomena, one also fulfills the aim of understanding all of the other mental and physical phenomena that occur at the same time.

## *The Case of Hearing*

As was explained above for the case of seeing, when we note hearing as "hearing" (smelling as "smelling," tasting as "tasting," touching as "touching"), one of the five phenomena that are distinct at the moment of hearing (smelling, tasting, or touching) becomes apparent in terms of its characteristic and so on. Thus we see and understand that phenomenon as it really is; this is "full understanding of the known." We also see and understand the characteristics of impermanence and so on, and see and understand the phenomenon as arising and passing away. These are "full understanding by investigation" and "full understanding by abandoning."

### *Ear sensitivity*

When one correctly understands the ear sensitivity (*sotapasāda*), one knows that it is sensitive or functional enough to detect a sound (characteristic); it brings a person or allows a person to hear a sound (function); it is the basis for hearing, the basis from which hearing results (manifestation); and its proximate cause is the kamma-generated solid ear. This is what "he understands the ear" (*sotañca pajānāti*) means in the *Satipaṭṭhāna Sutta*.[63]

### *Sound base*

When one correctly understands the sound base (*saddāyatana*), one knows that it becomes apparent in the ear (characteristic), it is heard (function), it is an object of hearing and experienced through hearing (manifestation), and it is based on the four primary material elements (proximate cause). This is what "he understands sounds" (*sadde ca pajānāti*) means in the *Satipaṭṭhāna Sutta*.

*Ear consciousness*

When one correctly understands ear consciousness (*sotaviññāṇa*), one knows that it arises in the ear or hears a sound (characteristic); it only takes sound as its object, or it is simply hearing (function); it is directed toward the sound (manifestation); and it is caused by paying attention, by the conjunction of the ear with sound, or by good or bad kamma (proximate cause).

## *The Case of Smell*

*Nose sensitivity*

When one correctly understands nose sensitivity (*ghānapasāda*), one knows that it is sensitive or functional enough to detect a smell (characteristic); it brings a person or allows a person to smell an odor (function); it is the basis for smelling, the basis from which smelling results (manifestation); and its proximate cause is the kamma-generated solid nose (proximate cause). This is what "he understands the nose" (*ghānañca pajānāti*) means in the *Satipaṭṭhāna Sutta*.

*Odor base*

When one correctly understands the odor base (*gandhāyatana*), one knows that it becomes apparent in the nose (characteristic), it is smelled (function), it is an object of smell and experienced through smelling (manifestation), and it is based on the four primary material elements (proximate cause). This is what "he understands odors" (*gandhe ca pajānāti*) means in the *Satipaṭṭhāna Sutta*.

*Nose consciousness*

When one correctly understands nose consciousness (*ghānaviññāṇa*), one knows that it arises in the nose or smells an odor (characteristic); it only takes odor as its object or it is simply smelling (function); it is directed toward the odor (manifestation); and it is caused by paying attention, by the conjunction of the nose with odor, or by good or bad kamma (proximate cause).

## *The Case of Taste*

When we consume food, we experience the quality of its flavor—sweet, sour, hot, bitter, salty, and so on. Thus when we eat something, we should note it as either "eating" or as "sweet," "sour," and so on, according to its flavor.

### *Tongue sensitivity*

When one correctly understands tongue sensitivity (*jivhāpasāda*), one knows that it is sensitive or functional enough to detect a flavor (characteristic); it brings a person or allows a person to taste a flavor (function); it is the basis for tasting, the basis from which tasting results (manifestation); and its proximate cause is the kamma-generated solid tongue. This is what "he understands the tongue" (*jivhañca pajānāti*) means in the *Satipaṭṭhāna Sutta*.

### *Flavor base*

When one correctly understands the flavor base (*rasāyatana*), one knows that it becomes apparent on the tongue (characteristic); it is tasted as something sweet, something sour, and so on (function); it is an object of taste, experienced through tasting (manifestation); and it is based on the four primary material elements (proximate cause). This is what "he understands flavors" (*rase ca pajānāti*) means in the *Satipaṭṭhāna Sutta*.

### *Tongue consciousness*

When one correctly understands tongue consciousness (*jivhāviññāṇa*), one knows that it arises on the tongue or tastes a flavor of sweetness, sourness, and so on (characteristic); it only takes flavor as its object, or it simply tastes (function); it is directed toward the flavor (manifestation);

and it is caused by paying attention, by the conjunction of the tongue with flavor, or by good or bad kamma (proximate cause).

Note that when we have a meal the sight of the food is seeing, the odor of the food is smelling, the touch of the food at our fingers, lips, tongue, throat, and so on is touching, as is moving the hands, opening and closing the mouth, chewing the food, and so on. Examining the food is considered thinking.

In this way, when noted as shown above in the case of seeing and such, we can understand all movements and activities in their true nature. Moreover, we can understand the mental constituents, such as contact, feeling, and so on, that are involved in moments of hearing, smelling, and tasting, in terms of their characteristics and such as well.

### *The Case of Touch*

We can experience touch throughout the whole body. The feet touch each other, the hands touch each other, and the hands touch the feet. The hands, feet, and hair touch the body, and the tongue touches the teeth and the palate. Mucus, saliva, food, and water touch the throat and the palate. Many organs and substances inside the body touch one another, such as food and internal air that touch the intestines. Blood, internal air, flesh, sinews, and bones touch one another. We are also always coming into physical contact with external things, such as our clothes, shoes, bed, pillow, blanket, the floor or ground, the wall, our umbrella or walking stick, stones and plants, the wind, sunlight, and water, tools and furniture, and so on. Animals and insects, such as mosquitoes and horseflies, touch us too. Aside from specific sensations, all touch must be noted as "touching" every time one notices it.

If the touching sensation is distinct as a pleasant or unpleasant feeling, then we should note it as it is. If it feels hot, note it as "hot, hot." If cold, note it as "cold, cold." If warm, note it as "warm, warm." If chilly, note it as "chilly, chilly." If lying down, note it as "lying, lying." If tired, note it as "tired, tired." If painful, note it as "pain, pain." If numb, note it as "numb, numb." If aching, note it as "aching, aching." If itchy, note it as "itchy, itchy." If stiff, note it as "stiff, stiff." If dizzy, note it as "dizzy, dizzy." If pleasant, note it as "pleasant, pleasant." In this way, we should note touch from moment to moment. Note the nature of these sensations of touch clearly, precisely, and accurately using everyday language and words that indicate ultimate realities.

*Body sensitivity*

When one correctly understands body sensitivity (*kāyapasāda*), one knows that it is sensitive or functional enough to detect physical sensation (characteristic); it brings a person or allows a person to touch a tangible object (function); it is the basis for touch, the basis from which touch results (manifestation); and its proximate cause is the kamma-generated solid body. This is what "he understands the body" (*kāyañca pajānāti*) means in the *Satipaṭṭhāna Sutta*.

*Tangible object base in general*

When one correctly understands the tangible object base (*photthabbāyatana*), one knows that it becomes apparent in the body (characteristic); it is felt as touching (function); and it is an object of touch, experienced through touch (manifestation).

*Tangible object base in particular: the primary material elements*

When one correctly understands the earth element, one knows that it is hard or rough, or soft or smooth (characteristic); it is the basis or foundation for all other physical matter (function); it receives or bears other physical matter (manifestation); and it is hard or soft because of the other three primary material elements—namely, it is hard due to solidity, cold, and pressure, and soft due to moisture, fluidity, and warmth (proximate cause).

Awareness of weight, whether heavy or light, is awareness of the earth element. However, pleasant and unpleasant physical sensations can be associated with any of the three elements of earth, fire, and air. The Abhidhamma commentary called *Aṭṭhasālinī* says:

> The earth element is defined by six qualities: hardness, softness, smoothness, roughness, heaviness, and lightness. On

> the other hand, the two qualities of pleasant and unpleasant (touch) are defined in terms of the three (discernable) primary material elements.[64]

When one correctly understands the fire element, one knows that it is hot, warm, or cold (characteristic); it matures or ripens matter (function); it softens matter (manifestation); and it is hot, warm, or cold because of the other three primary material elements (proximate cause).

When one correctly understands the air element, one knows that it is supporting, stiff, loose, or flabby (characteristic); it moves or shifts matter (function); it conveys to other places (manifestation); and it is stiff or loose because of the other three primary material elements (proximate cause). This is what "he understands tangibles" (*phoṭṭhabbe ca pajānāti*) means in the *Satipaṭṭhāna Sutta*.

### *Body consciousness*

When one correctly understands body consciousness (*kāyaviññāṇa*), one knows that it arises in the body or experiences touch (characteristic); it takes only touch as its object, or it is simply touch (function); it is directed toward the tangible (manifestation); and it is caused by paying attention, by the conjunction of the body with a tangible, or by good or bad kamma (proximate cause).

### *Physical pain*

When one correctly understands physical pain (*kāyikadukkha*), one knows that it is the feeling of an unpleasant tangible object (characteristic);[65] it withers or weakens its associated mental states (function);[66] it is painful or irritates the body (manifestation);[67] and it is painful because of body sensitivity, the fine fleshy tissue, or an unpleasant touch (proximate cause).[68]

*Physical pleasure*

When one correctly understands physical pleasure (*kāyikasukha*), one knows that it is the feeling of a pleasant tangible object (characteristic); it intensifies associated mental states (function); it is pleasant and enjoyable (manifestation); and it is pleasant because of body sensitivity, the fine fleshy tissue, or a pleasant touch (proximate cause).

## *Mindfulness of Breathing*

"Mindful he breathes in, mindful he breathes out."[69] According to this quote from the Pāḷi canon, every time we note the breath moving in and out as "in, out," we feel the touch of the air and are aware of the body consciousness. Thus awareness of the breath amounts to an awareness of touch. The observation of the in and out breath can serve as insight meditation.

If we observe the breath, we experience it as distension inside the nose. This is correct understanding of the characteristic of the air element, the characteristic of distension (*vitthambhanalakkhaṇā*). If we feel moving, movement, or motion, this is correct understanding of the function of the air element, the function of movement (*samudīraṇarasa*). And if we feel conveying, this is correct understanding of its manifestation, the manifestation of conveying (*abhinīhārapaccupaṭṭhāna*).

If we see the separate units of movement of the in and out breath as caused by the existence of the physical body, the nose, and the intention to breathe, this is correct understanding of the cause of its arising, referred to as:

> He abides contemplating in the body its nature of arising.[70]

If we see the separate units of movement of the breath disappear or that the breath cannot appear without the physical body, the nose, and the intention to breathe, this is correct understanding of the cause of its vanishing, referred to as:

> Or he abides contemplating in the body its nature of vanishing.[71]

When we note "in, out" with each breath, we do not take this process to be a person, a being, a woman, a man, me, or mine, but we see and understand it as a mere collection of movements that are felt. As it is said:

> Or else mindfulness that "there is a body" is simply established in him.[72]

The abdomen rises and falls as a result of the in and out breath. By noting this as "rising" and "falling," we are aware of tightening, loosening, or distending. This is correct understanding of the characteristic of the air element. If we are aware of movement and conveyance, this is correct understanding of the function and the manifestation of the air element. If we see that the rising and falling movements of the abdomen appear and disappear in separate units, this is correct understanding of arising and vanishing. In other words, we should perceive the actions and movements of our bodies in accord with the Pāḷi passage:

> He understands accordingly, however his body is disposed.[73]

In an ultimate sense the rise and fall of the abdomen characterized by tension, pressure, or movement is the air element. It is considered part of the physical aggregate (*rūpakkhandhā*), a tangible object (*phoṭṭhabba*), a tangible object element (*phoṭṭhabbadhātu*), and the truth of suffering (*dukkhasacca*). Thus the rise and fall of the abdomen is clearly an appropriate object of meditation for the development of insight.

Moreover, it is obvious from the last verse above that any bodily action or movement can be taken as an object for insight meditation. There is no way that this view can be considered incorrect. In fact, it is in accord with the Buddha's teaching and is highly beneficial in a variety of ways. By practicing insight meditation one acquires right view (*sammādiṭṭhi*) and true knowledge (*vijjā*), the defilements based on ignorance can be abandoned, and one can attain the end of unsatisfactoriness, that is, the fruit of arahantship (*arahattaphala*) and nibbāna.

I mention this point here not because the observation of the rise and fall of the abdomen is part of practice with the in and out breath (*ānāpāna*) but because the in and out breath itself produces the rise and fall of the abdomen. Actually, perception of the rise and fall of the abdomen constitutes contemplation of the body (*kāyānupassanā*), since it is both a physical movement and one of the elements. It can also be considered awareness of mental objects (*dhammānupassanā*), since it is included in the physical aggregate, the basis of the physical sense, and the truth of suffering.

## *The Four Primary Material Elements*

We can experience any one of forty-two parts of the body when sitting, standing, walking, or lying down. These include twenty parts that are dominated by the earth element,[74] twelve dominated by the water element,[75] four dominated by the fire element,[76] and six dominated by the air element.[77]

Each time a person touches one of these parts of the body, she notes it as "touching, touching," and so correctly understands that the earth element is experienced via the characteristics of hardness, softness, or smoothness (*kakkhaḷalakkhaṇā*); the fire element is experienced via the characteristics of heat, warmth, or cold (*uṇhattalakkhaṇā*); the air element is experienced via the characteristics of firmness, stiffness, or looseness (*vitthambhanalakkhaṇā*); and the air element is experienced via the function of movement, pushing, or pulling (*samudīraṇarasa*), and the manifestation of conveying (*abhinīhārapaccupaṭṭhāna*).

In reality we cannot directly experience the water element with the sense of touch. But given the power of this element, we can know its true nature with mind consciousness based on bodily sensations of the earth, fire, and air elements that arise in conjunction with the water element. Thus the water element is understood by noting touch. The water element is experienced via the characteristics of flowing or melting (*paggharaṇalakkhaṇā*). This type of sensation is especially noticeable when sweat, mucus, or tears flow, when spitting or swallowing phlegm or saliva, or when urinating. The function of the water element is experienced via expansion or dampening (*brūhanarasa*). We feel it mainly when we take a bath, have a drink, and so on. The manifestation of the water element is experienced via cohesion or holding together (*saṅgahapaccupaṭṭhāna*).

Thus every time we note a bodily sensation, we will be aware of the four primary material elements. We will understand that there is no person, being, woman, man, I, or mine, but only a collection of physical elements such as hardness, softness, heat, warmth, cold, tightness, looseness, movement, pulling, pushing, flowing, melting, wetness, expansion, and cohesion. This understanding is in accord with the following canonical passage:

> A bhikkhu reviews this same body, however it is placed, however disposed, by way of elements thus: "In this body there are the earth element, the water element, the fire element, and the air element."[78]

Note that awareness of the rise and fall of the abdomen is naturally in accord with this Pāḷi quote. Mindfulness of walking, bending, and other movements is also covered under this awareness of touch. However, the intention to walk, the intention to bend, and so on are an awareness of mind, so they will be explained in the upcoming sections on posture and clear comprehension.

### *How to Observe Thought*

I have previously explained that mental activities, such as thinking, considering, examining, reflecting, and so on, are referred to as mind-door processes. When one notes them as "thinking," "considering," "examining," "reflecting," and so on, one phenomenon, such as the mind door (*manodvāra*), mental object (*dhammārammaṇā*), mind consciousness (*manoviññāṇa*), mental contact, or feeling will be apparent in terms of its characteristic and so on. Thus one will see and understand one of these phenomena as it really is. This is full understanding of the known (*ñātapariññā*). One will also see and understand the characteristic of impermanence and so on, and will see and understand it as arising and passing away. These are full understanding by investigation (*tīraṇapariññā*) and full understanding by abandoning (*pahānapariññā*).

The commentaries and subcommentaries explain that "mind door" refers to both the life continuum and the mind unit that adverts to mental objects. Since the mind sensitivity of the heart is the basis for these, it is also figuratively called the mind door (*manodvāra*). Mental objects include the five sensitivities—the eye, ear, nose, tongue, and body sensitivities; the six kinds of subtle matter (*sukhumarūpa*)—the water element, femininity (*itthibhāvā*), masculinity (*pumbhāva*), the mind sensitivity of the heart (*hadaya*), vitality (*jīvita*), and nutrition (*āhāra*); and all mundane mental states, all mundane mental factors. These are all mental objects to be observed for the development of insight. Mind consciousness includes both wholesome and unwholesome thoughts, as well as registration (*tadārammaṇa*). The mental contact and feeling included here are those associated with mind consciousness.

### *The mind door*

When insight knowledge becomes extremely keen and pure, there are gaps between two consecutive notings. For example, when one bends the arm, each separate little movement of bending has to be noted as "bending, bending." When one is aware like this, gaps between the previous noting, the following intention, and the following bending movement become apparent. Over time it will seem as if fewer and fewer objects are noted or that there are gaps in one's noting. In fact, objects will not have become fewer and there are not gaps in one's noting. Instead, given the quickness of one's noting, the life continuum consciousness that falls between successive mental processes becomes apparent. Seeing the gap between two successive mental processes at that moment is called "understanding the life-continuum consciousness or the mind door."

Another mind door is the mind moment that adverts to an object. When one correctly understands adverting consciousness, one knows it as initial attention (characteristic), initial investigation (function), initial examination (manifestation), and the first moment of full consciousness following the life-continuum consciousness (proximate cause).

As mentioned before, the mind sensitivity of the heart is also metaphorically regarded as a mind door, since it serves as the basis for the mind. When one correctly understands the mind sensitivity of the heart, one knows that it is the basis of the thinking or noting mind (characteristic), it supports the existence of the thinking mind or noting mind (function), it receives or bears the thinking mind (manifestation), and it is caused by the four primary material elements (proximate cause). This is what "he understands the mind" (*manañca pajānāti*) means in the *Satipaṭṭhāna Sutta*.

*Mental objects*

Many varieties of mentality (*citta*) and mental constituents (*cetasika*) fall into the category of "mental objects." I have already explained awareness of certain mental objects, such as the five sensitivities of eye, ear, nose, tongue, and body, the water element, and the mind sensitivity of the heart. Certain other mental objects will be explained later, so I will not elaborate on them in detail here.

*Gender*

When one smiles or thinks with awareness of one's own gender, one experiences one's femininity or masculinity. When one correctly understands it, one knows that it has the nature of femininity or masculinity (characteristic); it shows femininity or masculinity (function); it manifests as the female or male structure of the body, its feminine or masculine features, the typical feminine or masculine occupations, and the typical feminine or masculine deportment (manifestation); and it is caused by the four primary material elements (proximate cause).

*Vitality*

A physical phenomenon called vitality (*jīvīta*) enlivens the five senses, the mind sensitivity of the heart, and gender. It becomes apparent along with these when one notes a sight, a sound, and so on, since it appears and disappears along with them. Before it disappears, it performs the function of enlivening the physical constituents, such as the eye sensitivity and so on. The process by which the eye sensitivity continuously generates new instances to replace old ones until one dies occurs because of and is sustained by vitality. When one correctly understands vitality, one knows that it maintains the physical constituents of the eye sensitivity and so on (characteristic), it makes the physical constituents of the eye sensitivity and so on occur (function), it supports the existence of the physical constituents of eye sensitivity and so on (manifestation), and it is caused by the four primary material elements (proximate cause).

*Nutrition*

When one feels physically strong and mentally alert after having eaten, nutrition becomes apparent. When one correctly understands nutrition, one knows that it has nutritive essence (*ojā*) (characteristic), it sustains the physical body (function), it strengthens the body (manifestation), and it is caused by food (proximate cause).

*Thinking consciousness*

When one correctly understands mind consciousness, one knows that it appears as thought, reflection, consideration, knowing, wandering, and so on (characteristic); it only takes mental objects as its object, or it is simply cognizing (function); it is directed toward mental objects (manifestation); and it is caused by attention or the combination of the mind sensitivity of the heart and mental objects (proximate cause).

*Mental contact*

When one correctly understands mental contact, one knows that it is mental contact between an object and the mind (characteristic); it strikes the object (function); it is the concurrence of the mind sensitivity of the heart, consciousness, and an object (manifestation); and it is caused by the appearance of an object (proximate cause).

*Feeling*

When one correctly understands the feeling of joy (*somanassavedanā*), one knows that it experiences a pleasant object or is delightful (characteristic), it partakes in pleasure (function), it is mental pleasure and enjoyment (manifestation), and it is caused by pleasant objects or mental peace and calm (proximate cause).

When one correctly understands the feeling of distress (*domanassavedanā*), one knows that it experiences an unpleasant object, is an unpleasant or frustrating mental activity, or is mental distress, sadness, sorrow, or worry (characteristic); it partakes in displeasure, dislike, or disgust with respect to an object (function); it is mental affliction, displeasure, or suffering (manifestation); and it is caused by the mind sensitivity of the heart and unpleasant objects (proximate cause).

When one correctly understands the feeling of neither displeasure nor pleasure (*upekkhāvedanā*), one knows that it is felt as neutral, neither unpleasant nor pleasant, neither happy nor unhappy (characteristic); it keeps the mind balanced between pleasure and pain (function); it is subtle or calm (manifestation); and it is caused by a consciousness without rapture or an object that is neither unpleasant nor pleasant (proximate cause).

### *Perception*

Perception, also called the aggregate of perception (*saññākkhandhā*), is the recognition, remembrance, and identification of an object so as not to forget it. It is especially obvious when one encounters a novel object or pays particular attention to someone or something. When one correctly understands perception, one knows that it perceives an object so as not to forget it (characteristic), it recognizes objects one has encountered previously (function), it is retained in one's memory the way it has been apprehended (manifestation), and it is caused by all apparent objects (proximate cause).

### *Mental formations*

The fifty mental factors other than feeling and perception are included in the aggregate of mental formations (*saṅkhārakkhandhā*). It includes all the mental phenomena that make things happen, such as seeing, hearing, and such, or going, standing, sitting, lying, bending, and such (see Appendix 3).

Among these fifty factors, I will only explain mental volition (*cetanā*) here, since it directs all the others. In this respect, mental volition is like a foreman who both performs his or her own duties while simultaneously directing coworkers in theirs. Another analogy is that volition is like a farmer who does his own work on the farm while also supervising workers. In the same way, volition makes the other mental constituents do their tasks as well. Volition is especially obvious when an urgent situation needs to be acted on very quickly and one feels as if one is urged and pushed to act.

When one correctly understands volition, one knows that it activates or stimulates the mental factors (characteristic); it acts, works, and accomplishes (function); it coordinates activities like a ruler who sentences someone to death or a donor who allows the goods he has offered to be taken away (manifestation); and it is caused by a wholesome or unwholesome attention or attitude (*manasikārapadaṭṭhānā*), ignorance of true happiness and suffering (*avijjāpadaṭṭhānā*), the sense bases and sense objects (*vatthārammaṇapadaṭṭhānā*), or consciousness (*viññāṇapadaṭṭhānā*) (proximate causes).

## *How to Note General Activities*

When walking, you should note each and every step as "walking, walking" or "stepping, stepping" or "right, left" or "lifting, moving, dropping." When your mindfulness and concentration grow strong, you will be able to note the intention to walk or the intention to move before starting to walk or move. At that point you will come to personally and thoroughly understand that the intention to walk occurs first, and that as a result of this intention, a sequence of movements happens, and that as these movements happen everywhere, all the physical phenomena that are called "body" move in separate little movements, arising and disappearing one after the other. This is called "walking." This is referred to in the following Pāḷi passage from the *Mahāsatipaṭṭhāna* and *Satipaṭṭhāna Suttas*:

> When walking, a bhikkhu understands "I am walking."[79]

And from the commentary to the Dīgha Nikāya:

> One understands that the intention to walk arises. This (intention) causes movement (i.e., the air element) to arise. This movement causes intimation to arise. Because these movements happen everywhere, all the physical phenomena that are called "body" move in separate little movements to the intended place. This is called "walking."[80]

This is not common knowledge. Those who have never practiced in this way or gained any knowledge may be dubious about the instruction: "When walking, a bhikkhu understands 'I am walking.'" I will explain this point here in accordance with the commentary.

One may wonder: "Doesn't even a dog or a fox understand it is walking when it is walking?" That is true. But the Buddha was not at all referring to this kind of common knowledge. Actually dogs, foxes, and ordinary people do not know their intention to walk or the movement that happens in separate little movements. They can't distinguish between mind and body and do not understand that the intention causes the movement to happen. They do not understand that there is only a sequence of successive intentions and successive movements that disappear and vanish one after the other. In fact, dogs, foxes, and ordinary people only know some of the time that they are walking, and this may be either in the beginning, the middle, or at the end of it; most of the time their minds wander elsewhere while they are walking.

Even when ordinary people occasionally know they are walking, they perceive it as an individual person who is walking, and they take that person to be unchanging. They think that they are the same person before, during, and after the walk. Even after walking a hundred miles, they think that they are certainly the same individual that they were before they left, even after having arrived at a different location. They think that they stay exactly the same as before. One cannot abandon the wrong view of a being, rid oneself of attachment to such a view, nor produce the insight knowledges with such an ordinary understanding. Making this kind of understanding the object of one's meditation or meditating based on such an understanding does not amount to practicing insight.

So this ordinary understanding is not meditation (*bhāvanākamma*). And since it is not a basis of insight meditation (*vipassanākamma*), this ordinary understanding cannot be called a basis or foundation for practice (*kammaṭṭhānā*). Since this understanding is not based on insight and mindfulness, it is not meditation on the foundations of mindfulness (*satipaṭṭhānabhāvanā*). One should understand that in the above passage, the Buddha did not intend the ordinary understanding that is common to dogs, foxes, and ordinary people.

However, if you note "intention" and "walking" whenever one walks, the intention that arises in the mind and the bodily movements that take place will be very distinct. Then you will not mix the mental process of intention with the body but will understand them as different processes. Likewise, you will not mix the bodily movements with the mind but will understand them as different processes. You will understand that the intention to walk causes the separate units of little movements to happen, and you will thereby understand that there are only separate units of intention and movement. Further, the intentions will not merge into the movements and the little separate movements will not merge into the next little movement but they will disappear one after the other. As the commentaries explain, you can see six or even more separate little movements in one pushing movement of the foot.

Based on this you will realize that saying "I am walking" or "he is walking" is purely conventional. There is in fact no individual person who walks; there is only the intention, followed by the movement of a collection of physical phenomena. No physical phenomenon lasts even for the twinkling of an eye. Everything is subject to impermanence, and because everything instantly arises and disappears, it is just a mass of unsatisfactoriness. You can judge it to be unsatisfactory based on personal experience. This understanding is called "clear comprehension without delusion" (*asammohasampajañña*), and it is one of the four kinds of clear comprehension. The understanding that arises from noting "intention" or "walking" belongs to clear comprehension of the domain (*gocarasampajañña*). The latter clear comprehension is the cause for the former. You should repeatedly cultivate and accomplish clear comprehension of the domain so that clear comprehension without delusion can spontaneously arise.

This is how one can abandon the view of a being and get rid of the attachment to that view by means of the insight knowledge developed by observing intention and bodily movements. In addition to becoming an object for counter-insight (*paṭivipassanā*), this causes insight knowledge to powerfully arise, so it is also called "a basis or foundation of practice." And since one's understanding is developed with mindfulness, it is called "meditation on the foundations of mindfulness." There is no doubt that the instruction "when walking, a bhikkhu understands, 'I am walking'" is the authentic word of the Buddha.

> This meditator's understanding helps him abandon the wrong view of a being and to eradicate the belief in self. Thus it is a basis or foundation (of practice) and also meditation on the foundations of mindfulness.[81]

According to this passage from the commentary, the phrases "the basis or foundation of practice" and "meditation on the foundations of mindfulness" are synonymous in an ultimate sense. But they are different in a technical sense. The mindfulness that penetrates objects such as the intention or the physical process of walking, for example, is called "a foundation of mindfulness" (*satipaṭṭhāna*). It is also called "meditation" (*bhāvanā*), since it must be developed. For these two reasons it is called "meditation on the foundations of mindfulness"—it is mindfulness that must be developed and that penetrates objects.

Insight knowledge is necessarily associated with mindfulness. There is no insight knowledge without mindfulness. In this regard, we should call it "meditation on the foundations of mindfulness" only when one's understanding is guided by mindfulness. This understanding is also called "the basis or foundation of practice," since it helps successive insight knowledges to powerfully arise, and "counter-insight," since it serves as a meditative object for the practice that follows. When the intention is noted, that very noting mind is noted in turn as "noting" or "perceiving." After that, one notes the resulting movement and then notes that noting mind. This is called "counter-insight meditation" (*paṭivipassanābhāvanā*).

In this way, beginning with the stage of insight knowledge of dissolution, insight grows stronger and stronger by taking the noting mind itself as an object to be noted. That is why the understanding that arises due to mindfulness of the mental and bodily processes involved in walking is called both "a basis or foundation for practice" and "meditation on the foundations of mindfulness."

## *Clear Comprehension*

### *In walking*

This Pāḷi instruction explains how clear comprehension without delusion (*asammohasampajañña*) arises:

> A bhikkhu is one who acts in full awareness when going forward and returning.[82]

The commentaries explain this as follows:

> Clear comprehension without delusion or clear comprehension of reality is the knowledge that there is no "I" or "self" behind activities. Understand it in the following way: ordinary people have deluded views about going forward and so on, such as "the self goes forward," "the self makes a forward movement," "I go forward," or "I make a movement." On the other hand, a bhikkhu (monk or meditator) who is going forward or backward understands that, when one intends to go forward, the intention and the movement it causes make movement to another place happen. As the movement instigated by the mind spreads everywhere, the collection of physical phenomena, the so-called body,[83] moves forward. While going forward, every time one lifts a foot, the earth and water elements become weak and ineffectual and the fire and air elements become strong and powerful. The same is true when pushing the foot down. When one releases momentum from pushing the foot forward, the fire and air elements become weak and ineffectual, and the

> earth and water elements become strong and powerful. This continues while dropping and pressing the foot.[84]

According to the subcommentary, lifting consists of dominant fire element followed by air element, moving forward and pushing consist of dominant air element followed by fire element, and releasing consists of dominant water element followed by earth element. Here we can say that the water element is heavier than the earth element, which is consistent with the *Aṭṭhasālinī*, a commentary on the Abhidhamma. Dropping and pressing consist of dominant earth element followed by water element. Thus when we are aware of lifting, the fire element is understood; when we are aware of moving forward and pushing, the air element is understood; when we are aware of releasing, the water element is understood; and when we are aware of dropping and pressing, the earth element is understood.

> While lifting, the mental and physical phenomena consisting of the intention to lift and the lifting movement do not carry over into the process of pushing. Likewise, the mental and physical phenomena happening while pushing do not carry over into the process of moving forward. Those happening while moving forward do not carry over into the process of releasing. Those happening while releasing do not carry over into the process of dropping. Those happening while dropping do not carry over into the process of pressing. They arise and disappear one after the other. Their distinct arising and disappearance are like sesame seeds bursting in a heated frying pan that make a sound like *pata-pata*. So who is going forward? Whose movement is it? In an ultimate sense, only selfless elements go forward, only elements stand, only elements sit down, only elements lie down. Thus along with the physical phenomena . . .
>
> > The preceding mind vanishes and the subsequent mind appears,[85] like the current of a river that ceaselessly flows forever.

> Thus is clear comprehension of reality when going forward and so on.[86]

Passages from the above commentary, such as "When one intends to go forward, the intention and the movement it causes make movement to another place happen" and "While lifting, the mental and physical phenomena consisting of the intention to lift and the lifting movement do not carry over into the process of pushing," are clearly not referring to the tranquility meditation of determining the four primary elements (*dhātuvavatthāna*) but to the practice of insight meditation. This is so because such understanding can only belong to insight meditators, not to tranquility meditators. The above passages from the commentary explain that when insight knowledge is strong, which is the clear comprehension of the domain, insight knowledge of clear comprehension of reality arises.

The word "element" here is opposite in meaning to "being" or "soul" (*jīva*). It refers to the mental and physical phenomena, the four primary material elements that are dominant during movement. Although all of the commentaries concerned with this instruction use the term "mass of bones" (*aṭṭhisaṅghāto*), it is unreasonable to conclude from this that the skeleton becomes apparent to an insight meditator. It is also unreasonable to conclude that a tranquility meditator who is contemplating the skeleton would gain insight knowledge of phenomena such as the intention to go forward and so on. So the correct phrase to use here would be "mass of physical phenomena" (*rūpasaṅghāto*) rather than "mass of bones." But even if one takes "mass of bones" to be the correct term, one must interpret it as an idiomatic reference to the repulsiveness of the body rather than as a literal reference to the physical skeleton.

Some teachers who use the tranquility method of meditating on particles instruct that one should observe the foot moving forward and so on by imagining it as particles of dust. But this is not correct, since the text instructs us to be aware of the air element that is dominant at the moment of moving the foot forward. When one is aware of this air element, one will experience it in terms of its ultimate characteristics of tension or pressure, its function of motion, or its manifestation as conveyance. If one understands any one of these aspects, one's awareness of the air element is accurate. Knowing the form of the foot to be particles is actually a concept, not an ultimate reality.

When you stand, sit, or lie down, note it as "standing," "sitting," or "lying down" in accordance with the Pāḷi texts.[87] When your mindfulness, concentration, and insight knowledge become powerful, you will be able to clearly understand the intention to stand and the air element that holds the standing posture by supporting it. This is also true for sitting. When you lie down, you will be able to clearly understand the intention to do so and the air and earth elements that manifest as the process of lying down. In this respect, there is a difference between a meditator's understanding and that of ordinary people. As the *Vibhaṅga-aṭṭhakathā* says:

> One bhikkhu walks with a wandering mind, thinking of something else, while another walks without abandoning the subject of meditation. The same is true of standing, sitting, or lying down. One bhikkhu does so with a wandering mind, while another does so without abandoning the subject of meditation.[88]

So in keeping with the Pāḷi line "a bhikkhu is one who acts in full awareness when going forward and returning," you should be aware of going forward, backward, or sideways or of bending or curling up when you do these things. When your practice becomes powerful, you will also become aware of the intention and the air element involved in moving forward, backward, or sideways, and so on.

*In seeing*

> ... who acts in full awareness when looking ahead and looking away.[89]

According to this line of Pāḷi, one should be mindful when one looks ahead, to the side, down, up, or back. When one looks one should note it as "looking." Thus one maintains one's awareness and does not abandon the subject of insight meditation. This is clear comprehension of the domain (*gocarasampajañña*).

> Not abandoning the subject of meditation is clear comprehension of the domain. It means understanding the domain of the object. When meditating on (the phenomena of the) aggregates, elements, or sense bases, one should do the looking ahead or sideways only in accordance with one's insight practice. However, when contemplating kasiṇa objects and so on, one should give first priority to one's tranquility meditation practice when looking ahead or sideways.[90]

So if a meditator practicing tranquility meditation wants to look at something or someone, he should do so without abandoning the subject of his meditation, like a cow that gives first priority to protecting her calf, even while she is eating. For an insight meditator, however, any object can serve as an object of insight meditation. So by noting the intention to look, insight knowledge of the four mental aggregates, two mental sense bases, and two mental elements can arise. Then by noting the movements caused by intention, such as opening the eyes, moving the eyes, or turning the head, insight knowledge of the physical aggregate, the physical sense bases, and the physical elements can arise. By noting the seeing consciousness, insight knowledge of the five aggregates, four sense bases, and four elements can arise. If thinking arises, similar insight knowledge can arise by noting this thinking.

Thus the objects of insight meditation are none other than the intention to look and so on. For this reason it is said that one should deal with the act of seeing in accordance with one's foundation of practice. A meditator practicing tranquility meditation does not need to deal with the act of seeing in a special way; he just changes the focus of his meditation object to seeing for a moment. The insight meditator, however, has to note whatever mental or physical phenomena are arising. By noting in this way, the intention to look and the air element (that manifests as movements of the eyes or head) will be clearly understood when one's insight knowledge becomes strong.

*In bending and stretching*

> . . . who acts in full awareness when flexing and extending his limbs.[91]

According to this Pāḷi passage, when one stretches, one should note it as "stretching." When shaking one's hands, when pushing and pulling, or when lifting, raising, and putting down, one notes them as "shaking," "pushing," "pulling," "lifting," "raising," or "putting down." When one's insight knowledge becomes strong one will clearly understand the intention to bend or to stretch and the air element that manifests in the bending or stretching movement. The commentary on the Mūlapaṇṇāsa of the Majjhima Nikāya relates the following story of an elderly monk to explain the clear comprehension of the domain:

> Once, an elderly bhikkhu who was speaking with his pupils bent his arm abruptly. He then returned his arm to its original position and bent it again slowly. His students asked the reason for this peculiar behavior, and he explained, "Since I began meditating, I've never bent my arm without mindfulness. But as I was speaking with you now, I forgot to do it mindfully. That's why I put my arm back and bent it again mindfully." His pupils were filled with admiration for his great mindfulness and said: "Well done, sir! You are a true bhikkhu!"

If, like this elderly monk, one bends and stretches one's limbs without abandoning the meditation subject by noting it as "bending" or "stretching," one understands the intentions and the movements of bending or stretching as separate little movements that happen one after the other. This is clear comprehension of the domain. When this comprehension becomes sharp, the understanding arises that it is not a self within this body that makes it bend or stretch, but it is the intention that causes tiny little separate movements to arise. Moreover, one sees that the intention to bend disappears before the actual bending movement takes place and that the bending movements also appear and disappear one after the other. Thus one understands that all phenomena are impermanent, unsatisfactory, and not-self. This is clear comprehension of reality.

You may wonder: "When noting 'bending' or 'stretching,' am I not simply seeing the conceptual name and form of my limb being bent and stretched?" In the beginning you will happen to note the conceptual names and forms of objects, but you will also see the movement as a manifestation of the air element. So at first your understanding will be mixed with concepts. However, when your mindfulness, concentration, and insight knowledge grow powerful and strong, you will no longer focus on concepts. Since you will only see the intentions and movements appearing and disappearing one after the other, clear insight knowledge can arise. I have explained this at the beginning of this chapter.

*In carrying or wearing*

> . . . who acts in full awareness when wearing his robes and carrying his outer robe and bowl.[92]

When one wears robes one notes it as "wearing." When one uses the alms bowl, cup, plate, or spoon, one notes it as "touching," "holding," "lifting," "putting down," and so on as appropriate. When one's insight knowledge becomes strong, mainly intentions and their resulting movements (that manifests as the air element), as well as the sensations and body consciousness, will become obvious.

*In eating, drinking*

> . . . who acts in full awareness when eating, drinking, consuming food, and tasting.[93]

When one eats, drinks, chews, licks, or swallows, one notes it as "eating," "drinking," "chewing," "licking," and "swallowing." When one's insight knowledge becomes strong, mainly the intention to eat and the resulting movement of eating (that manifests as the air element), as well as the sensation and tongue consciousness, will become obvious.

Some suggest that one should meditate on eating by contemplating the repulsiveness or foulness of food in accordance with the commentary that explains how to develop clear comprehension of reality. But that is actually a tranquility meditation—namely, contemplating ten aspects of the foulness of food, such as the trouble involved in obtaining it, the process of consuming it, and the foulness of it in the stomach when mixed with bile, phlegm, blood, and so on.

On the other hand, when one's clear comprehension of the domain matures through the practice of noting eating, chewing, swallowing, savoring, and so on every time one eats, one will also understand the repulsiveness of food. For some meditators the repulsiveness and foulness of food becomes apparent as they note while preparing or eating food. Such meditators grow very disgusted, stop eating, and remain seated there and note even though they have not yet eaten enough. This kind of experience is quite common among meditators even nowadays. Some meditators have this kind of experience while eating even when their practice has not yet matured. If, in such cases, one feels extremely disgusted by one's food, as if it were human waste, it isn't actually clear comprehension but merely aversion. The commentary presumably mentions comprehension of the foulness of food in connection with clear comprehension of reality because it often arises spontaneously when one's clear comprehension of the domain matures.

*In defecating and urinating*

> . . . who acts in full awareness when defecating and urinating.[94]

When one defecates or urinates, one notes it as "defecating" and so on. No object is regarded as good or bad in insight meditation. One must simply be aware of every phenomenon as it is. When one's insight knowledge becomes strong, primarily the intention to defecate or urinate and the resulting movements (that manifest as the air element), as well as the unpleasant sensations and body consciousness and so on, will become obvious.

*In walking, standing, sitting, falling asleep, waking, speaking, and keeping silent*

> . . . who acts in full awareness when walking, standing, sitting, falling asleep, waking up, talking, and keeping silent.[95]

The method of comprehension for walking, standing, and sitting has already been explained above. Regarding awareness of falling asleep, when one feels sleepy, one notes it as "sleepy," "nodding," "drowsy," "heavy," and so on. When one feels very sleepy, one lies down and while lying notes "lying, lying," and all other distinct mental and physical phenomena. When one wakes one tries to note that very mental state.

This can be difficult for the beginner. If you cannot note it yet, you should start noting the moment you remember to be mindful. Eventually, when your mindfulness strengthens, you will be able to catch the moment of waking. Then you will understand that the mental and physical phenomena that occur just prior to falling asleep do not carry over into sleep. The arising of those kinds of consciousness that cannot (consciously) think, note, see, hear, touch, and so on is called sleep. Likewise, the phenomena that occur during sleep do not carry over into waking. Here "waking" indicates the reemergence of fully conscious activities, such as thinking, noting, and so on. There is no self or "I" that falls asleep or wakes up. You will understand that there are no permanent or pleasing phenomena. This understanding is called clear comprehension of reality.

When one speaks, one notes "wanting to speak," and "speaking." It is quite difficult to note speaking thoroughly, so it's better not to speak unless it's really necessary. When one's mindfulness becomes strong, mainly the intention to speak and the resulting movements (that manifest as the air element), as well as the sensations of touch (that manifest as the earth element) will become obvious. When one stops speaking, note it as "wanting to stop," "stopping," and "being quiet," and then continue noting other obvious objects. When one's mindfulness becomes powerful, one understands that the phenomena in a moment of speech are gone the moment one is quiet and that the intention to stop speaking and the physical phenomena of not talking anymore vanish at that very moment. This understanding is clear comprehension of reality.

*Internal and external phenomena*

When clear comprehension of the domain becomes strong and grows keen, one understands that in going there is only the intention and a collection of physical phenomena that are moving in separate little movements one after the other. There is no self that goes. "I go" is actually a concept that people use out of convenience, just as people address strangers as "nephew," "grandchild," "auntie," or "grandfather" in order to be polite.[96]

When clear comprehension of reality arises, one understands that phrases like "he goes," "a woman goes," or "a man goes" are merely conventional expressions and that there is no being or self that goes. One comes to see that existence is the same for others as it is for oneself, in that it consists only of the intention to go and separate segments of bodily movements. This understanding is consistent with the Pāḷi passage:

> He abides contemplating the body as a body . . . externally.[97]

There is no need to observe phenomena in the continua of others by distinguishing them as separate continua. It sometimes happens that by noting "intention" and "going" in one's own continuum, clear comprehension of reality arises and one observes that the same is true in the continuum of another. So one alternates between observing internal and external phenomena. This accords with:

> He abides contemplating the body as a body . . . both internally and externally.[98]

*Appearance and disappearance*

Both the intention to go and its resulting physical movement appear and disappear instantly. This is understanding appearance and disappearance. While one notes one understands: These physical phenomena arise due to a cause; they could not arise if there were no cause. These physical phenomena arise due to the mind; they could not arise if there were no mind. These physical phenomena arise due to previous kamma;

they could not arise if there were no kamma. These physical phenomena arise due to ignorance; they could not arise if there were no ignorance. These physical phenomena arise due to attachment; they could not arise if there were no attachment. These physical phenomena arise due to nutrition; they could not arise if there were no nutrition. Thus one understands the appearance and disappearance of phenomena on the basis of what one sees and observes oneself and what one has learned. This accords with:

> He abides contemplating in the body its nature of both arising and vanishing.[99]

### *Accurate Awareness*

With each noting of "intention" and "going" one is aware that what exists is only physical phenomena that are moving, and not a being, person, self, woman, or man. It means that what appears to one's awareness is the uninterrupted and continuous occurrence of intentions and movements without the concept of a solid form or shape. When awareness begins to become very keen and sharp, some meditators examine and reflect on whether or not they still have a body, head, arms, or legs. Their awareness and insight knowledge progress step by step and grow increasingly keen and sharp owing to their accurate awareness. Each noting is free from attachment. This accords with:

> He understands accordingly however his body is disposed.[100]
> Thus is contemplation of the body (*kāyānupassanā*).

## Contemplation of Feeling

### *Pleasant Feeling*

> When feeling a pleasant feeling, a bhikkhu understands: "I feel a pleasant feeling."[101]

According to this passage from the *Satipaṭṭhāna Sutta*, pleasant bodily or mental feelings (*sukhavedanā*) should be noted as "pleasant," "comfortable," "good," or "happy." Then one will understand pleasant feeling as it is. I have fully explained how this understanding arises in the sections on how to note while seeing, touching, or thinking. The commentary on the Mūlapaṇṇāsa of the Majjhima Nikāya dispels skeptical doubt on this point for those who lack any distinctive insight knowledge. I will present the following explanation based on this commentary.

You may wonder: "Even a baby suckling its mother's milk understands the pleasantness of it, doesn't it?" This is true, but the Buddha is not referring to that kind of understanding at all. Like babies, ordinary people are usually not aware of their pleasant feelings. Most of the time their minds wander off and they are unaware of the feeling they are experiencing. Even when they do occasionally become aware of it, they know it on the basis of the "I" that feels pleasure. Not seeing its momentary nature, they take it to be something permanent and lasting. They cannot abandon the view in a being or self based on this kind of understanding. Consequently, when they focus on an object with this kind of understanding, insight knowledge does not arise. Thus this understanding is not an object of insight meditation and is therefore not called "a basis or foundation of practice." Since it is not an understanding based on mindfulness, it also does not give rise to the meditation on the foundations of mindfulness. So you should understand that the Buddha was not referring to the kind of understanding that babies and ordinary people have.

A meditator who uninterruptedly observes is aware of a pleasant feeling every time it arises, and so understands it as just another phenomenon in terms of its characteristics and so on. The meditator also sees that successive moments of pleasantness do not continue but rather disappear one after the other. Seeing things in this way, the concept of "continuity" cannot continue to conceal the fact that feelings are impermanent, unsatisfactory, and not-self. With this kind of understanding, one can abandon the view of a being or self. As I explained earlier, this is called "a basis or foundation of practice" and amounts to "meditation on the foundations of mindfulness." It was only with reference to this kind of understanding that the Buddha said, "When feeling a pleasant feeling, a bhikkhu understands: 'I feel a pleasant feeling.'"

When one's mindfulness becomes strong, one understands from one's own experience that expressions such as "I'm comfortable" and "I'm happy" are just conventional expressions. There is not really any "I" or "being" who feels comfortable or happy. All that exists are momentary mental states of comfort or happiness. That is why the commentary says:

> A person who, by focusing on an object that causes pleasure to arise, observes feeling only as feeling is one who knows that he is observing a pleasant feeling.[102]

## *Unpleasant Feeling*

Unpleasant physical feelings (*dukkhavedanā*), such as cramps, stiffness, aching, dizziness, heat, cold, numbness, pain, itchiness, and tiredness, are all classified as physical pain (*kāyikadukkha*). One should note them precisely and accurately as "cramp, cramp" and so on. Unpleasant mental experiences, such as sadness, frustration, worry, and fear, are classified as mental pain (*cetasikadukkha*) or distress (*domanassa*). These feelings should be noted by using ordinary language such as "sad, sad," "frustration, frustration," and so on. I have fully explained the way it is experienced and understood in the sections on how to note while seeing, touching, or thinking.

Some people think that one can only understand ultimate reality when using technical Pāḷi terms such as *rūpa, nāma, pathavī, āpo, phassa, vedanā, sukha, somanassa,* and so on. This is wrong. What matters most is to perceive the arising and passing away of mind and body as it really is. Technical terminology is not important. Pāḷi terms can be useful for Pāḷi scholars but not for other people. For the Burmese, the Burmese terms will serve their purposes best. English-speaking people should use English words.

If a Burmese person accurately notes pain as *narde* in Burmese, for example, he is bound to become aware of its true characteristic. What does it matter if one doesn't know the Pāḷi term for it? Will the insight knowledge one has gained be lost thereby? Not at all. Would knowledge of the correct Pāḷi term help improve one's insight knowledge? That is not possible. When a meditator's insight knowledge matures, he will be aware of the instantaneous arising and passing away of mental and physical processes such that there will not even be time to note by labeling or naming. At that point, one's insight knowledge improves; it does not decline. It is completely incorrect to think that one will understand ultimate reality only when one notes an object using a Pāḷi term.

### *Neither-Unpleasant-nor-Pleasant Feeling*

It is quite difficult to clearly experience neutral feelings (*upekkhāvedanā*), as they are neither unpleasant nor pleasant. The commentaries on the *Cūḷavedalla Sutta*[103] and the *Saṅgīti Sutta*[104] compare neither-unpleasant-nor-pleasant feeling (*adukkhamasukhavedanā*) to ignorance, since it too is too subtle to be noticed. And the commentary to the *Bahudhātuka Sutta*[105] also says that neutral sensation is like ignorance because it is not distinct. Both neither-unpleasant-nor-pleasant feeling and ignorance seem to be clear and easy to perceive with scriptural knowledge but not with empirical knowledge.

It is not as easy to notice ignorance as it is to notice attachment and aversion. In the same way, neither-unpleasant-nor-pleasant feelings are not as obvious as pleasant and unpleasant ones. We say that neither-unpleasant-nor-pleasant feeling and ignorance are difficult to understand and not distinct only in reference to how difficult it is to experience them empirically. With reference to these points, the commentaries on the *Sakkapañha Sutta*[106] and the *Satipaṭṭhāna Sutta*[107] say:

> Neither-unpleasant-nor-pleasant feeling is barely obvious, like an object in the dark. However, when both pleasant and unpleasant feelings are absent one can find the feeling to be neither. Thus one can inferentially know it as the opposite of those pleasant and unpleasant feelings.[108]
>
> "Barely obvious" here means that it is difficult to clearly see (neither-unpleasant-nor-pleasant feeling) with empirical knowledge. That is why the commentary says, "like an object in the dark."[109]

Although neither-unpleasant-nor-pleasant feeling is quite subtle, it can be an obvious contrast to pleasant and unpleasant feelings the moment they disappear. This type of realization is called "inferring a deer's footprint" (*migapadavalañjananaya*). The term comes from the example of inferring that a deer has stepped on a flat rock even though its footprint cannot be found there, because one sees its footprints on either side of the rock. Even though the deer's footprints cannot be found on the rock itself, we can draw the conclusion that the deer did indeed pass over it.

In the same way, as a meditator clearly experiences an unpleasant feeling and notes it as "pain, pain" and so on, the painful feeling may fade away. At that point, the unpleasant feeling is no longer apparent, but neither is a pleasant feeling yet apparent. But there will be another distinct object that the meditator continues to note. After a few minutes, a pleasant or unpleasant feeling may occur again, and the meditator will note it. Then the meditator will perceive that a neither-unpleasant-nor-pleasant feeling occurred during the interval between the preceding and succeeding feelings of pain or pleasure.

From experiences like this, one realizes that the neither-unpleasant-nor-pleasant feeling is very difficult to perceive in an obvious way. Since no mental phenomenon occurs without feeling, one can conclude that there must be neither-unpleasant-nor-pleasant feeling present when pleasant and unpleasant feelings are not apparent. This conclusion is reached via the method of "inferring a deer's footprint." Although neither-unpleasant-nor-pleasant feeling will not be obvious to beginning meditators, more sharp-minded or mature meditators can experience it empirically. I showed how it can be experienced and understood when I discussed how a meditator notes seeing or thinking.

### *Worldly Pleasure*

The happiness associated with external things that one loves or is fond of—one's spouse, children, clothing, property, estate, animals, gold, silver, and so on—or with internal things that one loves—one's eyesight, comfort, talents, skills, and so on—is called "worldly pleasure" (*sāmisasukha*). The Pāḷi term literally means "happiness that feeds on sensual pleasure," that is, happiness associated with sensual objects. It is also called "home happiness" (*gehasitasomanassa*), that is, happiness that dwells in the home of sensual satisfaction.

When one enjoys the beauty or sweet voice of one's spouse, for example, that visual object or sound arouses happiness. Or one may feel happy when thinking about a good time one had in the past. One should note all of these kinds of happiness as "happy, happy," according to the instruction:

> When feeling a pleasant feeling associated with a sensual object, one understands "I feel a pleasant feeling associated with a sensual object."[110]

### Unworldly Pleasure

A meditator whose awareness is constant and uninterrupted and whose insight knowledge is mature experiences the arising and passing away of the six sense objects arising at the six sense doors, and so understands their impermanent nature. Equating or relating this present object to other present objects or objects of the past, she comes to understand that they are impermanent, unsatisfactory, and changing all the time. This realization arouses a type of happiness called "unworldly pleasure" (*nirāmisasukha*)—happiness not associated with sensual objects. It is also called "happiness associated with renunciation" (*nekkhammassitasomanassa*). Regarding this kind of happiness, the Buddha says in the *Saḷāyatanavibhaṅga Sutta*:

> When, by knowing the impermanence, change, fading away, and cessation of forms, one sees as it actually is with proper wisdom that forms both in the past and now are all impermanent, suffering, and subject to change, joy arises. Such joy as this is called joy based on renunciation.[111]

The Buddha then repeats this same statement for all the other sense objects. Such happiness may grow so strong at the early stage of insight knowledge of arising and passing away that you cannot restrain it. In that case, simply be aware of it as it is by noting it as "happy, happy," in accord with this Pāḷi passage:

> When feeling an unworldly pleasant feeling, he understands "I feel an unworldly pleasant feeling."[112]

## *Worldly Displeasure*

When we do not get the desirable object we want, we feel disappointed and frustrated and think that we are unfortunate. Sometimes we may suffer distress when we think of our lack of sensual pleasures in the present or in the past. Such distress, sadness, frustration, worry, and so on is called "worldly displeasure" (*sāmisadukkha*)—unsatisfactoriness associated with sensual objects. It is also called "home distress" (*gehasitadomanassa*)—that is, the distress that dwells in the home of sensual dissatisfaction. Every time this sadness occurs, note it as "sadness," as this Pāḷi passage says:

> When feeling a worldly painful feeling, he understands "I feel a worldly painful feeling."[113]

## *Unworldly Displeasure*

When a meditator has reached the insight knowledges beginning with the knowledge of arising and passing away, and has spent quite a long time meditating, he may long to become a noble person (*ariya*) endowed with path knowledge (*maggañāṇa*) and fruition knowledge (*phalañāṇa*). But the meditator may feel disheartened, having not achieved what he wanted to achieve and thinking that he will be unable to attain path knowledge and fruition knowledge in this life. This distress is called "unworldly displeasure" (*nirāmisadukkha*)—unsatisfactoriness not associated with sensual objects, or "distress associated with renunciation" (*nekkhammassitadomanassa*). Every time this kind of distress or dissatisfaction arises, note it as it is, according to this Pāḷi passage:

When feeling an unworldly painful feeling, he understands "I feel an unworldly painful feeling."[114]

Regarding unworldly displeasure, the commentary illustrates it with the story of the erudite monk Mahāsīva. I will relate the story here briefly.

*The Story of Mahāsīva*

Venerable Mahāsīva was a great teacher who taught the Buddhist scriptures to eighteen Buddhist sects. It is said that under his guidance as many as thirty thousand monks were enlightened by attaining the path knowledge and fruition knowledge of arahantship.

One of these reflected on his spiritual achievement and found that it had innumerable virtues. He then investigated his teacher's virtues, using his psychic powers, thinking that they would be much superior. However, to his surprise, he found that his teacher was still an ordinary, unenlightened person. Then and there he flew to his great teacher by means of his psychic powers. His purpose was to remind his teacher that although the teacher was a refuge for many, he was not a refuge for himself.

He came down near his teacher's monastery and approached him. When asked the purpose of his visit, he said that he had come to hear a sermon from the teacher. However, the great teacher replied that he had no time to teach him just then.

He then asked the great teacher if he would teach him while he was waiting to go for alms food in the entranceway of the monastery. Again the teacher refused, saying that he would be busy with some other monks who were studying with him. The monk then asked if he could be taught while the great teacher was on his way to the village for alms. The great teacher again gave the same response.

The monk humbly continued to ask if he could be taught while the great teacher was adjusting his robes, taking his alms bowl out of the bag, or having rice gruel. Each time he received the same response. He asked if he could be taught while the teacher was on his way back from the village, after his lunch, during the afternoon rest, while preparing for bed, while getting up from bed, before washing his face, or while sitting in his room. On each of these occasions the teacher said that he would be busy.

The monk then made a pointed comment about his teacher's lifestyle, saying: "Venerable sir, you should take the time to practice meditation in the morning after having washed your face, when you go into your room to warm up your body. At the moment, you do not even seem to have time to die! Like a chair, you have been supporting others but not yourself. I give up my hope of hearing a sermon from you." So saying, he flew off into the sky.

The great teacher then realized that the monk had come not to learn anything from him but to remind him of what he should do. Early in the morning the next day the teacher left the monastery to practice, taking his alms bowl and robes with him. He did not inform any of his disciples about his journey, thinking: "For a person like me, it will not be difficult to attain the fruit of arahantship (*arahattaphala*). It will probably take two or three days to become fully enlightened."

The great teacher began practicing in a valley near a village two days before the full-moon day in July. However, he did not succeed in realizing enlightenment on the full-moon day as he had expected. Still he continued to practice, thinking: "I believed it would take two or three days to attain the fruit of arahantship, but it did not. So be it. I will continue to practice during the three months of the annual rains retreat (*vassa*). After the annual rains retreat, I will show them who I am."

By the end of the annual rains retreat, however, he had still not attained any path knowledge and felt ashamed, thinking: "I intended to reach the goal in two or three days, but even after three months I have not achieved anything. My fellow monks may conduct *pavāraṇā*[115] as arahants, but not I." As he considered this, tears rolled down his cheeks.

From then on, he put his bed away and spent all his time practicing intensively, using the three postures of sitting,

> walking, and standing. He did not lie down at all, thinking that it was a waste of time to lie down. Even so, after twenty-nine years he still had not attained enlightenment. On every *pavāraṇā* day for twenty-nine years, tears rolled down his cheeks. On the thirtieth *pavāraṇā* day, he again found himself without any experience of path knowledge and fruition knowledge, and again wept over his failure to gain enlightenment, regretting that he could not yet join his fellow monks as an arahant at the *pavāraṇā* ceremony. However, this time he also heard someone else crying nearby and called out to know who it was.
>
> "It is I," answered a celestial being, "a deva, venerable sir."
>
> "Why are you crying here?" asked the monk.
>
> "Because I hope, sir," replied the deva, "to attain two or three stages of path knowledge and fruition knowledge just by crying."
>
> Feeling humiliated, the great monk admonished himself, "Even devas are laughing at me! This is not the way to behave." He then set aside his regret, calmed his mind, and developed insight knowledge, stage by stage, until finally attaining enlightenment, the fruit of arahantship.

Venerable Mahāsīva presumably took so long to complete his practice because he practiced insight by contemplating phenomena on a large scale, the same reason it took Venerable Sāriputta longer to attain arahantship than it did Venerable Moggallāna. The subcommentary says that it took that long for his insight to mature. This must refer to the development of insight knowledge over a wider range of phenomena than what is strictly necessary for the attainment of arahantship.

Venerable Mahāsīva was so learned that he had memorized the entirety of the canonical texts, so it is reasonable to conclude that his noble deeds (*pāramīs*) and insight knowledge were more than sufficient to realize arahantship on a small scale, as was the case with the hermit Sumedha, the Buddha-to-be, whose noble deeds and insight knowledge were sufficient to have become an enlightened disciple under Dīpaṅkarā Buddha.

### *Worldly Neither Displeasure nor Pleasure*

Ordinary, spiritually blind people (*andhaputhujjana*) often feel neither happy nor unhappy when they encounter a sensual object that is neither unpleasant nor pleasant. However, they are not aware of this, cannot give up the object, and relate to it with attachment. This kind of feeling is called "worldly neither displeasure nor pleasure" (*sāmisa-adukkhamasukha*), "home equanimity" (*gehasita-upekkhā*), or "equanimity associated with delusion" (*aññāṇupekkhā*). Insight practitioners often experience it, but it is difficult to notice since it is not distinct. When you notice it, note it according to the following Pāḷi passage:

> When feeling a worldly neither-painful-nor-pleasant feeling, he understands "I feel a worldly neither-painful-nor-pleasant feeling."[116]

### *Unworldly Neither Displeasure nor Pleasure*

When one's insight meditation practice is purified from the corruptions of insight, any of the six sense objects that arise will become very distinct and neither-unpleasant-nor-pleasant feeling becomes very distinct in the face of penetrating insight knowledge. At the stage of insight knowledge of equanimity toward formations, it becomes even more distinct. This neither-unpleasant-nor-pleasant feeling is called "unworldly neither displeasure nor pleasure" (*nirāmisa-adukkhamasukha*). It is also called "neutral feeling associated with renunciation" (*nekkhammassita-upekkhā*). Note it accordingly, based on the following:

> When feeling an unworldly neither-painful-nor-pleasant feeling, he understands "I feel an unworldly neither-painful-nor-pleasant feeling."[117]

### *Realizing Feelings*

The method for contemplating feelings is the same as the method for contemplating external and internal phenomena previously explained in the section on contemplation of the body.

When one notes feelings, one sees that they instantaneously arise and pass away. This is realization of the arising and passing away of feelings. One also realizes that one feels happy, unhappy, or neutral owing to pleasant, unpleasant, or neither-unpleasant-nor-pleasant objects, respectively, and that one does not have those feelings in the absence of such objects. One further realizes that a feeling arises owing to a previous action, ignorance, and attachment, and that in the absence of a previous action, ignorance, and attachment no feeling arises. Therefore, one realizes the causes of arising, disappearance, and nonarising of feelings as described by the Pāḷi passage:

> He abides contemplating in feelings their nature of both arising and vanishing.[118]

Every time one notes a feeling accurately, one realizes that there is no person or being, no "I" or "mine," and no woman or man that feels, but simply a feeling that is pleasant, unpleasant, or neither unpleasant nor pleasant. In other words, one is able to perceive the feeling independent of any conceptual forms or shapes—that is, free from conditioned solid images. In this way, one's mindfulness and insight knowledge improve and attachment weakens, as stated in the Pāḷi passage:

> Mindfulness that "there is feeling" is simply established in him.[119]

This is the contemplation of feelings (*vedanānupassanā*).

## Contemplation of Mind

### *Mental States*

Craving, lust, and desire are called "mind affected by lust" (*sarāgacitta*). When this state of mind occurs, note it as "desire, desire." It may disappear when you note it just once or twice. If it persists, continue to note it repeatedly until it finally fades away. When the mind is free from wanting and liking, it becomes pure and clear, a mind unaffected by lust (*vītarāgacitta*). You should note this state of mind as it is, as described in the Pāḷi passage:

> Here a bhikkhu understands mind affected by lust as mind affected by lust, and mind unaffected by lust as mind unaffected by lust.[120]

Anger, frustration, hate, hostility, and cruelty are called "mind affected by hate" (*sadosacitta*). When one of these occurs, note it as "angry" and so on. It may disappear when you note it just once or twice. If it continues, note it repeatedly until it disappears. Eventually it will vanish completely and then the mind becomes pure and clear, a mind unaffected by hate (*vītadosacitta*). You should also note this state of mind as it is, according to the Pāḷi passage:

> He understands mind affected by hate as mind affected by hate, and mind unaffected by hate as mind unaffected by hate.[121]

The mind that is simply confused or restless, in the grip of ignorance or delusion, is called "mind affected by delusion" (*samohacitta*). Sensual thoughts, hypocrisy, and delusions of identity are considered states of mind rooted in desire and affected by delusion (*lobhamūla samohacitta*). Unpleasant states of mind, such as fear, worry, grief, sadness, aversion, jealousy, and regret, are all states of mind rooted in hate and affected by delusion (*dosamūla samohacitta*). When any of these states of mind occur, note them as they really are. When these states of mind have come to an end, the mind becomes pure and clear, a mind unaffected by delusion (*vītamohacitta*). You should also note as it is, according to the Pāḷi passage:

> He understands mind affected by delusion as mind affected by delusion, and mind unaffected by delusion as mind unaffected by delusion.[122]

When experiencing any of these other states of mind, a meditator should also note them accordingly: an indolent state of mind (*saṃkhittacitta*); a distracted state of mind (*vikkhittacitta*); a concentrated state of mind (*samāhitacitta*); an unconcentrated state of mind (*asamāhitacitta*); a liberated state of mind, when the noting mind is temporarily liberated from mental defilements (*vimuttacitta*); and an unliberated mind, when there is no awareness and the wandering mind is subject to mental defilements (*avimuttacitta*).

The following four states of consciousness occur only to those who have achieved jhāna, so they are not relevant for a practitioner of pure insight meditation: a developed state of mind (*mahaggatacitta*), an undeveloped state of mind (*amahaggatacitta*), an inferior state of mind (*sa-uttaracitta*), and a superior state of mind (*anuttaracitta*).

The observation of states of mind as they are from moment to moment is called contemplation of mind (*cittānupassanā*). If one focuses on the enumeration or itemization of states of mind, considering that there are eight types of mind rooted in lust, that they are called mind affected by lust, and so on, this is not true contemplation of the mind but only conceptualization. This is why the commentary says:

> The moment a state of mind arises one observes either one's own mind or another's mind, or sometimes one's own mind and sometimes another's mind. This is called "contemplating mind as mind."[123]

If one notes a state of mind the moment it occurs, one understands: It has the characteristic of knowing an object (*vijānanalakkhaṇā*). It sees, hears, smells, tastes, or touches, and although it appears and disappears along with its mental factors, it is like a forerunner to perceive the object—it has the function of leading its mental factors (*pubbaṅgamarasa*). It manifests continuously, one moment after the other (*sandahanapaccupaṭṭhāna*). Its proximate causes are a physical basis, an object, mental contact, feeling, and so on (*nāmarūpapadaṭṭhāna; vatthārammaṇapadaṭṭhānā*).

## *Realizing Mind*

The method for the contemplating of mind is the same as the method for awareness of external and internal phenomena previously explained in the section on contemplation of the body.

When one notes a state of mind, one sees that it instantaneously arises and passes away. This is realization of the arising and passing away of mind. One also realizes that a particular state of mind arises only in the presence of such conditions as its specific mental factors, a physical basis, past actions, delusion, and attachment. Without these conditions, that state of mind does not arise. This is realization of the cause of states of mind that are arising and passing away, as described in the Pāḷi passage:

> He abides contemplating in mind its nature of both arising and vanishing.[124]

Every time one notes a state of mind, one realizes that there is no person or being, no "I" or "mine," and no woman or man that knows, but only awareness of an object. In other words, one is able to perceive the mind independent of conditioned conceptual images. Thus one's mindfulness and insight knowledge improve and attachment weakens, as stated in the Pāḷi passage:

> Or else mindfulness that "there is mind" is simply established in him.[125]

This is contemplation of the mind (*cittānupassanā*).

## Contemplation of Mental Objects

### *The Five Hindrances*

The desire for and enjoyment of sensual pleasures is called "the hindrance of sensual desire" (*kāmacchandanīvaraṇa*). It also includes desire for attainment of *jhāna* or for realization of path, fruition, and nibbāna. The desire for spiritual attainment can become sensual desire. When sensual desire arises, note it as it is.

> [There being sensual desire in him, a bhikkhu understands:] "There is sensual desire in me."[126]

Anger, frustration, hatred, cruelty, and hostility are included in what is called "the hindrance of aversion" (*byāpādanīvaraṇa*). One should be aware of these, as they truly are, the moment they occur. The hindrance caused by the sluggishness, dullness, and lack of energy of the mind and mental factors is called "the hindrance of sloth and torpor" (*thīnamiddhanīvaraṇa*). Be aware of these, as they truly are, the moment they occur. Mental restlessness is called "restlessness" (*uddhacca*). Note it as it is the moment it occurs. Regret and remorse are called "regret" (*kukkucca*). Note it as it is the moment it occurs. This is the way to note, according to the Pāḷi passage:

> [There being ill will in him. . . . There being sloth and torpor in him. . . . There being restlessness and remorse in him, a bhikkhu understands:] "There is ill-will . . . sloth and torpor . . . restlessness and remorse in me."[127]

Skeptical doubt about the Buddha's omniscience, about the attainments of path, fruition, and nibbāna, about the enlightenment of disciples, or about the fact that there is no person or being but only the law of cause and effect,[128] or doubts about whether one is practicing the correct method, whether the practice will lead to path, fruition, and nibbāna, whether one's teacher's instructions are correct, or whether anyone has ever become enlightened using this method is called "doubt" (*vicikicchā*). When you experience such doubt, note it as it is the moment it takes place, according to the following Pāḷi passage:

> [There being doubt in him, a bhikkhu understands:] "There is doubt in me."[129]

These mental hindrances may disappear when you note them once, twice, or several times. You should also note mental states free from hindrance as they are:

> [There being no sensual desire in him, a bhikkhu understands:] "There is no sensual desire in me."[130]

Sensual desire arises out of unwise attention. You will be able to note it when your insight knowledge matures. You will also experience the disappearance of sensual desire when you are aware of it. This awareness is wise attention. You may sometimes also become aware of unwise attention soon enough to prevent sensual desire from arising. The same applies for the other hindrances. When you note sloth and torpor, for example, and they disappear, you may feel alert for the rest of the day and night. Thus you will come to see the cause of mental hindrances. You will realize that unwise attention is what arouses sensual desire and the other hindrances, and wise attention is what dispels them.

### *Wise Attention*

Any awareness that arouses wholesomeness should be regarded as wise attention or right attitude (*yoniso manasikāra*). Here I will elaborate on wise attention as it relates specifically to insight meditation.

In the case of insight meditation, wise attention consists of noting or observing mental and physical phenomena the moment they take place, in terms of their specific and general characteristics. When one's empirical knowledge of mental and physical phenomena matures, one will then inferentially realize the nature of phenomena that one has never experienced by comparing them with those one has. This is also wise attention. Therefore wise attention is attention that leads to the attainment of higher insight knowledges and path knowledge and fruition knowledge. As the commentaries say:

> Wise attention is the (right) method and the (right) way of attention; wise attention is seeing what is impermanent as impermanent, seeing what is unsatisfactory as unsatisfactory, seeing what is not-self as not-self, and seeing what is unappealing as unappealing.[131]

Insight knowledges, path, fruition, and nibbāna are the true prosperity that an insight meditator hopes to gain. Thus "wise attention" is awareness of phenomena as they truly are, contemplation of the characteristics, impermanence, and so on of mental and physical phenomena.

An insight meditator need only know distinct mental and physical phenomena as they really are; he needn't experience a person, a being, an "I," a woman, or a man. A meditator needs to understand the general characteristics of impermanence and so on that help remove mental defilements; he needn't experience the appearance or apparent existence of permanence, satisfaction, self, and attractiveness. When a meditator experiences any of the six sense objects through the six sense doors, the mind units called the "five-sense-door-adverting" (*pañcadvārāvajjana*) or the "mind-door-adverting" (*manodvārāvajjana*) arise and are aware of those sense objects in such a way that they are only perceived as impermanent mental and physical phenomena. This type of "adverting mind" is then followed by an insight impulsion. Both of these are regarded as wise attention, since they lead toward right understanding of mental and physical phenomena and path knowledge and fruition knowledge. As the subcommentary on the *Satipaṭṭhāna Sutta* explains:

> Wise attention is a state of mind guided by wisdom that rightly understands the specific and general characteristics, function, and so on of wholesome mental states. It is called "wise attention" because it is the right way of paying attention. The adverting mind is also considered wise attention like that (wisdom-guided) state of mind.[132]

According to this subcommentary, both the adverting mind and the insight impulsion that arise in preceding mental processes should be considered wise attention, since they produce wholesome states of mind in the mental processes that follow.

### *Unwise Attention*

> Unwise attention (*ayoniso manasikāra*) is not the (right) method and is not the (right) way of attention; unwise attention is seeing what is impermanent as permanent, seeing what is unsatisfactory as satisfactory, seeing what is not-self as self, and seeing what is unappealing as appealing.[133]

Taking the mental and physical phenomena that appear at the six sense doors to be permanent, satisfactory, self, and attractive is unwise attention. In fact, any instance of unmindfulness should be regarded as unwise attention because it may lead to notions of permanence and so on.

Let's say, for example, that we fail to note an instance of seeing the moment it occurs. Because we do not stop with the mere process of seeing, we begin to think about who it is that one sees or about the fact that we have seen the person before. Or a bit later we reflect: "That person was in that place a moment ago, and now he is in this place," or "It is I who am thinking about that person after having seen him." Having these kinds of thoughts indicates that we harbor a perception of permanence. Or we may happily consider: "I see a woman. I see a man. He is well. It is nice to meet her." Or we may take the object and our eye consciousness to be a person, a being, or an "I." Or we may take it to be nice and attractive. It is unlikely that we will see impermanence and the other characteristics at such times, and even if we were to pay attention, impermanence and so on would not clearly appear to us. It goes without saying that we would stand no chance of attaining path and fruition under such circumstances. Any state devoid of mindfulness is considered to be unwise attention because it bears no benefit and doesn't result in attainment of insight knowledge or path and fruition. Unwise attention is the cause for any kind of unwholesomeness.

We should also consider both the adverting mind and all unwholesome impulsions that arise in preceding mental processes to be unwise attention in such cases, since they produce unwholesome states of mind in the mental processes that follow. Within a single mental process, the adverting mind should be considered unwise attention when it leads to unwholesomeness. Ordinary people are generally inclined toward sense objects that arouse mental defilements. As soon as the object appears at one of the six sense doors, the adverting mind arises based on unwise attention, as if it wonders whether the object is lovely or terrible. This kind of adverting mind is comparable to someone who is afraid of ghosts and jumps at any noise in the night, or to someone who is so eager to meet a dear friend that one mistakes a random passerby for that friend. In the case of the process at the five sense doors,[134] after consciousness adverts, receiving and investigating moments of consciousness arise, followed by a determining consciousness that decides whether the object is lovely or terrible. This is how kammic impulsions arise based on greed, hatred, and delusion. Also in the case of the process at the mind door, unwholesome kammic impulsions arise depending on the attention paid to the object when consciousness adverts to it and takes it to be something lovely or terrible. This is how unwholesome mental states arise due to unwise attention.

In brief, wise attention refers to mindfulness in the case of insight meditation. Attention that supports mindfulness is also considered wise attention. The wandering mind is unwise attention and produces mental hindrances. One should be aware of these two kinds of attention, according to the Pāḷi passage:

> He also understands how there comes to be the arising of unarisen sensual desire, and how there comes to be the abandoning of arisen sensual desire, and how there comes to be the future non-arising of abandoned sensual desire.[135]

Regarding future nonarising of abandoned hindrances: the first path knowledge uproots skeptical doubt; the third path knowledge uproots aversion and regret; and the fourth path knowledge completely removes sensual desire, sloth and torpor, and mental restlessness.

The various knowledges of the path that cause the complete uprooting of their respective hindrances can only be known at the moment of reviewing knowledge that occurs only after attaining the respective path knowledge. Before that, one can only understand them based on scriptural knowledge. Using scriptural knowledge, one can determine that one has not yet attained a particular path knowledge because its hindrances still arise. This helps one to make greater efforts to attain the various path knowledges.

### *The Five Aggregates*

There is no particular method for contemplating the aggregates. As mentioned before, those for whom the noting of materiality is suitable are able to thoroughly understand them when they note "seeing," "hearing," and so on. But those for whom the contemplation of the sense bases (*āyatana*) or elements (*dhātu*) is suitable will understand them when they note "seeing" and so on. This will also serve the purpose of those for whom contemplation of mental and physical phenomena is suitable.

If one notes "seeing, seeing" at the moment of seeing and is aware of one's eye sensitivity or the visual object, then one is aware of the physical aggregate. If one is aware of a pleasant, unpleasant, or neither-unpleasant-nor-pleasant feeling connected with the visual object, one is aware of the aggregate of feeling. If one is aware of recognizing the visual object, one is aware of the aggregate of perception. If one is aware of mental formations arising, such as mental contact with the visible object, the volition to see it, greed, faith, and so on, one is aware of the aggregate of mental formations. If one is aware of eye consciousness, one is aware of the aggregate of consciousness. Being aware of the aggregates in these ways is consistent with the Pāḷi passage:

> [Here a bhikkhu understands:] "Such is material form . . . such is feeling . . . such is perception . . . such are the formations . . . such is consciousness."[136]

The same applies to hearing and so on. If one notes "bending" while bending a limb, one is aware of the physical aggregate in the form of the bending movement, the mental aggregate of consciousness in the form of the intention to bend, and mental formations connected with bending, such as the contact between the mind and the physical process and the volition that drives the physical process. The aggregates of feeling and perception are only obvious some of the time. When they are, one is aware of the pleasant or unpleasant nature associated with the intention to bend and of the perception that recognizes the experience. The same applies for stretching, walking, and so on.

In this way knowledge that discerns mental and physical phenomena arises. One thoroughly understands that the physical aggregate is just this: changing for the worse. Feelings are just feeling, perception is just perceiving, mental formations are just performing their functions, and consciousness is just knowing the object. This is not merely an enumeration or itemization of the five aggregates but an empirical realization based on moment-to-moment awareness, consistent with the Pāḷi passage above, "Such is material form, such is feeling . . ." The commentary gives the following explanation:

> "Such is material form" indicates (realization of physicality in this way): "Such is material form. It consists of this much and no more." One understands material form based on its unique characteristics. The same applies for feelings, and so on.[137]

*The appearance and disappearance of physical phenomena*

Every time one notes physical phenomena, one sees that they are instantaneously appearing and disappearing. For example, when seeing, we see that eye sensitivity and the visible object momentarily appear and disappear. This is the insight knowledge of arising and passing away that realizes the characteristic of arising (*nibbattilakkhaṇā*) and the characteristic of disappearance (*vipariṇāmalakkhaṇā*).

People believe that mental and physical phenomena are good and beautiful. They cannot see that they are unsatisfactory, bad, and unattractive. They do not understand that the complete cessation of these mental and physical phenomena is peaceful and good. This not knowing is ignorance. Because of this ignorance, people were attached to mental and physical phenomena in past lives and committed wholesome or unwholesome deeds in an attempt to make them pleasant. These wholesome and unwholesome actions are kamma. Wholesome kamma is the cause of this human life. An insight meditator has already accepted the law of kamma after having learned that kamma brings both mental and physical good or bad results. One also empirically realizes the causes of mental and physical phenomena and their appearance and disappearance while practicing insight. Thus a meditator's understanding is a combination of empirical and scriptural knowledge.

By way of reflection one understands: "This physical body has arisen in this life because ignorance was present in a past life; it could not have arisen without ignorance. This physical body has arisen in this life because attachment and craving were present in a past life; it could not have arisen without attachment and craving. This physical body has arisen in this life because wholesome and unwholesome deeds were performed in a past life; it could not have arisen without wholesome and unwholesome deeds. This physical body has arisen in this life because of nourishment in this life; it could not have arisen without nourishment."

According to the *Paṭisambhidāmagga*, this realization is regarded as inferential knowledge of the arising and passing away of phenomena. One will also realize the immediate causes of physical phenomena in one's present existence—that the physical process of bending the hand is caused by the intention to do so, for example. The bending would not occur without the intention. Also, physical sensations of heat or cold are caused by environmental conditions of heat or cold. The physical experience of being hot or cold would not occur without those conditions. As the Pāḷi text says:

> Such is material form, such is its origin, such is its disappearance.[138]

*Feeling, perception, and formations*

Comfort, pleasure, and happiness are called "pleasant feeling" (*sukhavedanā*). Discomfort, unpleasantness, and sadness are called "painful feeling" (*dukkhavedanā*). A feeling that is neither unpleasant nor pleasant is called "neutral feeling" (*upekkhāvedanā*). When one notes these feelings, one sees that they instantaneously arise and disappear. This is the insight knowledge of arising and passing away that realizes the characteristics of appearance and disappearance of phenomena.

By way of reflection, one understands: "These feelings have arisen in this life because ignorance was present in a past life; they could not have arisen without ignorance. These feelings have arisen in this life because attachment and craving were present in a past life; they could not have arisen without attachment and craving. These feelings have arisen in this life because wholesome and unwholesome deeds were performed in a past life; they could not have arisen without wholesome and unwholesome deeds. These feelings have arisen in this life because of nourishment in this life; they could not have arise without nourishment.

This realization is regarded as inferential knowledge of the arising and passing away of feelings. The same is true for the aggregates of perception and mental formations. As the Pāḷi text says:

> Such is feeling, such is its origin, such is its disappearance.[139]

*Consciousness*

When one notes consciousness as "seeing," "hearing," "intention to bend," "intention to stretch," "knowing," and so on, one sees that it instantaneously arises and disappears. This is the insight knowledge that realizes the characteristic of the arising and the characteristic of the disappearance or passing away of phenomena.

By way of reflection, one understands: This consciousness has arisen in this life because ignorance was present in a past life; it could not have arisen without ignorance. This consciousness has arisen in this life because attachment and craving were present in a past life; without attachment and craving, it could not have arisen. This consciousness has arisen in this life because wholesome and unwholesome deeds were performed in a past life; it could not have arisen without wholesome and unwholesome deeds. This consciousness has arisen in this life because of nourishment in this life; it could not have arisen without nourishment.

This realization is regarded as inferential knowledge of the arising and passing away of consciousness. Because there is an object, consciousness arises; without it consciousness would not arise. Because there is a preceding consciousness, the following consciousness arises; without it consciousness would not arise. As the Pāḷi text says:

> Such is consciousness, such is its origin, such is its disappearance.[140]

According to the commentary, insight knowledge of arising and passing away arises in fifty ways: each aggregate is realized in terms of its appearance, disappearance, four causes of appearance, and four causes of disappearance,[141] making ten ways for each aggregate. Therefore the five aggregates are realized in fifty ways, altogether. But what is most important is realizing this understanding in ten ways—that is, seeing each of the five aggregates in terms of its appearance and disappearance.

## *The Six Senses*

### *Seeing*

At the moment of seeing we can experience various sense bases and elements and mental and physical phenomena, such as the eye sensitivity that is the eye base (*cakkhāyatana*) and the eye element (*cakkhudhātu*), the visual object that is the form base (*rūpāyatana*) and the form element (*rūpadhātu*), and the mind base (*manāyatana*).

We can also experience bases and elements associated with the mental process of sight. These arise in the following order: the element of eye consciousness (*cakkhuviññāṇadhātu*), the mind element (*manodhātu*) comprised of a mind moment that adverts to the object (*āvajjana*) and a mind moment that receives the sense object (*sampaṭicchana*), followed by the mind consciousness element (*manoviññāṇadhātu*) comprised of a mind moment that investigates the sense object (*santīraṇa*), a mind moment that determines the sense object (*votthapana*), mind moments of kammic impulsion (*javana*), and a mind moment that registers the sense object (*tadārammaṇa*).[142]

All the mental factors are called the mental-object base (*dhammāyatana*) and the mental-object element (*dhammadhātu*). Some of these are: mental contact (*phassa*) with a visual object, feeling (*vedanā*), perception (*saññā*), volition (*cetanā*), desire (*lobha*), aversion (*dosa*), and faith (*saddha*).

Consciousness and the mental factors are called *nāma* because they "go" or "bend" toward the visual object.[143] The eye sensitivity and the visual object cannot bend toward the object. They are called *rūpa* because they undergo alteration and are deformed when they meet with adverse physical conditions.[144] Thus, depending on one's disposition, every time one notes seeing as "seeing," one understands phenomena in terms of either the four bases, the six elements, or in terms of being mental (*nāma*) and physical (*rūpa*).

*Hearing, smelling, tasting, touching*

At the moment of hearing, the bases and elements and mental and physical phenomena that we can experience are the ear sensitivity that is physical, the ear base (*sotāyatana*), and the ear element (*sotdhātu*); the sound that is physical, the sound base (*saddāyatana*), and the sound element (*saddādhātu*). The mental process of hearing is mental and can be subdivided in terms of bases into its mind base and mental-object base, or in terms of elements into its ear-consciousness element (*sotaviññāṇadhātu*), its mind element, its mind-consciousness element, and its mental-object element.

At the moment of smelling we can experience the nose sensitivity that is physical, the nose base (*ghānāyatana*), and the nose element (*ghānadhātu*); the odor that is physical, the smell base (*gandhāyatana*), and the odor element (*gandhādhātu*). The mental process of smelling is mental and can be subdivided in terms of bases into its mind base and mental-object base, or in terms of elements into its nose-consciousness element (*ghānaviññāṇadhātu*), its mind element, its mind-consciousness element, and its mental-object element.

At the moment of tasting we can experience tongue sensitivity that is physical, the tongue base (*jivhāyatana*), and the tongue element (*jivhādhātu*); the flavor that is physical, the flavor base (*rasāyatana*), and the flavor element (*rasadhātu*). The mental process of tasting is mental and can be subdivided in terms of bases into its mind base and mental-object base, or in terms of elements into its tongue-consciousness element (*jivhāviññāṇadhātu*), its mind element, its mind-consciousness element, and its mental-object element.

At the moment of touching we can experience body sensitivity that is physical, the body base (*kāyāyatana*), and the body element (*kāyadhātu*); the bodily sensation that is physical, the tangible-object base (*phoṭṭhabbāyatana*), and the tangible-object element (*phoṭṭhabbadhātu*); the mental process of touching that is mental and can be subdivided in terms of bases into its mind base and mental-object base, or in terms of elements into its body-consciousness element (*kāyaviññāṇadhātu*), its mind element, its mind-consciousness element, and its mental-object element.

Thus, depending on one's disposition, every time one notes hearing as "hearing" and so on, one understands the phenomena in terms of the four bases or six elements, or in terms of being physical and mental.

### *Thinking*

At the moment of thinking we can experience the following bases and elements, or physical and mental phenomena: the mental process of simply taking an object that is mental, the mind base (*manāyatana*), and the mind-consciousness element (*manoviññāṇadhātu*).

We can also experience mental factors that are comprised of mind objects and mind bases, such as mental contact with the object, feeling, perception, volition, concentration, initial application, sustained application, determination, energy, rapture, will, desire, aversion, delusion, wrong view, pride or conceit, jealousy, regret, sloth and torpor, restlessness, skeptical doubt, nongreed, goodwill or benevolence, compassion, sympathetic joy, faith, mindfulness, moral shame and fear of consequences, wisdom, calm or tranquility, lightness and agility, and so on.

There are also physical phenomena associated with thinking that are mental-object bases and mental-object elements, such as the heart base (*hadayavatthu*) that is the physical base for thoughts and the feminine faculty (*itthindriya*) and masculine faculty (*purisindriya*) that bring about male and female traits, respectively.

Thus, depending on one's disposition, when one notes the thinking mind—the intention to bend or stretch one's limbs, thinking, wandering, considering, noting, observing, and so on—one understands phenomena in terms of the two bases, or two elements, or in terms of being mental and physical. A mental object can be either conceptual or ultimate. If it is ultimate, one can understand it in terms of its bases, elements, or in terms of being mental and physical.

### *The Ten Fetters*

There are ten fetters: (1) lust (*kāmarāga*), the desire for internal or external sensual objects; (2) anger (*paṭigha*), frustration, hatred, wanting someone to die; (3) arrogance (*māna*), thinking highly of oneself, and competing with others; (4) wrong view (*diṭṭhi*), the view of a "self" or personal identity that either lasts forever or is annihilated after death; (5) doubt (*vicikicchā*); (6) wrong belief (*sīlabbataparāmāsa*), the belief that rituals or ritualistic behavior can lead to liberation; (7) desire for existence (*bhavarāga*), the desire for and enjoyment of a good life; (8) envy (*issā*); (9) stinginess (*macchariya*), not wanting others to have the same prosperity and reputation as oneself; and (10) ignorance (*avijjā*), not knowing the true nature of mind and body—this fetter accompanies all the others.

When any of these ten fetters are present in a person, he will assume a new existence following death in the previous one and cannot be freed from the unsatisfactoriness of repeated existences. This is why they are called fetters—they bind us to the unsatisfactoriness of repeated existences. The ten kinds of fetters arise in our mind if in a moment of seeing we fail to be aware of the eye sensitivity, the visual object, or eye consciousness, or if in a moment of hearing we fail to be aware of the ear sensitivity, sound, or ear consciousness, and so on. When a fetter occurs, we should note it as it is.

If sensual desire arises and one notes it as it is, for example, one will become aware of the unwise attention that is arousing that sensual desire. By noting it as it is, one will then become aware of the wise attention that dispels that sensual desire. When one's practice matures, there are times when one will become aware of unwise attention as soon as it occurs and, by noting it, the sensual desire will disappear without having been fully developed. This is why the Pāḷi text says:

> Here a bhikkhu understands the eye, he understands forms, and he understands the fetter that arises dependent on both; and he also understands how there comes to be the arising of the unarisen fetter, and how there comes to be the abandoning of the arisen fetter.[145]

Reviewing knowledge (*paccavekkhaṇāñāṇa*) is the knowledge that arises immediately after path and fruition, and it reflects on the five factors of path, fruition, nibbāna, mental defilements that have been uprooted, and those that have not yet been uprooted. One can reflect on path and fruition that uproot the fetters only in a moment of reviewing knowledge, according to the Pāḷi phrase:

> And how there comes to be the future nonarising of the abandoned fetter.[146]

For general knowledge, however, one should know that the first path knowledge uproots the view of personality (*sakkāyadiṭṭhi*), skeptical doubt regarding the Buddha's teachings (*vicikicchā*), belief in rites and rituals as a path to liberation (*sīlabbataparāmāsa*), envy or jealousy (*issā*), and avarice or stinginess (*macchariya*); the second and third path knowledges uproot the gross and subtle forms, respectively, of sensual desire (*kāmarāga*) and aversion (*paṭigha*); and the fourth and final path knowledge eradicates pride or conceit (*māna*), desire for existence (*bhavarāga*), and ignorance (*avijjā*).

Note that not every apparent instance of stinginess is necessarily a sign of the fetter of stinginess. Even though the first path knowledge uproots stinginess, this doesn't mean that a stream enterer becomes so generous that she will give away anything she has. Apparent stinginess can occur owing to attachment to belongings, as well as to stinginess. Stinginess is the kind of stinginess or avarice that is so strong one cannot bear the thought of or approve of another person possessing or using one's belongings. A stream enterer is free from this kind of stinginess but not from attachment to property.

Remember that there were wealthy laymen and laywomen as well as kings and queens during the Buddha's time who attained the first three stages of enlightenment: stream enterer, once returner, and nonreturner. There surely must have been thieves or those holding opposing views to the Buddha's teaching who demanded property from such people under threat of force. If these noble persons had given whatever was requested, they would have lost all their wealth. Even the household of the merchant Anāthapiṇḍika experienced theft. If the merchant had always given whatever was asked of him, no one would have had cause to commit such a crime. So unwillingness to give is not necessarily the fetter of stinginess. On the other hand, feeling jealous at the thought that another person will possess or use one's own possessions is considered stinginess. Simply being attached to one's own property is not stinginess, but rather desire. Moreover, not giving what one shouldn't give is neither stinginess nor attachment to one's belongings. The female arahant Uppalavaṇṇā, for example, refused bhikkhu Udāyī's request for her underrobe. Uppalavaṇṇā was not only free from desire and stinginess but from all defilements as well. She simply refused the request because her underrobe was not something fit to be given away.

## *The Seven Factors of Enlightenment*

### *Mindfulness*

Beginning with the stage of insight knowledge of arising and passing away, one's practice is less and less disturbed by the hindrances, and one firmly establishes mindfulness of objects to be noted. It seems as if mental and physical objects that arise instantaneously and disappear spontaneously present themselves to the noting mind. Immediately after one object has been noted, another object appears. The noting mind seems to sink into the object and the object seems to sink into the noting mind. The commentary says that this noting is characterized by a mental state that "dips" its mental constituents into the object. This quality of mindfulness is the enlightenment factor of mindfulness (*satisaṃbojjhaṅga*), since it leads to path knowledge.

### *Investigation*

When one notes an object, one understands the characteristics of the mental or physical phenomena associated with it. One also sees the sudden arising and disappearance of these mental and physical phenomena. Furthermore, one clearly sees their characteristics of impermanence, unsatisfactoriness, and not-self. This understanding is the enlightenment factor of investigation (*dhammavicayasaṃbojjhaṅga*).

### *Energy*

When one notes an object, one should apply moderate effort or energy. If one begins one's practice with too much energy, one will later become overzealous and restless, and one's noting will not be as good as it could be. On the other hand, if one begins one's practice with too little energy, one's effort will not be strong enough for one's noting, and the mind will become lethargic and dull. So one should apply moderate effort in practice, reducing the effort when it's too strenuous and boosting energy when it's too weak. Then one will be neither restless due to excessive effort nor lethargic due to deficient energy. One will be mindful of each object that arises without missing any objects. This kind of energy is considered the enlightenment factor of energy (*vīriyasambojjhaṅga*).

### *Delight and calm*

Experiencing delight with every noting mind is the enlightenment factor of delight (*pītisaṃbojjhaṅga*). The mental calm or tranquility that results from effortless practice is the enlightenment factor of tranquility (*passaddhisambojjhaṅga*). These qualities of delight and calm are very obvious, especially at the beginning of insight knowledge of arising and passing away, at which point one feels greater delight and tranquility than one has ever felt before, verifying the Buddha's statement:

> The delight in Dhamma surpasses all delights.[147]

In all activities such as walking, standing, sitting, lying down, bending, stretching, and so on, one will feel well in body and mind. Due to delight, one may feel as if swaying back and forth in a hammock. Due to calmness, one may not note any object, feeling as if one is gazing at it or just sitting calmly. These mental states of delight and tranquility only occur occasionally, beginning with insight knowledge of dissolution, but they often gain momentum with insight knowledge of equanimity toward formations.

### *Concentration*

The mind focuses on each object as one notes it, sticking to it without wandering off, firmly concentrated on it. This type of concentration enables one to understand mental and physical phenomena in terms of both their unique characteristics and their universal characteristics of impermanence and so on. This kind of "momentary concentration" involved in each and every moment of noting is considered the enlightenment factor of concentration (*samādhisaṃbojjhaṅga*).

### *Equanimity*

The mind is balanced and equanimous as it notes each object. This balanced state of mind (*tatramajjhattatā*) is called the enlightenment factor of equanimity (*upekkhāsaṃbojjhaṅga*). It is quite difficult to empirically understand this kind of equanimity or to explain it to somebody else. However, one can easily understand it through one's own experience with the knowledges beginning with insight knowledge of arising and passing away.

## *Balancing Spiritual Faculties*

### *Faith and wisdom*

When a meditator sees only the arising and passing away of mental and physical phenomena with each noting, he may repeatedly think and reflect (on this matter) based on his strong faith or confidence. For example, one may marvel that there is no person or being but only mental and physical phenomena that arise and immediately pass away without lasting for even the blink of an eye. One may think it so true that phenomena are impermanent, unsatisfactory, and conditioned that one believes that the Buddha knew everything. One may also think how true what the Buddha and teachers say is. However, as one ponders this with confidence and appreciation, one may forget to be aware of that very mental state of confidence, as well as other phenomena that are arising and passing away. This is excessive faith in the Dhamma that interferes with noting.

Those meditators whose wisdom is excessive may think and reflect quite often. For example, one may wonder whether one is noting a physical or a mental phenomenon, whether it is mental contact or feeling, whether one notes an object effectively, whether one is experiencing its characteristic, function, and so on, or whether one is seeing its arising, disappearing, or impermanence, and so on. Whenever such a meditator has a clear experience in practice, she is likely to compare it with familiar scriptures, her own opinions, or other people's accounts. However, as a meditator thinks about these things, she forgets to be aware of those very mental states of thinking and reasoning, as well as other phenomena that are occurring from moment to moment. This is excessive analysis or reasoning that interferes with noting.

Due to the power of equanimity, which is by nature balancing, faith and wisdom become balanced such that neither faith nor analysis become excessive. Having faith and wisdom, one just notes all the arising objects without thinking and analyzing. As a result, one is able to note and clearly understand all mental and physical phenomena as they occur.

### *Energy and concentration*

When energy is excessive one strives too much. One may end up searching for an object to note or be concerned that one cannot note objects effectively or that one might miss objects to note. Sometimes one may end up thinking about how effectively one will note objects in the future, or how often one missed objects in the past. The mind cannot become well concentrated with all this excessive worry, and it will just be restless. Because of this restlessness one will not be able to be thoroughly aware of each arising mental and physical phenomena. Thus does excessive effort result in weak concentration and unclear experience when practicing. This is excessive effort that interferes with noting.

When concentration is excessive, however, the noting mind may remain on just one object for a long time. Because other objects do not appear to the mind, one does not strive to note other objects. As one continues to just note in a relaxed way without exerting effort, one's effort will weaken. This is like the weakening of effort that occurs when one repeats a chant that one has memorized by rote. As a result, the object and the noting mind grow cloudy or vague, sloth and torpor begin to prevail, and one cannot be thoroughly aware of each arising mental and physical phenomena. This is excessive concentration that interferes with noting.

Due to the power of equanimity, which maintains balance between the faculties of effort and concentration, one will be able to note objects clearly from moment to moment. Even though many objects may occur, the mind will not grow restless. All the appearing mental and physical phenomena will be noted, as if by themselves, and the mind will remain steadfastly on the objects that one is aware of. Then one will think that no objects have been missed and that one is aware of all the objects occurring.

*Balanced practice*

Equanimity and balance between faith and wisdom and between energy and concentration, and balancing these mental faculties, is called the enlightenment factor of equanimity. When this equanimity matures, mental factors such as mindfulness are balanced, strong, and distinct. Then one does not have to look for an object, it will readily appear after the previous object has been noted. The object will be noted without exerting much effort, as if the noting process flows smoothly of its own accord. The mind will remain steadfastly on any object that occurs, and one will experience mental and physical phenomena in terms of their individual and universal characteristics.

At this stage you should maintain balance by refraining from analyzing your experiences or increasing or decreasing your effort. Allow the practice to proceed evenly without making any changes. Then you will be able to be aware of that balanced mental state itself, and you will experience the seven factors of enlightenment involved, as the instruction says:

> [There being the mindfulness enlightenment factor in him, a bhikkhu understands:] "There is the mindfulness enlightenment factor in me."[148]

When one's practice does not go smoothly, and the enlightenment factors are no longer present due to excessive effort, failure to note objects, and so on, realize that the enlightenment factors are not present while noting "unsteady," "forgetting," "thinking," and so on. As the instruction says:

> [And there being no mindfulness enlightenment factor in him, he understands:] "There is no mindfulness enlightenment factor in me."[149]

The proximate causes for the arising of the enlightenment factors are previous mindfulness and wise attention, such as the determination to arouse the enlightenment factors or reflecting on an object that arouses faith. One also understands what arouses the enlightenment factors, according to the Pāḷi passage:

> And he also understands how there comes to be the arising of the unarisen mindfulness enlightenment factor.[150]

Only when one realizes the arahant path and becomes fully enlightened do all of the enlightenment factors become fully developed. One understands the completion of their development with reviewing knowledge, immediately following full enlightenment. As the Pāḷi passage says:

> And how the arisen mindfulness enlightenment factor comes to fulfillment by development.[151]

## *The Seven Types of Suffering*

There are four noble truths, namely: (1) the noble truth of suffering (*dukkhāriyasacca*), the truth about unsatisfactoriness that noble ones understand; (2) the noble truth of the origin of suffering (*samudayāriyasacca*), the truth about the origin of unsatisfactoriness that noble ones understand; (3) the noble truth of the cessation of suffering (*dukkhanirodhaariyasacca*), the truth about the cessation of unsatisfactoriness that noble ones understand; and (4) the noble truth of the path leading to the cessation of suffering (*dukkhanirodhagāminīpaṭipadā-ariyasacca*), the truth of the path leading to the cessation of unsatisfactoriness understood by noble ones. These four truths are called "noble truths" because they are only experienced by noble beings. In brief, they are referred to as the truth of suffering (*dukkhasacca*), the truth of origin (*samudayasacca*), the truth of cessation (*nirodhasacca*), and the truth of the path (*maggasacca*).

The emergence of the first mental and physical phenomena in an existence is called "birth" (*jāti*), the continued occurrence and maturing of those phenomena is called "aging" (*jarā*), and the disappearance of the last mental and physical phenomena in an existence is called "death" (*maraṇa*). The dynamics of birth, aging, and death are suffering (*dukkha*),[152] since they cause us mental and physical distress in each existence. Suffering means that the phenomena are not good, are devoid of anything that could be enjoyed, and are repulsive. Thus it is said:

> Birth is suffering, aging is suffering, death is suffering.[153]

### *Suffering of pain*

The various kinds of physical pain, such as aches, pains, and so on, and different kinds of mental pain, such as sadness, sorrow, and so on, are all called the "suffering of pain" (*dukkhadukkha*) or obvious suffering. These types of mental and physical phenomena are obviously distressing.

### *Suffering of change*

Even though they are pleasant the moment they occur, pleasant mental and physical feelings—what we call comfort, happiness, and so on—are considered to be suffering of change (*vipariṇāmadukkha*) because we feel distressed when they vanish or something goes wrong with them. The more pleasant a feeling is while it exists, the more distressing it is when it disappears.

It's like taking a fall: the greater the height we fall from, the more painful the injury will be, even to the point of death. It's also like having to part from the people or things that we love: the more attached to a person we are, the more painful it is to leave them. The pleasant feeling that we had when we were with them turns to distress when it comes time to part. Such is the nature of all pleasant feelings. This kind of suffering is also like an evil demon appearing in the guise of a lovely angel: if we knew the true nature of the angel, we would fear and detest it. This is why pleasant feelings are called the "suffering of change."

*Suffering of conditioned phenomena*

Because they are subject to impermanence, neither-unpleasant-nor-pleasant feeling and all worldly mental and physical phenomena, except attachment,[154] are called "suffering of conditioned phenomena" (*saṅkhāradukkha*). This kind of suffering permeates all the other kinds of suffering. Suffering of change includes pleasant and unpleasant feelings as well. The Pāḷi text says:

> And I have also said: "Whatever is felt is included in suffering." That has been stated by me with reference to the impermanence of formations.[155]

Pleasant feeling is distinctive and we feel distressed when it disappears. So we can say that we are more afraid and distressed by the suffering of change than we are by the suffering of conditioned phenomena. Unpleasant feeling is also distinctive, in that it is more obviously painful and so we are more afraid and distressed by it than we are by other types of suffering—it is the worst of all suffering. This is why commentators deal with these two kinds of suffering separately, even though each can be included in the category of "suffering of conditioned phenomena."

When regarding the truth of suffering in the context of insight practice, we must thoroughly understand what it is to suffer conditioned phenomena. We enjoy internal and external phenomena because we mistakenly believe them to be permanent. If we understand that they are conditioned and impermanent, we will no longer take them to be permanent and satisfactory; instead we will regard them as fearful and distressing.

*Hidden and manifest suffering*

Physical pain that is not externally apparent, such as headaches, earaches, toothaches, and mental distress, such as worry caused by want, or worry, frustration, or sadness caused by aversion, are called "hidden pain or distress" or "hidden suffering" (*paṭicchannadukkha*). Other people can perceive this kind of suffering only when its victims communicate it, and not otherwise. This is also referred to as "obscure pain or distress" or "obscure suffering" (*apākaṭadukkha*). Physical pain caused by external injuries or afflictions is called "manifest pain" or "manifest suffering" (*appaṭicchannadukkha*) or "plain pain" or "plain suffering" (*pākaṭadukkha*).

### *Explicit and implicit suffering*

Unpleasant feelings are explicit suffering (*nippariyāyadukkha*) or apparent suffering. But other types of suffering—such as repeated rebirth, aging, and so on—are implicit suffering (*pariyāyadukkha*) because they are not painful in an apparent way yet lead to suffering nonetheless. It is for this reason that, among the seven kinds of suffering, birth, aging, and death are called the "the truth of suffering."

## *The Four Noble Truths*

### *The truth of suffering*

The scriptures say: "Birth (repeated rebirth) is suffering, aging is suffering, death is suffering." If we were to lose our relatives, friends, health, wealth, moral conduct, or moral beliefs, or if we were punished, tortured, or thrown into jail, we would suffer sorrow (*soka*). Out of strong sorrow, lamentation (*parideva*) arises. Unbearable and inconsolable despair is a form of aversion called "tribulation" (*upāyāsa*). All forms of physical pain are called "suffering." Ordinary mental pain is called "distress" (*domanassa*).

Sorrow, suffering, and mental distress are called true suffering because they cause us to suffer pain and because they produce future mental and physical suffering. Lamentation and inconsolable mental despair is called true suffering only because the result is mental and physical suffering due to it being inferred suffering. To have to associate with persons or things we dislike is also suffering, as is being separated from what we love or like. Craving what we cannot obtain is suffering too.

These three forms of suffering are called true suffering because they produce various kinds of mental and physical pain.

If we fail to be aware of the five aggregates—materiality, feeling, perception, mental formations, and consciousness—that are involved in seeing, hearing, and so on, they become objects of clinging and wrong beliefs. This is why they are referred to as "aggregates subject to clinging" (*upādānakkhandhā*). If these aggregates subject to clinging exist, these seven forms of suffering, beginning with repeated birth, can arise; suffering cannot arise when they do not exist. Thus these five aggregates are true suffering since they are subject to impermanence and the other kinds of suffering mentioned here. This is why the Buddha said:

> In brief, the five aggregates subject to clinging are suffering.[156]

### *The truth of origin*

The phenomena that we can directly experience in a moment of seeing, hearing, and so on are called the five aggregates subject to clinging and are true suffering. Attachment to and enjoyment of them is craving. Because of craving, we long for a better life now and in the future, and to this end we perform wholesome and unwholesome actions of body, speech, and mind, which form wholesome and unwholesome kamma. We have performed countless kammas throughout our lives.

In the last moment of this life when we are on our deathbed, one of those kammas, or an image that was impressed in our memory when we performed a kamma (*kammanimitta*), or an image of the new life we will go to (*gatinimitta*) will arise in the mind. When our present life ends, rebirth—the first emergence of the five aggregates in the next life—will immediately follow, taking the same mental image as the one that appeared last to us on our deathbed.[157] It is like the fear that one experiences in a dream that lingers even after one wakes up. The relationship between death and relinking is similar to the relationship between actually seeing something and then thinking about what was seen—both take the same sense object in different ways. A yogi will be able to understand this.

From relinking until death, the five aggregates subject to clinging constantly occur and will do so repeatedly throughout our next life, just as they do in this life. We see something, for example, and then think about what we have seen, then we hear something, and so on. In this way the five aggregates affected by clinging happen continuously. The first emergence of the five aggregates subject to clinging in a new life is the suffering of birth, their repeated occurrence and maturing is the suffering of aging, and their last disappearance is the suffering of death. Any sorrow, lamentation, and so on that we experience before death is, of course, also suffering. The five aggregates subject to clinging that continuously arise based on seeing, hearing, and so on are also suffering.

The truth of suffering is produced by kamma, which is in turn initiated by craving—attachment to and craving for the five aggregates subject to clinging. If one eliminates craving, new kamma cannot be formed, nor can the kamma that has already been formed give rise to a new life. So craving is the origin of all kinds of suffering, beginning with the arising of the five aggregates subject to clinging in each life. The moment we see something, for example, we become attached to the five aggregates subject to clinging that are involved in seeing because we mistakenly believe them to be pleasurable. This craving is the truth of the origin of suffering (*samudayasacca*). That is why it is said:

> It is craving, which brings renewal of being, [and] is accompanied by delight and lust, . . . [158]

*The truth of cessation*

When we attain nibbāna by means of path knowledge, we will truly understand that all arising and disappearing mental and physical phenomena are utterly suffering. Therefore craving for these mental and physical aggregates will no longer arise, and we will thus no longer experience rebirth. In other words, mental and physical phenomena will cease. This is the cessation of all suffering or nibbāna without residue (*anupādisesanibbāna*). The term "cessation" here means that the aggregates no longer arise. Thus the commentaries call it nibbāna without residue. Nibbāna as the cessation of craving and the cessation of the mental and physical aggregates is called the truth of cessation (*nirodha*). Path knowledge takes nibbāna as its object. This is the truth of the cessation of all suffering (*nirodhasacca*).

> It is the remainderless fading away and cessation of that same craving.[159]

*The truth of the path*

The noble eightfold path—including right view and so on—that directly takes nibbāna as its object is the truth of the path.

In short, all of the mental and physical phenomena that arise and pass away in ordinary people are suffering and the causes of suffering: attachment, desire, or craving is the truth of the cause of suffering, and everything else is the truth of suffering. The cessation of both the objects of awareness and the awareness of them is the truth of the cessation of suffering. The mental state of experiencing that cessation is the truth of the path.

## Mindfulness of the Four Noble Truths

### *Truths in the Round of Existence and Truths Beyond It*

Among the four noble truths, one should observe only the two in the round of existence (*vaṭṭasacca*)—suffering and the cause of suffering—for the development of insight. One can only intellectually appreciate and know the two truths beyond the round of existence (*vivaṭṭasacca*)—cessation of suffering and the path to cessation of suffering—so one must simply aspire to them. By doing so, awareness of these two truths is fulfilled. According to the commentary:[160]

> Out of the four truths, the first two are in the round of existence (*vaṭṭa*), while the latter two are beyond the round of existence (*vivaṭṭa*). Among them, only the two truths in the round of existence become meditation subjects for a monk; he does not observe the two truths that are beyond the round of existence. Regarding the two truths in the round of existence, a monk

should learn from a teacher, in brief, that the five aggregates subject to clinging are suffering and that craving is its origin; or he should learn in detail that the five aggregates subject to clinging are such and such. A meditator does the work of insight by repeatedly reflecting on this.

Regarding the other two truths, a monk simply hears or learns that the truth of the cessation of suffering is a dhamma to be wished for since it is a good dhamma; it is a dhamma to be liked because it is a noble dhamma; it is a dhamma that nurtures the heart and it is a dhamma to be cherished. The truth of the path to the cessation of suffering is a dhamma to be wished for, to be liked, and to be nurtured. Thusly he also does the work of insight. Then when he finally penetrates the four noble truths at the moment of path knowledge, he thoroughly realizes them once and for all.

One penetrates the truth of suffering by fully understanding it, penetrates the truth of the cause of suffering by abandoning it, penetrates the truth of the cessation of suffering by experiencing it, and penetrates the truth of the path to the cessation of suffering by developing it. One realizes the truth of suffering by fully understanding it, realizes the truth of the cause of suffering by abandoning it, realizes the truth of the cessation of suffering by experiencing it, and realizes the truth of the path to the cessation of suffering by developing it.

Thus one initially understands the first two mundane truths by learning, listening, discussing, memorizing, and observing them. The truth of the cessation of suffering and the truth of the path to the cessation of suffering are understood only by hearing about them. Later, at the moment of path knowledge, one functionally accomplishes the three truths of suffering, the cause of suffering, and the path, and one penetrates the truth of the cessation of suffering by taking it as one's object.[161]

Cessation and path are not to be observed for the purpose of developing insight. Ordinary people cannot take supramundane phenomena as sense objects. They also cannot help noble ones, having realized any of the various knowledges of the path, to further eradicate mental defilements. The commentary uses the phrase "to be wished for, to be liked, and to be nurtured" merely to illustrate the enthusiasm and aspiration to realize the supramundane truths of cessation and the path to cessation. Just as one expresses one's intent with the resolve, "Through this practice may I be liberated from aging and death,"[162] so too one need only aspire to realize these two truths. However, one needn't excessively wish for it or repeatedly think about it. Otherwise it may encourage craving and wrong views and disturb one's practice. I explained this point in chapter 2 of the *Manual of Insight* in regard to the first hindrance to liberation. As the subcommentary says:

> The two truths in the round of existence can become meditation subjects because one can experience them through their own characteristics. But this is not so of the two truths beyond the round of existence—cessation and the path to cessation—because ordinary people cannot take them as sense objects and they serve no purpose when taken as sense objects by noble ones. So the phrase "to be wished for, to be liked, and to be nurtured" is used to incline the mind toward the truth of cessation of suffering and the truth of the path to the cessation of suffering, and not to promote obsession with them on the basis of craving and wrong view. One must simply aspire to realize the two truths that are beyond the round of existence.[163]

## *How Suffering Is Realized*

Noting each mental and physical phenomenon that arises, one understands the unique characteristics of each respective phenomenon. One understands the changeable and oppressing characteristics of the body, as well as its characteristic of bending toward the objects of the mind. One understands the characteristics of torment (*bādhanalakkhaṇā*) as being tortured by arising and disappearance, unpleasant feelings, and mental distress and physical pain for the one they afflict.

When they realize the characteristic of arising and disappearing, even those who have no intellectual knowledge whine as their insight knowledge matures, saying: "All that exists are these continually arising and disappearing phenomena! They disappear and then they are gone. Whatever I note is not satisfactory. There is no peace so long as these phenomena continue. Because these phenomena exist there is suffering. When will they cease to exist?" This is consistent with the following passages:

> Here a bhikkhu understands as it actually is: "This is suffering." . . . [164] Except for craving, all phenomena in the three worlds[165] are suffering. One understands them as they really are.[166]
>
> The phrase "as they really are" means that one understands them in an ultimate sense [that is, as torment in the form of unpleasant feeling, mental and physical distress, and impermanence]—in other words, in terms of their individual natures of changeability, hardness, and so on.[167]

The phrase "all phenomena in the three worlds" in the commentary refers only to animate phenomena in the three worlds and not to inanimate ones. Inanimate physical material is not the noble truth of suffering. The reasons for this are: inanimate phenomena do arise and pass away, and although they can be called impermanent and suffering, they are not caused by craving and path knowledge does not bring them to an end. One can still observe external objects, such as clothing and so on, to evaluate the impermanence and impersonality of external objects, so that mental defilements do not arise because of them, and so that they easily become internally distinct. Although external objects arise by themselves at the six sense doors and should be observed, we cannot say that these inanimate, external objects are "full understanding of the noble truth of suffering" (*pariññeyya-ariyadukkhasacca*).

Among the phenomena that occur in the lives of living beings, we need only understand the four noble truths in ourselves. The reasons for this are: When the truth of suffering arises because of one's craving, it arises only in oneself; it cannot arise in another person. When suffering arises in somebody else due to his craving, it arises only in him; it cannot arise in oneself. Furthermore, one's truth of the path that leads to the cessation of suffering can only lead to the cessation of one's own suffering and craving; it cannot lead to the cessation of another person's suffering and craving. And another person's path can only lead to the cessation of his or her suffering and craving; it cannot lead to the cessation of one's own suffering and craving. Furthermore, noble ones experience their individual truths of the cessation of craving and suffering; they cannot experience another person's four noble truths. After having experienced their own four noble truths, they can inferentially understand others' truths.

Therefore, although one can attain path and fruition by being aware of something external, the most important thing is to understand the four internal truths.

Pāḷi texts such as the *Satipaṭṭhāna Sutta* give priority to the awareness within oneself by mentioning it first. The following excerpts from the Pāḷi texts, commentaries, and subcommentaries illustrate this point:

> As to that end of the world, friend, where one is not born, does not age, does not die, does not pass away, and is not reborn—I say that it cannot be known, seen, or reached by traveling. However, friend, I say that without having reached the end of the world there is no making an end to suffering. It is, friend, in just this fathom-high carcass endowed with perception and mind that I make known the world, the origin of the world, the cessation of the world, and the way leading to the cessation of the world.[168]
>
> Here, "the world" refers to the truth of suffering, "the origin of the world" refers to the truth of the cause of suffering, "the cessation of the world" to the truth of the cessation of suffering, and "the way leading to the cessation of the world" refers to the truth of the path to the cessation of suffering. By saying, "However, friend, I say that without . . ." and so on, [the Buddha indicates that he does not recognize] the four noble truths in inanimate phenomena, such as a log or the trunk of a tree, but only in this very body constituted of the four primary material elements.[169]
>
> One's own suffering and craving are what cease, so cessation

> is regarded as internal and belonging to oneself. Thus the phrase "one's own four truths" is used. Understand the phrase "another's four truths" in the same way.[170]

Thus inanimate phenomena are not the noble truth of suffering, since according to the Pāḷi texts and commentaries the four noble truths pertain only to animate phenomena. Also, even though the truth of the cessation of suffering is technically an external phenomenon, the subcommentary above clearly says that it should be regarded as part of one's own or someone else's four noble truths. Although everyone possesses all four noble truths, one can only penetrate into and realize one's own craving by eradicating it, one can only penetrate into and realize the cessation of one's own suffering and craving by experiencing it, and one can only penetrate into and realize one's own path by developing it. No one can abandon anyone else's craving, experience anyone else's cessation, or develop anyone else's path. So the important thing is to be aware of one's own four noble truths.

### *How the Origin of Suffering Is Realized*

Noting each mental and physical phenomenon that arises, one understands craving and desire when one is mindful of them. This is an empirical understanding of craving in the present moment. However, present craving is not the origin of present suffering. It is the origin of suffering in a future life that will be produced by the kamma one does in this life. Similarly, the craving or sense desire that formed when one performed kamma in past lives is the origin of present suffering.

Due to attachment to oneself or to sense pleasure, one performed wholesome and unwholesome deeds in past lives just as one does in this life. That kamma has been generating one's mental and physical phenomena since one was born into this life. One cannot empirically know one's past craving; one can only know it inferentially by comparing it to one's present craving. The craving that one can know empirically in the present and past craving differ only in terms of being present or past, they do not differ in terms of their characteristic. One can even say that they are the same because they manifest in the continuum of the same individual. It is like saying that we see a mountain or the sea even though we see only a small part of either. If one is aware of one's present craving, one can understand the truth of craving as the cause of suffering. In any event, one can also be inferentially aware of past craving, beginning when one's knowledge that discerns mental and physical phenomena matures.

A meditator can empirically observe the cause-and-effect relationship between mental and physical phenomena: only when there is an intention to bend does the bending movement occur, only when it is cold does cold manifest in the body, only when there is a visible form and functioning eye does eye consciousness arise, only when there is a mental object does thought occur, only when there is a previous mind moment does a following mind moment occur.

This realization becomes more obvious at the higher levels of insight that lead to path knowledge. At that point, one understands that the mental and physical phenomena that one observes are not devoid of causes and that these mental and physical phenomena that have been occurring since birth only happen due to causes. One easily understands that the cause of this life is the wholesome kamma one performed in a past life. This understanding is based on one's faith in kamma and its effects. Thus one gains right understanding regarding kamma.

Thus one uses analytical knowledge (*cintāmaya*) and theoretical knowledge (*sutamaya*) based on empirical knowledge (*bhāvanāmaya*) to realize that craving is the origin of this life. One realizes that—driven by craving and sense desire—one performed wholesome and unwholesome deeds in past lives, just as one does in the present life. That past kamma based on craving then generated this present life, as explained in the commentarial passage:

> It gives rise to this very suffering (mental and physical phenomena), and so "Craving in previous lives is the origin of this present suffering."[171]

This is an inferential understanding of the origin of this present life's suffering. Note that the long explanation given here is only for the sake of general knowledge. In practice, of course, it will not take a meditator very long to understand. Immediately after one understands, one can continue noting objects in the present moment as usual.

*Obvious but difficult to see*

The first two truths are quite obvious because they are always present in us. They are not very profound or obscure. However, it is extremely difficult to understand that they are simply distressing or unsatisfactory and that craving is their origin. This is not obvious at all. The difficulty in understanding obvious phenomena lies in the fact that we are not mindful of them or do not pay attention to them. As the Burmese saying goes: "We cannot see even a cave without attention." So if we are mindful and pay attention to phenomena, we are bound to understand them as they really are through insight knowledge. Later at the peak of insight, with path knowledge, this understanding will become firm and irreversible.

> The truth of suffering[172] is obvious once it appears. If a stump, stake, or thorn hurts one, one cries out, "It hurts!"[173] The truth of the origin of suffering [that is, craving] is also obvious when one experiences the desire to do something, to eat, and so on. But these two truths are profound when understood in terms of their specific characteristics. Thus these two truths are profound because they are difficult to observe and understand.[174]
>
> The expression "difficult to see" means that even though the truth of suffering and the truth of craving as the cause of suffering are quite obvious the moment they appear, they are so profound that it is impossible to use normal intelligence to see them in terms of their characteristics and functions. We can see them only with the profoundly developed wisdom that reaches its peak with realization of noble path knowledge.[175]

## *How Cessation and Path Are Realized*

As the commentary says, the last two truths, cessation and path, are extremely profound since they never happen to ordinary people—we cannot empirically understand and see them. As mentioned before, all that a beginning meditator needs to do with respect to these two truths is to incline the mind toward them, having heard that they are noble. It is not necessary to contemplate and think about them.

However, at the stage of insight knowledge of arising and passing away, a meditator may spontaneously start to reflect and understand that the five aggregates would not exist if there were no ignorance, craving, volition, nutriment, mental contact, or mental and physical phenomena. Beginning from the stage of insight knowledge of dissolution, a meditator may spontaneously start to reflect and understand that as long as mental and physical processes—such as seeing, hearing, touching, thinking, observing, and so on—exist, there will be no peace. Only when these processes no longer exist will there be peace. This is an intellectual understanding of cessation during insight practice. As the *Paṭisambhidāmagga* says:

> Arising is torment; nonarising is peace.[176]

At the stage of insight knowledge of desire for deliverance (*muñcitukamyatāñāṇa*), we may not want to observe mental and physical phenomena, since we see only the negative aspects of the phenomena we note. Some meditators may even stop observing them. However, as the momentum of practice is still there, mental and physical phenomena appear as usual and meditators are aware of them without the need to exert much effort to observe them. Eventually meditators may understand that phenomena do not cease without observing them; peace only comes with the experience of the peace of nibbāna, and that only happens when we note as usual. This is an intellectual understanding of path during insight practice.

This is how all four truths are understood by observing them during the practice of insight meditation.

## *Cultivating Mundane Understanding*

To understand the four noble truths means to fully understand suffering, to abandon craving, to experience cessation, and to develop the path. Thus one really understands these truths only when one abandons craving, experiences cessation, and develops the path. The four functions of fully understanding, abandoning, experiencing, and developing are simultaneously fulfilled with each and every noting. So we can say that the four noble truths are understood with each noting.

### *Suffering*

The mental and physical phenomena that one is aware of when one notes are all suffering of conditioned phenomena. Their constant arising and passing away is oppressive and so they are the truth of suffering. When one's insight matures and one experiences them in terms of their unique characteristics and universal characteristics—impermanence and so on—one thoroughly understands them. This is why one also accomplishes the function of fully understanding (*pariññākicca*).

### *Craving and cessation*

The more one is accurately aware of mental and physical phenomena, the weaker the illusions of permanence, satisfaction, and personality become for one. Thus one's craving for phenomena diminishes. When one's understanding prevents craving from arising, that craving is abandoned. This accomplishes the function of abandoning (*pahānakicca*) craving, which in turn prevents clinging or grasping (*upādāna*), kamma, and its effect of consequent rebirth. This is the truth of temporary cessation (*tadaṅganirodhasacca*) in the context of insight meditation practice. It amounts to the cessation of craving and suffering for that moment of noting. Thus one accomplishes the function of directly experiencing (*sacchikiriyākicca*) cessation with each noting. In the case of path knowledge, however, "directly experiencing" refers to taking nibbāna as one's object. In the case of insight practice, one does not experience cessation by taking it as one's object; one accomplishes only the function of cessation.

### *Path*

Understanding mental and physical phenomena as they really are, in terms of their individual and universal characteristics, is right view. There are also right intention (*sammā-saṅkappa*), right effort (*sammā-vāyāma*), right mindfulness (*sammā-sati*), and right concentration (*sammā-samādhi*). The mental processes involved in noting are considered right speech (*sammā-vācā*), right action (*sammā-kammanta*), and right livelihood (*sammā-ājīva*), since it is the opposite of wrong speech, wrong action, and wrong livelihood. I will explain this in detail later. This is the mundane noble eightfold path. Because one develops the truth of the path leading to the cessation of suffering with every noting, noting functions to develop the path (*bhāvanākicca*). As the *Visuddhimagga* says:

> When one sees mental and physical phenomena arising and passing away [with fully developed knowledge of arising and passing away], that is the mundane noble eightfold path. Thus the truth of the path leading to the cessation of suffering exists in one.[177]

Thus because the four functions are accomplished in every noting, one understands the four [mundane] truths while noting mental or physical phenomena when they arise. Since all four functions are simultaneously accomplished with one noting, a person who develops mindfulness will gradually attain the supramundane truth of the path leading to cessation of suffering when insight knowledge becomes penetrating and mature. At that point, the four noble truths will be simultaneously fully understood with path knowledge. The commentary explains the phrase "attainment of the true way" [from the *Satipaṭṭhāna Sutta*] as follows:

> The phrase "attainment of the true way" means realizing the noble eightfold path. The mundane practice of mindfulness, developed before path, leads to the attainment of supramundane path knowledge.[178]

## *Cultivating Supramundane Understanding*

### *Suffering: the first noble truth*

We cannot take suffering as an object during path knowledge, but we fully understand it at the moment of path. The reason for this is that when the path is accomplished by experiencing nibbāna as the cessation of all conditioned phenomena, one realizes that both noted phenomena and the noting mind, like all phenomena, are suffering and not peace. One realizes that they are subject to impermanence, even though they appear permanent, satisfying, and personal. We can compare it to losing our sense of direction and getting lost: we may have no idea where to find a particular town, city, road, pond, or lake when we do not know which direction is east or west and so on, but once we regain our sense of direction, we will know how to find the town or city, and so on, without confusion.

Another simile is moving from a place that is extremely hot to a place that is less hot: in comparison we may think, "It's cool here!" If we then went to a third place that was even less hot, we would also think, "Now, this place is really cool!" But when we finally arrived at a place that was actually cool, we would know, "Oh, it really is cool here!" and realize that the prior places were actually hot. In the same way, a person who has never practiced insight meditation thinks that all mental and physical phenomena are good, except unpleasant feelings. He takes places that are not so hot to be cool places. An insight meditator understands that the mental and physical phenomena he observes are unsatisfactory but takes his awareness of that to be something good. This is like taking a less hot place to be a cool place. At the moment of path knowledge, he experiences nibbāna and so is able to understand that all conditioned mental and physical phenomena are not peaceful. This is like having finally arrived at the coolest place and fully realizing that all the other places were hot.

We can find many similar examples in ordinary life. For example, when we encounter an exceptionally wonderful view, fragrant scent, sweet voice, delicious flavor, pleasant touch, good friend, lovely town, and so on, we realize that those one has previously known were not really so wonderful. In the same way, even though suffering is not directly an object of path, the path knowledge penetrates into and realizes suffering with full understanding, since it accomplishes the function of understanding.

An ordinary person cannot definitively decide that all mental and physical phenomena are impermanent, unsatisfactory, and not-self using scriptural knowledge or the power of reasoning. They can only accomplish this with wisdom developed through direct, personal experience. So ordinary people who rely on scriptural knowledge or the power of reasoning cannot overcome skeptical doubt. Often the more they analyze phenomena, the more confused they become.

On the other hand, noble ones who have attained full understanding by means of the path (*maggapariññā*) can definitively decide that all mental and physical phenomena are impermanent, unsatisfactory, and not-self. Unlike ordinary people they do not take mental and physical phenomena to be permanent, satisfactory, and personal, and so cannot become attached to these phenomena. The more they contemplate phenomena, the clearer their understanding of impermanence, unsatisfactoriness, and not-self becomes. So even though a person who has attained the first level of path knowledge is still attached to sense pleasures and strives to enjoy them, she no longer has any intentions toward unwholesome deeds that would lead to the lower realms of existence.

This is the supramundane understanding of suffering.

### *Craving: the second noble truth*

As mentioned above, attachment and craving can no longer arise when one is clearly aware of mental and physical phenomena. Due to the first path, attachment or craving that generates kamma that would lead to the lower realms and more than seven rebirths in a blissful destination (*sugati*) can no longer arise. Due to the second path, attachment or craving that generates gross sense desire (*kāmarāga*) and more than two rebirths can no longer arise. Due to the third path, subtle sense desire and attachment to or craving for sensual pleasure can no longer arise. Due to the fourth path, attachment to or craving for existence in the fine-material realm or immaterial realm can no longer arise.

We can liken this to the situation of a poor person who has become a millionaire, king, or queen—such a person would no longer be attached to or crave for his life as a poor person. Another example is that of a person who had a wicked and blameworthy spouse but now has a respectful and blameless spouse: as soon as the person understands the virtues of her new spouse and the vices of her former spouse, she no longer loves the former spouse.

This nonarising of attachment and craving is called both "penetration by abandoning" (*pahānappaṭivedha*) and "realization by abandoning" (*pahānābhisamaya*) because of [the realization and penetration that occur with] path knowledge. The realization of the abandonment of craving means it is a straightforward and penetrating one, even though path knowledge does not take the craving as its object. This abandoning or nonarising is referred to as "penetration" (*paṭivedha*) and "realization" (*abhisamaya*) because it fulfills the function of understanding. The subcommentary explains:

> Having abandoned, one knows. That is why it is called "penetration by abandoning" (*pahānappaṭivedho*).[179]

Noble ones fully understand that attachment to mental and physical phenomena is the cause of suffering, whereas ordinary people mistake it for pleasure. We can compare this with a person who used to be a heavy smoker but is no longer attached to smoking after coming to understand that smoking is an unhealthy and useless habit.

This is the supramundane understanding of craving, the origin or cause of suffering.

### *Cessation: the third noble truth*

Both the mental and physical phenomena being noted and the noting mind are obvious in a moment of insight practice. The alteration and deformation of these mental and physical phenomena in accordance with their arising and passing away are also obvious. Further, their respective functions and unique characteristics are as obvious as material substance, the body, or a sign are.

But at the moment of path knowledge and fruition knowledge, those mental and physical phenomena are cut off and cease so that only their peaceful nature is obvious. There is no arising and passing away in this state of peace (or cessation), so it is devoid of alteration and deformation. It is also devoid of material substance, body, forms, shapes, and signs. Therefore, at the moment of path knowledge, one takes the truth of cessation called nibbāna as one's object and experiences it as the characteristic of peace (*santilakkhaṇā*), as the function of deathlessness (*accutirasa*), and as the manifestation of the signless (*animittapaccupaṭṭhāna*). This is "penetration through direct experience" (*sacchikiriyāpaṭivedha*) and "realization through direct experience" (*sacchikiriyābhisamaya*). Unlike intellectualization, this experience of the cessation of phenomena is very clear, like seeing a precious jewel in one's hand.

Immediately after one realizes path knowledge, reviewing knowledge that sees nibbāna as devoid of conditioned phenomena and peaceful arises. Noble ones understand that nibbāna is devoid of arising and passing away, and thus it is free from alteration and deformation—is permanent—and devoid of material substance, form, shapes, and signs.

It is like knowing a cool place when one enters a cool and shady place after having been out in a hot place. Or it is like appreciating that one's disease has disappeared when one recovers from a chronic disease.

This is the supramundane understanding of the cessation of suffering.

*Path: the fourth noble truth*

When one practices insight in order to bring about the noble eightfold path, which is the truth of the path leading to the cessation of suffering, one takes nibbāna as one's object, so the truth of the path leading to the cessation of suffering arises in oneself. This is "penetration of the path through development" (*bhāvanāpaṭivedha*) and "realization of the path through development" (*bhāvanābhisamaya*). It is impossible to understand the path through the path itself, just as it is impossible to touch one's finger using that same finger. As soon as a person finds the solution to a problem that he has been pondering, for example, he exclaims, "I've got it, I know!"

After understanding has come about, one recollects it, thinking,

"Before I experienced the peace of nibbāna, the suffering of mental and physical phenomena had not yet ceased. Only with the occurrence of this understanding have the suffering of mental and physical phenomena ceased and been cut off. Thus this understanding is the right path leading to the cessation of suffering."

This is the supramundane awareness of the path leading to the cessation of suffering. Thus the four noble truths are simultaneously understood by taking cessation as one's object and by accomplishing the function of understanding the other three. This point can be checked in the commentarial explanations.

### *How to Develop the Noble Eightfold Path*

If one wants to become a noble one and understand the four noble truths, one must develop the truth of the path leading to the cessation of suffering. If one wants to bring about the supramundane path knowledge, one must develop, with insight practice, the mundane path that includes right view and so on, by noting all arising mental and physical phenomena as explained before. The reason for this is that the path of insight (*vipassanāmagga*) is the cause, the decisive supporting condition (*upanissayapaccaya*) for the resulting conditionally arisen state (*upanissayapaccayuppanna*), the supramundane path.

Thus when the mundane path of insight is not adequately developed, the supramundane path cannot arise. When the path of insight is adequately developed up to the stage of insight knowledge of adaptation, the supramundane path arises by itself without one deliberately exerting much effort. As the *Visuddhimagga* says:

> If one wants to accomplish the first path, there is nothing else to do. Practicing insight meditation [until adaptation] is all one need do.[180]

If one wants to realize path knowledge, one need only practice insight. Thus the mundane path of insight should also be included in the truth of the path that one must develop (*bhāvetabbāmaggasacca*). As the *Sammohavinodanī*[181] says:

> This is the supramundane noble eightfold path, which together with the mundane path [i.e., insight] is called "the path that leads to the cessation of suffering" (*dukkhanirodhagāminīpaṭipadā*).[182]

The eight factors that are included in path consciousness are called "the supramundane path" (*lokuttaramagga*). However, it cannot lead to the cessation of suffering without insight. In other words, this path, which has nibbāna as its object, cannot occur in isolation from the development of insight. That is why the supramundane path and the mundane path together are considered the truth of the path, the truth of the path that leads to the cessation of suffering. The *Visuddhimagga-mahāṭīkā* says:

> The mundane paths are implicitly included, since [the supramundane paths] cannot take place without developing [mundane] concentration and insight.[183]

*How to develop the path factors seclusion, dispassion, and cessation*

In its instructions on developing path factors, the Saṃyutta Nikāya says: "Here, Ānanda, a bhikkhu develops right view, which is based on seclusion, dispassion, and cessation, maturing in release. He develops right intention . . . right speech . . . right action . . . right livelihood . . . right effort . . . right mindfulness . . . right concentration, which is based on seclusion, dispassion, and cessation, maturing in release. It is in this way, Ānanda, that a bhikkhu who has a good friend, a good companion, a good comrade, develops and cultivates the noble eightfold path."[184]

> The term "seclusion [from defilements]" means that one develops right view based on temporary seclusion (*tadaṅgaviveka*), perpetual seclusion (*samucchedaviveka*), and liberation-related seclusion (*nissaraṇaviveka*). To elaborate: in a moment of insight practice, a meditator who is seeking the noble path develops right view based on temporary seclusion in the form of temporarily abandoning defilements and liberation-related seclusion in the form of the aspiration for nibbāna. At

> the moment of path knowledge, the meditator develops right view based on perpetual seclusion in the form of completely abandoning defilements and liberation-related seclusion in the form of taking nibbāna as an object. Understand the terms "dispassion" and "cessation [of defilements]" in the same way, as they have the same meaning.
>
> However, there are two kinds of release (*vossagga*): release that abandons defilements (*pariccāgavossagga*) and release that rushes to nibbāna (*pakkhandanavossagga*). The first kind of release abandons defilements temporarily in a moment of mindful noting and permanently at the moment of path knowledge. The second kind of release rushes to nibbāna by aspiring to it in a moment of mindful noting and by taking it as an object at the moment of path knowledge. Here, both meanings of release serve to explain the mundane and supramundane together.
>
> Thus right view both abandons defilement and rushes into nibbāna. The compound "maturing in release" (*vossagga-pariṇāmiṃ*) refers to both insight, which is maturing, and path, which is fully mature, as abandoning defilements and rushing into nibbāna. The point is that a bhikkhu who practices meditation develops the path in such a way that right view matures [in moments of practicing insight] and becomes fully mature [at the moment of path knowledge] to abandon defilements and to rush into nibbāna. The same is true of the other seven path factors.[185]

There are five kinds of seclusion (*viveka*), dispassion (*virāga*), and cessation (*nirodha*): temporary (*tadaṅga*), liberation-related (*nissaraṇa*), perpetual (*samuccheda*), stopping (*vikkhambhana*), and repeated (*paṭipassaddhi*).

Because there are no latent defilements connected with sense objects at the levels of insight knowledges beginning with knowledge of dissolution, defilements have no opportunity to become obsessive or transgressive. In the context of insight meditation, seclusion from defilements is called "temporary seclusion" (*tadaṅgaviveka*), dispassion toward the defilements is called "temporary dispassion" (*tadaṅgavirāga*), and cessation of the defilements is called "temporary cessation" (*tadaṅganirodha*).

Every time one notes, one understands mental and physical phenomena as they really are. This is insight right view, which is accompanied by insight right thinking or aiming at an object, insight right effort, insight right mindfulness, and insight right concentration. The remaining mental states led by volition constitute right speech, right action, and right livelihood. These eight insight path factors that arise with each noting are referred to as "seclusion-based" (*vivekanissita*), "dispassion-based" (*virāganissita*), and "cessation-based" (*nirodhanissita*) because they are based on the above-mentioned temporary seclusion, dispassion, and cessation. Here "based" means only that each noting leads to seclusion, dispassion, and cessation with regard to the three kinds of defilement; it does not mean that seclusion, dispassion, and cessation are taken as objects.

Nibbāna is called "escape" (*nissaraṇa*) because it is escape from the cycle of defilement, kamma, and resultant (*vipāka*) mental and physical phenomena. Because nibbāna is also seclusion, dispassion, and escape from defilements, it is called "escape by means of seclusion" (*nissaraṇaviveka*), "escape by means of dispassion" (*nissaraṇavirāga*), and "escape by means of cessation" (*nissaraṇanirodha*). The above-mentioned insight path factors arise only for those who aspire to experience nibbāna and who note mental and physical phenomena every time they arise. Those who enjoy life and do not aspire to attain nibbāna do not practice, and so the insight path factors do not arise for them. Thus these path factors are called "based on nibbāna" due to bearing the aspiration to attain it. For this reason, too, they are based on the seclusion of nibbāna, the dispassion of nibbāna, and the cessation of nibbāna. In this case, at the time of noting, one does not take nibbāna as one's object. It is only referred to as "based on nibbāna" because of the aspiration to experience nibbāna.

This is like performing an act of generosity with the aim of attaining nibbāna. The intention that arises during the act of offering takes the offering as its object, not nibbāna. Yet because the action was done with the aim of attaining nibbāna it is called "a nibbāna-based wholesome action" or "a wholesome action based beyond the round of rebirth" (*vivaṭṭanissita*). In the same way, although one takes the presently arising mental and physical phenomena as one's object, insight is called "nibbāna-based" because one notes with the aspiration to attain nibbāna. Thus an insight meditator who notes every arising mental and physical phenomenon is said to develop the insight path factors that are based on temporary seclusion, temporary dispassion, and temporary cessation, as well as escape by means of seclusion, dispassion, and cessation. As I have said, this is the truth of temporary seclusion that one can experience with insight practice.

The seclusion, dispassion, and cessation through the four supramundane knowledges of the path (in connection with the complete eradication of the respective defilements at each path) are called "perpetual seclusion" (*samucchedaviveka*), "perpetual dispassion" (*samucchedavirāga*), and "perpetual cessation" (*samucchedanirodha*). Because the supramundane path factors accomplish the seclusion, dispassion, and cessation of the defilements by eradicating them completely, they are called "nibbāna-based seclusion," "nibbāna-based dispassion," and "nibbāna-based cessation." Further, because they also take nibbāna (which is called "escape by means of seclusion," "escape by means of dispassion," and "escape by means of cessation") as their object, they are called "escape-based seclusion," "escape-based dispassion," and "escape-based cessation."

### *Maturing in release*

The insight path factors are in the process of maturing in order to abandon the defilements. Because these path factors arise only for those who aspire to attain nibbāna, the process of maturing also includes release in nibbāna by way of aspiring to it. Therefore it is called "maturing in release" (*vosaggapariṇāmī*).

When the meditator notes every arising mental and physical phenomenon she is said to develop the *vipassanā* path factors. The supramundane path factors are brought to full maturity in order to completely abandon their respective defilements. They are also brought to full maturity so that one will be released into nibbāna by taking it as one's object. This is why it is called "maturing in release."

Here "fully mature" means that at the moment of path knowledge, one need not exert effort in order to take nibbāna as one's object or to abandon the defilements. Taking nibbāna as one's object and eradicating the defilements happen by themselves, due to the momentum of the preliminary path (*pubbabhāgamagga*) gained through the development of the insight path factors [up to insight knowledge of adaptation]. A person who wants to jump over a wide ditch, for example, begins running toward it from some distance away and needn't make further efforts once she has leaped from the brink of the ditch; she will simply be carried to the other side by momentum. This is difficult to understand!

### *The morality path factors*

Insight practice includes the morality path factors of right speech, right action, and right livelihood. The commentaries on Abhidhamma and Khuddaka Nikāya explain:

> The same is true of the other seven path factors.[186] The three factors of right speech and so on refer to abstinence and mental volition. In the case of path, however, they refer only to abstinence.[187]

Refraining from immoral conduct in speech, action, and livelihood is abstinence. This constitutes moral conduct, consisting of right speech, right action, and right livelihood. Actively engaging in wholesome speech, actions, and thoughts involves wholesome intention, and is accordingly also referred to as "right speech" and so on. However, at the time of path knowledge, only the mental factors connected with abstinence are called "right speech" and so on. Since insight meditation falls within the realm of wholesome thought, the intention involved in wholesome mental states constitutes right speech and so on. In the case of insight knowledge and the various knowledges of the path, however, the abstinence involved is not the same as that involved in ordinary moral conduct.

> In the Pāḷi text called *Sikkhāpadavibhaṅga*,[188] a moral precept is defined, in an ultimate sense, as abstinence, intention, and

> associated dhammas (*sampayuttadhammā*). Of these three, only abstinence and intention are mentioned here, as they are the dominant factors. In other words, refraining from telling a lie, and so on, is abstinence, while telling the truth, and so on, is intention.[189]

*Contemplation of the four truths*

According to the commentary, insight meditation is called "contemplation of the four truths" (*catusaccakammaṭṭhāna*) because it leads to attainment of the path knowledge that understands the four noble truths by observing mental and physical phenomena (i.e., suffering and craving) with the aim of attaining the various knowledges of the path and nibbāna, and because it produces the special happiness of bliss of the knowledges of path and fruition that comes from meditation aimed at understanding the four noble truths.

> Insight meditation that leads to the understanding of the four noble truths, or insight meditation that is practiced with the aim of experiencing the four truths, is called "contemplation of the four truths" and becomes the cause for the meditator's special happiness of bliss of the knowledges of path and fruition.[190]

*The example of mindfulness of in and out breath*

The commentary says that any meditation that is practiced according to one of the twenty-one sections mentioned in the *Satipaṭṭhāna Sutta* leads to knowledge that is the fruit of arahantship (*arahattaphala*), and is considered to be contemplation of the four noble truths. The practice of mindfulness of in and out breath (*ānāpānasati*) is considered here as an example:

> Mindfulness of the in and out breath is the truth of suffering. Previous craving is its origin. The cessation of both is nibbāna. The path knowledge that fully understands suffering, abandons craving, and takes nibbāna as its object is the truth of the

> path leading to the cessation of suffering. By means of contemplating the four noble truths one gradually becomes more purified and reaches the cessation of defilements. Thus this in and out breath practice becomes the cause for a monk's liberation from the cycle of suffering through knowledge that is the fruit of arahantship (*arahattaphala*).[191]

If a meditator notes the in and out breath in harmony with this text, she will experience the air element or the sensation of touch every time she notes. This is the awareness or mindfulness that is considered the preliminary insight path. Because it is necessary for attainment of the supramundane path, it is included figuratively under development of the path. But since it is mundane, this mindfulness is not really part of the truth of the path to the cessation of suffering but is actually part of the truth of suffering. Contemplation of the four noble truths is insight practice that is only aimed at the definite noble truths. Thus in the explanation of how contemplation of the four noble truths occurs, the commentators say that mindfulness belongs only to the truth of suffering.

The passage above says: "Mindfulness of the in and out breath is the truth of suffering." Mindfulness is singled out as the truth of suffering, but this is only a figure of speech based on the fact that mindfulness is the dominant factor involved. Actually, all of the mental and physical phenomena associated with mindfulness are also the truth of suffering. This includes the consciousness and mental factors that accompany mindfulness, the physical body on which mindfulness depends, and the air element or sensations of touch from the in and out breath that mindfulness takes as its object. Mindfulness, along with all of these mental and physical phenomena, is seen in a moment of insight and fully understood as the truth of suffering at the moment of path knowledge. This process that is mindful of previous mindfulness and its accompanying mental factors is called "counter insight."

> The craving that was the origin of the body is also the origin of mindfulness, since mindfulness arises dependent on that body. If there were no craving, the body could not come into existence, and neither could mindfulness. Thus it is said:

> "Previous craving is its origin." Just as "conditioned phenomena is the origin of consciousness" refers to all mundane states of consciousness that originated from those conditioned phenomena, in line with the discourses.[192]

All mental and physical phenomena, beginning with the moment of relinking consciousness, are results of one of the wholesome volitional deeds performed in previous lives. The cause of those wholesome volitional deeds was the craving for life and the results of actions. Thus craving is regarded as the origin of all mental and physical phenomena in one's present life.

In the Pāḷi passage above, this is compared to the use of the word "consciousness" in the expression "conditioned phenomena are the origin of consciousness." "Consciousness" refers only to "resultant" consciousness—consciousness that is the direct result of previous conditioned phenomena. However, by extension, it includes all other types of consciousness: wholesome, unwholesome, and functional (*kriyācitta*). This is so because these other types of consciousness all originate in turn from the resultant consciousness.

Likewise, the craving that we harbored in previous lives has been generating the cycle of mental and physical phenomena, including mindfulness, throughout our present life. This is why craving is said to be the origin of mindfulness. It is said that mindfulness is the truth of suffering and that its origin, craving in previous lives, is the truth of the cause of suffering. Although it is impossible to be empirically aware of craving from a past life, we can inferentially realize it when our insight practice matures enough to perceive craving in the present life. Every time we note craving in the present, we are said to see the truth of the cause of suffering, because both past and present craving have the same characteristics and belong to the same individual person.

Nibbāna, which is the cessation of the truth of suffering as well as the cessation of craving (the cause of suffering), is called "the truth of the cessation of suffering." The eight supramundane path factors that accomplish the function of fully understanding the truth of suffering and abandoning craving as its cause, while taking nibbāna as its object, are called the "truth of the path to the cessation of suffering." As a meditator, all that one need do with regard to cessation and path is to appreciate their nobility and arouse the aspiration to attain them. Thus according to the *Visuddhimagga*:

> It is certain that I will be liberated from the cycle of rebirth, aging, sickness, and death through this practice.[193]

When, based on the previous aspiration for cessation and the path, a person observes the presently arising in breath and out breath or any other mental and physical phenomena [that constitute the truth of suffering and the truth of the cause of suffering], she is said to practice the insight meditation called contemplation of the four noble truths (*catusaccakammaṭṭhāna*). This person attains the cessation of all defilements by gradually going through the levels of purification (*visuddhi*), beginning with purification of view, and the four kinds of purification of knowledge and vision (*ñāṇadassanavisuddhi*), beginning with the first path knowledge (see Appendix 4). This means that the person has become an arahant. The commentators in the above quotes have explained this.

## The Moment of Path Knowledge

At the moment of the four various knowledges of the path that are also called "the purification of knowledge and vision," one simultaneously understands the four noble truths. I have already explained how they are realized, but I will offer some further explanation here.

### How one understands suffering

Path knowledge experiences nibbāna, which is the cessation of all mental and physical phenomena (such as constantly arising and disappearing in breath and out breath or mindfulness). Due to this experience, one fully understands without confusion that all these phenomena (that is, the in breath and out breath, mindfulness, dependent material phenomena, constantly arising and disappearing mental and physical phenomena, and conditioned phenomena) are suffering and not peaceful.

*How one understands craving*

When one has fully understood that all conditioned phenomena are unsatisfactory, craving for these conditioned mental and physical phenomena no longer arises. This absence is penetration by abandoning (*pahānappaṭivedha*) and realization by abandoning (*pahānābhisamaya*).

*How one understands cessation and path*

By taking nibbāna—the cessation of all conditioned phenomena—as one's object, path factors such as right view arise distinctly in oneself. Experiencing nibbāna at that moment is penetrating or realizing the truth of cessation. The arising of the path factors, the truth of the path leading to the cessation of suffering while taking nibbāna as one's object, comes about by observing objects such as the in and out breath. This is called "penetration through development" and "realization through development."

## Other Objects of Meditation

So far, I have explained how, by observing the in and out breath as her basic object, an insight meditator becomes enlightened, up to the attainment of knowledge that is the fruit of arahantship (*arahattaphala*). The commentary gives similar explanations of how to develop the four noble truths and become an arahant for the twenty other sections of the text that deal with alternate objects of meditation, such as the bodily postures and so on. The only difference among these various practices is the primary object of mindfulness. I will briefly mention the different objects here.

- "Bodily postures" (*iriyāpatha*) refers to awareness of bodily postures, such as walking, standing, sitting, and lying down, as the truth of suffering.
- "Clear comprehension" (*sampajañña*) refers to awareness of moving forward or back, bending and stretching the limbs, and so on as the truth of suffering.

- "Attention to repulsiveness" (*paṭikkūlamanasikāra*) refers to awareness of the thirty-two parts of the body—hair on the head, body hair, nails, teeth, skin, and so on—as the truth of suffering. However, this awareness is a form of tranquility meditation, not insight. Body parts, such as hair, are conceptual objects and not absolute realities. Therefore the objects of the awareness cannot be included in the truth of suffering.
- "Attention to the elements" (*dhātumanasikāra*) refers to awareness of the four primary material elements as the truth of suffering.
- "Charnel ground contemplation" (*sīvathika*) refers to awareness of a swollen corpse and so on as the truth of suffering.
- "Contemplation of feeling" (*vedanānupassanā*) refers to awareness of feeling as the truth of suffering.
- "Contemplation of mind" (*cittānupassanā*) refers to awareness of mind as the truth of suffering.
- "Hindrances" (*nīvaraṇa*) refers to awareness of hindrances as the truth of suffering.
- "Aggregates subject to clinging" (*upādānakkhandhā*) refers to awareness of the five aggregates as the truth of suffering.
- "Sense bases" (*āyatana*) refers to awareness of the sense bases and fetters as the truth of suffering.
- "Factors of enlightenment" (*bojjhaṅgā*) refers to awareness of the factors of enlightenment as the truth of suffering.
- "Four noble truths" (*ariyasaccā*) refers to awareness of the truth of suffering and the truth of craving as the cause of suffering, and the awareness of the truth of the cessation of suffering and the truth of the path to the cessation of suffering, in the form of the aspiration to attain it, as the truth of suffering.

Among these twenty sections, only mindfulness is explicitly said to be the truth of suffering. However, as explained above, this is only a figurative way of speaking and refers to the fact that mindfulness is the dominant factor involved. Actually all of the accompanying mental factors, physical and mental objects, and the physical bases associated with mindfulness are also the truth of suffering that insight knowledge and path knowledge must realize. Thus, when one practices insight using these meditation subjects, in order to attain path knowledge and nibbāna one should be aware of: the meditation object itself, such as the body posture, and so on; one's awareness of the object; mental factors that accompany one's awareness; the physical basis of that awareness, if it is obvious; and the present craving that is similar to past craving, which was the origin of the present phenomena.

When one's insight knowledge matures, one will automatically become inferentially aware of the past origins of phenomena. So one need not exert effort or reflect on them. If one practices in this way, one will be practicing the form of insight meditation that is called "contemplation of the four noble truths." Going through the different levels of purification, one will attain the defilement-free state of arahantship.

In accordance with the commentary, this is briefly how a person who practices any of the twenty-one sections mentioned in the *Satipaṭṭhāna Sutta* develops contemplation of the Four Truths and attains the knowledges of path and fruition up to the knowledge that is the fruit of arahantship (*arahattaphala*).

## The Benefits of Mindfulness

After having attained all the four stages of path knowledge and fruition knowledge, a person who practices according to the *Satipaṭṭhāna Sutta* becomes purified of all mental defilements such as lust, aversion, and delusion; overcomes all forms of worry and grief, as well as weeping and lamentation; overcomes all forms of physical suffering and mental suffering—there is no more physical suffering after having entered *parinibbāna* and there is no more mental suffering after having attained knowledge that is the fruit of arahantship (*arahattaphala*); attains the four various knowledges of the path, which are also called "right conduct" (*ñāya*); and understands nibbāna, which is the cessation of all kinds of suffering.

## The Only Way

The Buddha praised the mindfulness practice of the foundations of mindfulness as follows:

> Bhikkhus, this is the [only way][194] for the purification of beings, for the surmounting of sorrow and lamentation, for the disappearance of pain and grief, for the attainment of the true way, for the realization of nibbāna—namely, the four foundations of mindfulness."[195]

This passage explicitly states that mindfulness is the only way to purify the mind of mental defilements and realize nibbāna. So being mindful of the body, feelings, mind, and mind objects, which are all ultimate realities, is certainly contemplation of the four noble truths, the development of insight, and the preliminary path. The development of the four efforts, five mental faculties, seven factors of enlightenment, eight path factors, and so on are all included in this mindfulness practice. No practice can lead to nibbāna without mindfulness of the body, feelings, mind, and mind objects. This is the commentarial explanation of this point:

> The phrase "this is the only way" means that this path is the only path; it is not a divided path or two paths. [196]
>
> The term "only way" means the one-and-only path, as there is no other path besides mindfulness that leads to nibbāna. One may wonder: "Why does 'path' refer only to mindfulness practice when there are many other paths?" It is true that there are many other paths, but all are embraced by mindfulness practice, which is indispensable. That is why wisdom, effort, and so forth are mentioned in the *Niddesa*, while only mindfulness is mentioned in the *Uddesa*, according to the inclination of the Dhamma audience (*veneyyajjhāsaya*). The phrase "not a divided path" indicates that there is not any other path and that it is impossible that this path does not lead to nibbāna.[197]

Furthermore, the commentaries say that it is only through path knowledge based on mindfulness that the countless buddhas, silent buddhas, and noble followers have been purified of mental defilements. It is impossible to arouse wisdom without noting the body, feelings, mind, and mind objects. It is also due to path knowledge based on mindfulness that some people in the Buddha's time attained the knowledges of path and fruition by listening to just a single verse of discourse. So it should be clear in one's mind that the only practice that leads to knowledge of path and fruition is the mindfulness practice of contemplating the body, feelings, mind, and mind objects, which are ultimate realities.

### *The Buddha's Acknowledgment*

The Buddha acknowledged that a person of middling intelligence, wisdom, or understanding (*majjhimapaññāneyya*) who practiced in harmony with one of the twenty-one methods would become an arahant or a nonreturner within a maximum of seven years and after a minimum of seven days:

> If anyone should develop these four foundations of mindfulness in such a way for seven days, one of two fruits could be expected for him: either final knowledge here and now, or if there is a trace of clinging left, nonreturn.[198]

In the *Bodhirājakumāra Sutta*,[199] the Buddha acknowledged that a person of sharp intelligence, wisdom, or understanding (*tikkhapaññāneyya*) can even become fully enlightened within a night or a day:

> When a bhikkhu who possesses these five factors of striving finds a tathāgata to discipline him, then being instructed in the evening, he might arrive at distinction in the morning; being instructed in the morning, he might arrive at distinction in the evening.[200]

These are the five factors of striving: (1) faith in the Buddha, Dhamma, Saṅgha, one's meditation teacher, and the meditation method, (2) sufficient health to digest the food one eats, (3) enough honesty to state the facts of one's experience to one's teacher and fellow meditators without boasting about virtues that one is not endowed with or trying to conceal one's shortcomings, (4) the determination to persist in one's efforts until one becomes fully enlightened, even if the result is that one's flesh and blood wither away, leaving only skin, sinew, and bones, and (5) arousing insight knowledge of the arising and passing away of mental and physical phenomena.

"May you be able to attain the knowledge of path and fruition and reach nibbāna within seven years, or seven days, or even within one night or day." These words are not the words of an ordinary person but of the Buddha, who understood by himself all phenomena as they really are. Because he said only what was true and beneficial, they are the words of the Sugata, as the Buddha was called. Therefore may you all be endowed with faith and the aspiration to become free from the cycle of suffering.

> The buddhas do not speak ambiguously [they only speak what is true]; the victorious ones do not speak fruitlessly [they only speak what is beneficial].[201]

If one has faith that the Buddha speaks only what is true and beneficial, and having faith in the two acknowledgments, then one should aspire like this: "If I am a person with sharp intelligence, wisdom, and understanding, I will become fully enlightened even within one night or one day. If I am a person with middling intelligence, wisdom, and understanding, I will become fully enlightened within seven days, or within fifteen days, or within seven years."

With this aspiration may you be able to practice mindfulness meditation.

## *Suitable Contemplations*

The *Satipaṭṭhāna Sutta* and its commentary state that one can attain the final fruition knowledge by practicing in harmony with one of the twenty-one meditations (that is, the contemplation of the in and out breath, and so on). However, this does not mean that the knowledge of path and fruition can be attained only by practicing exclusively according to one particular section without following the practices in any of the other sections. When asked about this, the Buddha taught bhikkhu Uttiya and others to develop all four foundations of mindfulness.[202] Practicing in that way, they attained arahantship.

Saying that one is bound to attain the knowledge that is the fruit of arahantship (*arahattaphala*) by practicing in line with one of the twenty-one meditations refers to the contemplation of an object from one particular section as a primary object. It does not mean that one should contemplate only a particular object mentioned in a particular section and ignore any objects mentioned in other sections, however obvious they may be. If one did this, it would lead to a sense of permanence, satisfaction, personality, and beauty in regard to those mental and physical phenomena that are not noted.

These days it is quite difficult to accurately determine which particular meditation object is most suitable for a particular person. However, based on my own experience, the contemplation of the body as a primary object is suitable for most people. That is why, in the next chapter, I will explain how to practice the four foundations of mindfulness using contemplation of the body as the primary object. I will present the foundations in the order that they should be practiced rather than the order in which they are taught. In conclusion, I offer this wish:

> May you all be able to observe mental and physical phenomena as instructed, using one or more of the contemplations that are suitable for your own particular inclination and disposition, and quickly attain the knowledges of path and fruition, nibbāna, by going through the stages of insight knowledge.

Here ends the chapter regarding the development of mindfulness.

# Practical Instructions

In this chapter, I will explain how to practice insight meditation and experience path knowledge and fruition knowledge from a practical perspective. So I will use everyday language rather than technical terminology.[203] I will also not be including many textual references or quotations. If readers have any doubts on a subject, they can refer to the supporting material and references included in earlier chapters of the *Manual of Insight*.

## Preparations for Practice

If a meditator aspires to attain path knowledge and fruition knowledge and nibbāna in this very life, he should cut any impediments during the time of meditation practice through the following preparations.

Purify moral conduct[204] and cultivate the wish: "May my moral conduct be supportive of path knowledge." If you suspect that you may have ever committed some offense toward an enlightened person, you should apologize for the mistake. If you cannot go see that person to apologize, you should offer the apology in front of a teacher.

Entrust yourself to the Buddha's wisdom in order to be free from fear in the event that frightening objects appear during intensive practice. You should also entrust yourself to a teacher's care so that the teacher may guide you without any hesitation. This may not be necessary if you are already following a teacher's instructions respectfully.

Reflect on the merits of nibbāna, which is completely free from any mental or physical suffering; path knowledge, which eradicates defilements and leads directly to nibbāna; and insight practice, which will surely lead to the attainment of path knowledge and nibbāna. You should find inspiration by remembering that the path of insight you are practicing is the same path that the Buddha, arahants, and all of the noble ones have followed.

You should then bow to the Buddha, reflecting on as many of his attributes as you know. After this, it is recommended that one cultivate loving-kindness toward all living beings, beginning with the devas that guard the monastery. If possible, you should then contemplate death and the impurity of your own body.

Finally, you should sit with legs crossed, or in any other sitting posture that is comfortable, and observe as explained below.

## The Basic Practice

### *The Primary Object*

The meditator should focus the mind on the abdomen. You will feel it rising and falling. If you don't feel this clearly, place a hand on the abdomen and its rise and fall will become obvious after a while. When breathing in, you will experience the rising movement of the abdomen. Note this as "rising." When breathing out, you will experience the falling movement. Note this as "falling."

While doing this you may reflect that observing the form or concept of the abdomen is not what you ought to be doing. This is not a cause for worry. Initially, of course, it is almost impossible to avoid a conceptual sense of solid form. So in the beginning, you must observe objects on a conceptual level. That is the only way that your concentration, awareness, and insight knowledge will mature. In due time, however, insight knowledge will break through to the absolute reality beyond concepts.

True insight practice is an awareness of all of the mental and physical phenomena that constantly arise at the six sense doors. However, because concentration and awareness are not strong enough in the beginning, it will be difficult to observe all the phenomena that constantly arise. You will not be skillful enough to follow all of the objects, or may get caught up in searching for an object to note. For these reasons, you should initially focus just on the rise and fall of the abdomen that occurs all the time and is noticeable enough to observe without much difficulty. Later, when your practice matures, you will be able to note objects as they arise.

So you should concurrently and continuously note the movements of the abdomen as "rising" and "falling" from moment to moment. A meditator should do this mentally, not audibly. Do not make the breath more vigorous than usual so as to make the rise and fall more distinct; neither slow down nor speed up the breath. If a meditator changes his natural pattern of breathing, he may get tired quickly and not be able to note properly. Just breathe in and out normally and regularly, and observe concurrently.

*A textual note*

The rise and fall of the abdomen is a manifestation of the air element, one of the types of tactile, physical phenomena. When observing the rise and fall, you will experience pressure and movement, which are characteristics of the air element, in accord with the following Pāḷi passages:

> Bhikkhus, attend carefully to form. Recognize the impermanence of form as it really is.[205]
>
> Bhikkhus, a bhikkhu sees as impermanent form that is actually impermanent: that is his right view.[206]

This is stated in discourses contained in the Khandhasaṃyutta of the Saṃyutta Nikāya. And it is also in accordance with the contemplation of mind objects (the five aggregates) in the *Mahāsatipaṭṭhāna Sutta*.

> Bhikkhus, attend carefully to tactile objects. Recognize the impermanence of tactile objects as it really is.[207]
>
> Bhikkhus, a bhikkhu sees as impermanent tactile objects that are actually impermanent: that is his right view.[208]
>
> By directly knowing and fully understanding the eye . . . the mind, by developing dispassion toward [tactile objects] and abandoning them, one is capable of destroying suffering.[209]
>
> When one knows and sees [tactile objects] as impermanent, ignorance is abandoned and true knowledge arises.[210]

This is stated in discourses contained in the Saḷāyatanasaṃyutta of the

Saṃyutta Nikāya. It is also in accordance with the contemplation of mind objects (the six bases) in the *Mahāsatipaṭṭhāna Sutta*.

> Now both the internal air element and the external air element are simply the air element. And that should be seen as it actually is with proper wisdom thus: "This is not mine, this I am not, this is not my self."[211]

This is as stated in the discourses dealing with the elements. It is also in accordance with the contemplation of the body (elements) in the *Mahāsatipaṭṭhāna Sutta*.

Moreover, the air element is part of the materiality aggregate subject to clinging (*rūpa-upādānakkhandha*) and is therefore included in the truth of suffering. It should be seen as it really is, in accord with the Buddha's teaching:

> This noble truth of suffering is to be fully understood.[212]

This is in accordance with the discourses dealing with the noble truths. It is also included in the contemplation of mind objects (the four noble truths) in the *Mahāsatipaṭṭhāna Sutta*.

Therefore, observing the rise and fall of the abdomen is clearly consistent with the teaching of the Buddha, because one understands the pressure and movement of the air element as it really is. With regard to the observation of the in and out breath as explained in the previous chapter, it is said:

> He understands accordingly however his body is disposed.[213]

### *Distracting Thoughts*

As you continually note the rise and fall of the abdomen, various kinds of thoughts will arise. When this happens, you note them using everyday language. For example, when you find yourself thinking, note it as "thinking, thinking." If you daydream, note it as "daydreaming, daydreaming." If you imagine something, note it as "imagining, imagining."

If you find yourself considering something, note it as "considering, considering." When the mind wanders off, note it as "wandering, wandering." If you imagine traveling to some other place, note it as "traveling, traveling." If you imagine meeting someone, note it as "meeting, meeting." If you imagine speaking with someone, note it as "speaking, speaking." Whenever you imagine seeing something or someone, repeatedly note it as "seeing, seeing," until the mental image disappears. Then immediately return to noting the rise and fall of the abdomen.

### *Physical Discomfort*

While noting the rise and fall of the abdomen, you may feel like you want to swallow or spit out the saliva in your mouth. This should be noted as "wanting to swallow," or "wanting to spit." If a meditator actually swallows or spits, he notes it as "swallowing, swallowing" or "spitting, spitting" and immediately returns to noting the rise and fall of the abdomen. If you want to lower your head, note it as "wanting to lower." If you bend the neck to lower the head, note it as "bending, bending" while continuing to focus on every movement involved. Do this slowly, not quickly. Follow the same procedure when bringing the head back up again. Afterward, go right back to the primary object of the rise and fall of the abdomen.

When an uncomfortable stiffness arises in any part of the body, focus only on the stiffness and continuously note it as "stiffness, stiffness." Keep your noting concurrent with the actual sensation. The stiffness may slowly fade away, or it may grow even more intense. If it becomes unbearable and you want to shift your posture, note that mental state as "wanting to shift, wanting to shift." If you actually shift your posture, continue to note each of the physical movements involved in that process. When you want to lift a limb, for example, note it as "wanting to lift." Then, when you actually lift it, note each movement as "lifting, lifting." When stretching it, note that as "stretching." When bending it, note that as "bending." When lowering it again, note that as "lowering." Do not make any of these movements quickly, but rather make them slowly and steadily. If you feel something touching any part of the body during the movement, note it as "touching." When you are done shifting your posture, or if the stiffness fades away without shifting your posture, immediately return to noting the rise and fall of the abdomen.

If you feel heat somewhere in your body, focus the mind on it and concurrently and continuously note it as "heat, heat." If it fades away, return to noting the rise and fall of the abdomen. If it becomes unbearable and you want to shift your posture, note it as "wanting to shift." If you actually shift your posture, concurrently and continuously note the entire process of lifting each limb as described above. Afterward, immediately return to noting the rise and fall of the abdomen. A meditator does not leave any gap in the flow of noting.

When a meditator feels a bodily itch, he focuses on it and steadily and continuously notes it as "itching, itching." While noting it in this way, the itch may fade away. If it does, return to noting the rise and fall of the abdomen. If the itch becomes unbearable and you either want it to disappear or to scratch it, note it as "wanting to disappear" or "wanting to scratch." If a meditator wants to raise her hand to scratch, she notes it as "wanting to raise." As you actually raise your hand, note it as "raising." Do this slowly and steadily. When touching the itchy part of your body, note it as "touching." As you scratch, every time your hand or fingers move back and forth note it as "scratching." When you feel like you want to stop scratching, note it as "wanting to stop." When you want to put your hand back down, note it as "wanting to put down." A meditator then notes "lowering, lowering" as she actually lowers the hand. When you feel the touch of your hand coming to rest back in its place, note it as "touching." Immediately afterward, a meditator returns to noting their primary object, the rise and fall of the abdomen.

When any kind of unpleasant sensation arises and becomes distinct, a meditator focuses his mind on it and notes it accurately and steadily using everyday language such as "pain, pain," "numb, numb," "ache, ache," "tired, tired," or "dizzy, dizzy." When you note it in this way, it may fade away or increase. If noted with patience and perseverance, it often fades away. If it becomes unbearable, ignore it and take extra care to concurrently and continuously note the rise and fall of the abdomen.

## *Odd Experiences*

As concentration grows stronger, you may experience unbearable pain in your body. You may feel strong pressure, as if an airbag were being inflated inside your chest, a sharp pain, as if being stabbed with a dagger, a stinging pain, as if being pricked with many small needles, or an overall irritation, as if insects were crawling all over your body. You may feel fierce heat, severe itchiness, unbearable aching, extreme cold, or a variety of other unpleasant sensations.

If a meditator becomes frightened and stops noting when any of these kinds of extreme sensations occur, he will find that they immediately disappear. But they will generally reappear when his noting becomes strong again. A meditator should not be afraid of encountering any of these kinds of experiences. These are not signs of some serious disease; they are ordinary sensations that we often have in our bodies. We rarely notice them, however, because our attention is usually occupied with more obvious sensations. It is actually the strength of our concentration that makes them obvious in this way. So you needn't worry that something is wrong. Simply continue to note the sensation in order to overcome it. If a meditator stops noting, he may end up encountering the same kind of sensation every time concentration becomes strong. If you note it with patience and perseverance, though, at some point it will suddenly disappear for good.

If you feel like your body wants to sway, note it as "wanting to sway." If your body starts to actually sway, note it as "swaying, swaying." If you find yourself swaying unintentionally, you should not be afraid of it, nor should you encourage it. You simply continue noting it, steadily and gradually, as "swaying, swaying," confident that it will disappear if noted. If the swaying becomes very strong, you can practice while sitting against a wall or other firm support, or while lying down; the swaying will soon cease entirely. Follow the same procedure if you experience trembling in the body.

Sometimes you may get goose bumps or a chill may run up your back or through your whole body. You needn't be afraid of this; it's just rapture brought on by your meditation. Sometimes any sound you hear may cause fear to arise. You needn't fear this either; it's just that your sensitivity to mental contact has become very keen as a result of strong concentration. Any time you feel like rearranging your limbs or posture, first note the intention to do so, and then note every single successive movement involved as well. A meditator should not move quickly. He should move slowly and steadily.

## *Getting a Drink*

When you are thirsty, note it as "thirsty." If you intend to stand up to get a drink, note it as "intending to stand up." As a meditator prepares to stand up, she notes all of the physical movements involved using everyday language. When standing up, focus on the gradual rise of the body and note it as "standing up, standing up." Move slowly and steadily. When you have risen and are standing, note it as "standing, standing." If you happen to see or look at something or someone, note it as "seeing" or "looking." When you want to get some water, note it as "wanting to go." While you are actually going, note every step as "stepping, stepping" or "right, left." Follow each step mindfully from the moment the foot is lifted until it is dropped back down again. When walking slowly, or during formal walking meditation, note two parts of each step: either "lifting, moving," "lifting, dropping," or "moving, dropping." Once you can easily note two parts of each step, switch to noting three parts: "lifting, moving, dropping."

When you look at and see the container of drinking water, note it as "looking, seeing." When standing still in front of it, note that as "standing, standing." When reaching for a cup, note that as "reaching, reaching." When touching the cup, note that as "touching, touching." When taking hold of the cup, note that as "holding, holding." When pouring water into the cup, note that as "pouring, pouring." When lifting the cup of water to the mouth, note that as "lifting, lifting." When the cup touches the lips, note that as "touching, touching." When feeling the coldness of the water, note that as "cold, cold." When drinking and swallowing the water, note that as "drinking, swallowing." When feeling the coldness of the water in your throat or stomach, note it as "cold, cold." When putting the cup down, note that as "putting down, putting down." When lowering the hand, note that as "lowering, lowering." When the hand touches the body, note that as "touching, touching."

When the intention arises to turn and go back to your seat, note it as "intending to turn," and as you turn, note it as "turning, turning." As you walk back to your seat, note each step in the same way described above. When you intend to come to a stop and stand still, note that as "intending to stand," and then note "standing, standing" as you stand. If you remain standing for some time, you can note the rise and fall of the abdomen along with the standing posture as "rising, falling, standing." When you intend to sit down, note that as "intending to sit." If you need to position yourself on your seat, note that in a similar manner. If you need to turn, note it as "turning."

As you lower yourself to sit, note it as "sitting down, sitting down," with awareness of the weight of the body gradually being lowered. Do everything slowly and steadily. Once you are seated, you will need to arrange your hands and legs again. Carefully note all of the movements involved, using everyday language. Then if there are no other obvious objects to note, return to noting the primary object, the rise and fall of the abdomen, as usual.

### *Going to Bed*

When you want to lie down, note it as "wanting to lie down." As you prepare the bed, note all of the movements of the arms and legs as "lifting," "stretching," "repositioning," and so on. As you lie down, focus on the whole body as it gradually lies down and note it as "lying down, lying down." When feeling the touch of the pillow and bedding, note it as "touching, touching." When finally lying, note the movements of the arms, legs, and body, and note any adjustment of your lying posture as well. Do this slowly and mindfully. Then if there is nothing else to note, focus on the rise and fall of the abdomen, continuously noting it.

As a meditator lies in bed noting the rise and fall of the abdomen, he may feel some unpleasant sensations, such as stiffness, heat, pain, itchiness, and so on. If you do, note these mindfully in the same way you do in sitting meditation. Carefully note any distractions, such as swallowing, thinking, imagining, and so on, as you would at other times.

If you want to turn over, bend or stretch your limbs, or adjust your position in any other way, first note the intention and then note every single movement involved without missing any. When there is nothing else in particular to note, return to noting the primary object, the rise and fall of the abdomen. If you feel sleepy, note it as "sleepy, sleepy." If your eyelids feel heavy, note that as "heavy, heavy." When your meditation matures, sleepiness disappears and the mind becomes clear again. If that happens, note it as "clear, clear" and return to noting the rise and fall of the abdomen. If sleepiness has not disappeared, do not stop noting; simply continue noting the rise and fall of the abdomen or any other object without any intention of falling asleep. When your body gets really tired you will eventually fall asleep in the middle of noting.

Sleep is a prolonged period of the "life continuum" or "functional" consciousness. This is the same kind of consciousness that arises during the first and last moments of our lives. This type of consciousness is so subtle that its sense objects cannot be known. Life-continuum consciousness also occurs between successive moments of full consciousness while we are awake. It occurs, for example, between moments of seeing and thinking, hearing and thinking, and so on. However, it does not last long enough for us to notice on such occasions. When we sleep it lasts long enough that we notice it, but we still cannot detect its characteristics or its object. So it is not possible to note any objects when we are asleep.

### *Getting Up*

As soon as you wake up, note it as "waking up, waking up." At the beginning of your practice you will find it difficult to catch the first moments of waking. If a meditator is not yet able to note right from the moment of waking up, she should start noting whatever object arises from the time she remembers to note. If you find yourself thinking, note it as "thinking, thinking" and then continue to note the rise and fall of the abdomen. If a sound awakens a meditator, she notes it as "hearing, hearing." If there is nothing else to note, she continues noting the rise and fall of the abdomen.

Turn over, bend, and stretch slowly and mindfully, while noting each movement using everyday language. If you think about what time it is, note it as "thinking, thinking." If you feel that you want to get up, note it as "wanting to get up." Note without any gap all of the movements involved in the process of getting out of bed. Focus on the body getting up and note it as "getting up, getting up." If a meditator sits afterward, she notes it as "sitting, sitting." Then she returns to noting the primary object, the rise and fall of the abdomen.

If you wash your face or bathe, note every single action involved, without any gap. For example, note looking at and seeing the bathing bowl, reaching for it, picking it up, scooping up the water, pouring the water over the body, the coolness of the water, rubbing the body, and so on.[214] You should also note any other activities, such as putting on clothes, making the bed, opening or closing the door, arranging your things, and so on, without any gap.

### *Eating a Meal*

When having a meal and looking at the plate, note it as "looking" or "seeing." When gathering a morsel of rice, note that as "gathering, gathering." As the morsel is lifted to the mouth, note that as "lifting, lifting." If you lower your head, note it as "lowering, lowering." As your fingers touch your lips, note it as "touching, touching." As your mouth is opening, note it as "opening, opening." As you place the morsel of rice into your mouth, note it as "placing, placing." As you close your mouth, note it as "closing, closing." As you lower your hand, note it as "lowering, lowering." If you raise your head again, note it as "raising, raising." Each time you chew the food, note it as "chewing, chewing." As you taste the flavor of the food, note it as "tasting, tasting." When swallowing the food, note it as "swallowing, swallowing." If you feel the food passing through your throat and digestive tract, note it as "touching, touching."[215]

In this way, a meditator meticulously notes during the entire process of eating. At the beginning of practice when you are not yet able to note things as they arise, there will be many gaps in your noting. There will also be many instances when you cannot be aware of or note your intention to move the body. A meditator shouldn't feel frustrated by this! If a meditator has the attitude to note meticulously and carefully, he will be able to note and observe more and more. As your understanding matures, you will be able to easily note even more objects than I have explained here.

### *Increasing the Number of Objects*

After about a day, you are likely to feel that simply noting the rise and fall of the abdomen is too easy. You may find that there is a gap or break between the movements of rising and falling. In that case, a meditator should switch to noting three objects, adding the sitting posture itself as a third object. You will then be noting: "rising, falling, sitting; rising, falling, sitting; . . ." In the same way that you note the rise and fall of the abdomen, you must now be aware of the sitting posture of the body and note it as "sitting." If lying down, note the three objects of "rising, falling, lying."

If a meditator still finds that there are gaps while noting these three objects, he can add a distinct sensation of touch in any part of the body as a fourth object and note "rising, falling, sitting, touching." If you are not comfortable with this approach, then you can note "rising, sitting, falling, sitting" instead. If lying down, the four objects to note are "rising, falling, lying, touching" or "rising, lying, falling, lying." If the breath becomes so subtle that you cannot clearly feel the rise and fall of the abdomen, you can note the sitting or lying posture or touch points. A meditator can note four, five, or six touch points, one after the other.

### *General Objects*

While you are carefully noting phenomena within the body, such as the rise and fall of the abdomen and so on, there is no need to note ordinary seeing or hearing. Careful noting of the rise and fall of the abdomen and so on fulfills the aim of noting and understanding seeing or hearing; it is simply seeing or hearing. However, if you intentionally look at something or someone, note it as "looking, looking" and then continue to note the primary object. Even if you don't do it intentionally, if you happen to see an object like a woman or a man, note "seeing, seeing" two or three times and then continue to note the primary object. If you intentionally listen to a sound, note "listening, listening" and then continue to note the primary object. If you hear a distinct sound, such as people talking, a song, a loud noise, dogs barking, birds chirping, or chickens clucking, and so on, note "hearing, hearing" two or three times and then continue to note the primary object.

If you do not note these other distinct objects that capture your attention, you cannot be clearly aware of the primary object. You may also get caught up in thinking about them and mental defilements will be aroused. In that case, you should note "thinking, thinking" and then return to the primary object. If a meditator forgets to note bodily phenomena or thought, he should note "forgetting, forgetting" and then continue to note the primary object.

If the breath becomes very subtle and the movements of rising and falling are no longer distinct, note "sitting, touching" if practicing in the sitting posture or "lying, touching" if lying down. When noting "touching," direct the mind toward four, five, or six different sensations of touch.

## *Mental States*

If a meditator has been practicing for a long time and is not making any progress, he may become lazy. Note that as "lazy, lazy." When mindfulness, concentration, and special insight knowledges have yet to arise, you may assume that noting gets you nowhere, and so doubt will arise. Note this as "doubting, doubting."

At times, a meditator may hope for smoother practice or some special experience. Note that as "hoping, hoping." If you reflect on previous practice, note it as "reflecting." If you wonder whether the object is mental or physical, note that as "wondering." Sometimes when practice doesn't go smoothly, you may feel frustrated. Note that as "frustrated, frustrated." Sometimes when you find that practice is going well, you may feel happy. Note that as "happy, happy."

A meditator should note all mental states in this way, whenever they arise, and then continue to note the primary object.

### *Diligence*

You should note each and every thought, whether wholesome or unwholesome. You should note each and every physical movement, whether large or small. You should note each and every feeling that arises in the body or mind, whether pleasant or unpleasant. You should note each and every mental object, whether wholesome or unwholesome. If there is nothing else in particular to note, then note the primary object, the rise and fall of the abdomen when sitting or the lifting, moving, and dropping of the foot when walking. Note these objects uninterruptedly and continuously.

In this way, you should continuously and uninterruptedly note all day and all night, except during the hours of sleep. Before long the meditator will be able to observe all mental and physical phenomena the moment they arise and disappear. Thus you will gradually come to experience insight knowledge of arising and passing away as well as higher stages of insight knowledge.

## Insight

### *Mind and Body*

When a meditator practices noting as described above, and his mindfulness, concentration, and insight mature, he will find that the noting mind and the noted objects occur in pairs. You will observe, for example, both the physical phenomena (body) involved in the rise of the abdomen and the mental phenomenon (mind) that notes it; the physical phenomena involved in the fall of the abdomen and the mental phenomenon that notes it; the physical phenomena involved in lifting the foot and the mental phenomenon that notes it; the physical phenomena involved in moving the foot forward and the mental phenomenon that notes it; the physical phenomena involved in dropping the foot and the mental phenomenon that notes it; and so on.

When practice is going well, you will see the rise and fall of the abdomen and the mind that notes it separately in this way. Thus you will be able to distinguish between mental and physical phenomena, or mind and body. It will seem like the noting mind rushes toward noted objects. This is awareness of the mind's characteristic of inclining toward its objects (*namanalakkhaṇā*). The clearer your observation of physical objects becomes, the more obvious the noting mind will become. The *Visuddhimagga* says:

> Whenever physical phenomena become clear, unambiguous, and obvious to a meditator, the mental phenomena associated with those physical sense objects will also become obvious to her of their own accord.[216]

When ordinary people experience this realization of mind and body in meditation, they are pleased and tend to have thoughts such as: "Nothing exists but mind and body. There is only the rising of the abdomen and the mind noting it, only the falling of the abdomen and the mind noting it, only the sitting posture and the mind noting it, only the bending movement and the mind noting it. What we call a human being is nothing but these two kinds of phenomena. Except for these two phenomena there is nothing else. Also what we call a woman or man is only these two phenomena. Except for these two phenomena there is no independent person or being."

When people with scriptural knowledge clearly experience physical sense objects, the sense bases, and the knowing mind, they are pleased and tend to reflect on it in this way: "It really is true that there are only mental and physical phenomena. In a moment of noting, what I really experience are the noted physical phenomena and the noting mind. The same is true at other times, too. There is no 'woman,' 'man,' or other living being that exists independent of these phenomena. The mental and physical phenomena of the present moment are all that really exist. These phenomena are commonly called a person, being, woman, or man, but those are just names. In reality, there is no independent person, being, woman, or man, only the mental and physical phenomena I experience while noting them."

When these kinds of reflections arise, note the mental state of reflection itself as "reflecting, reflecting" then return to the primary object and note it uninterruptedly.

## *Cause and Effect*

As practice matures further, the intention to move becomes obvious by itself when you intend to move your body. As soon as an intention arises, you will easily be aware of it. At the beginning of practice, even if you note "intending to bend," you will not be able to have clear awareness of the intention to bend your arm. However, when practice matures, you will be clearly aware of the intention to bend without confusing it with anything else. Any time you want to change your bodily posture, first note the intention and then note the actual movements involved.

When first beginning to practice, you change your bodily posture, often without noticing it. Because you don't notice, you tend to think, "The body is fast; the noting mind is slow." But as empirical knowledge matures, it will seem as if the noting mind welcomes objects in advance. You will be able to note the intention to bend or stretch, sit, stand, or walk, and so on, and notice the different movements involved in bending and so on as well. Then you will realize, "The body is slow; the noting mind is quick." You will experience for yourself that only after the intention to move has arisen can the movement of bending, stretching, and so on take place.

When you feel hot or cold, note "hot, hot" or "cold, cold." As you note, you will be able to experience the heat or cold getting stronger. When you note while eating, you will be able to experience your strength being replenished. After you have noted an object, do not return to the primary object if another object arises. A meditator should stay with a newly arisen object and note it uninterruptedly. Moreover, while noting mental images (such as images of the Buddha or an arahant) or physical sensations (like itchiness, heat, aching, or pain), another object may arise even before the object being presently noted has disappeared. In this case, you should change to the new object and continue to note it uninterruptedly.

By noting every object that occurs, you will experience that the noting mind arises whenever there is an object. Moreover, at times the rise and fall of the abdomen will become so subtle that you cannot note them. Then you will realize that the noting mind cannot arise if there is no object. In this case, you should switch to noting "sitting, touching" as the primary object if you are sitting, or "lying, touching" if you are lying down, rather than noting "rising, falling." You can also alternate between various touch points. For example, after noting "sitting" once, you can note the touch point of the right foot as "touching." Then note "sitting" again, followed by the touch point of the left foot. In this manner, you can alternate among four, five, or six touch points. Furthermore, when noting "seeing" or "hearing" you will clearly understand that when the eye and a visible form are present you experience seeing, and when the ear and a sound are present you experience hearing.

Thus, as you note various objects, you will clearly understand the different causes that give rise to different effects. For example, the intention to bend or stretch results in the movement of bending or stretching; a cold or hot environment results in cold or hot physical sensations; eating nutritious food results in the survival of the physical body; the presence of objects to note, such as the rise and fall of the abdomen, results in the noting mind; attention to mental objects results in the mental states of thought or imagination; the presence of visible objects of form or audible objects of sound results in eye consciousness or ear consciousness; and the presence of the physical phenomenon of the eye or ear also results in eye consciousness or ear consciousness. A meditator also comes to understand clearly that the volitional actions he has performed in past lives give rise to pleasant or unpleasant feelings in the present. Mental and physical phenomena have happened throughout this present life since birth because of past volitional actions. These phenomena have no creator. They arise in accord with the law of cause and effect.

When these realizations happen, you needn't stop noting in order to intellectualize or reflect on them. These realizations will occur suddenly and of their own accord as you note. Note these realizations as "realizing, realizing" or "comprehending, comprehending" or "reflecting, reflecting" and then return to continuously noting the primary object.

After realizing how the law of cause and effect or the interaction of mind and body operates in this life, you will comprehend how it operated in past lives and how it will operate in future lives as well. You may reflect: "The mental and physical phenomena of past and future lives had, or will have, the same causes as these present phenomena. There is neither an independent person, a being, nor a 'creator' that exists in relation to them, but only the law of cause and effect."

These kinds of reflections tend to occur more often for people of high intelligence and less often for those of average intelligence. The more intelligent the person, the broader her comprehension tends to be. However, a meditator should simply note these reflections and return to the primary object. If you make continuing to note a higher priority than engaging in reflection, you will spend less time reflecting and your practice will develop faster. Just a few moments of reflection will suffice.

### *Effects of Concentration*

As concentration grows particularly strong, you may experience a variety of unpleasant feelings, such as itchiness, heat, aches and pains, a feeling of heaviness or tightness, and so on. These often disappear immediately if you stop noting and tend to reappear when noting is resumed. Such feelings are not a sign of any kind of disease. The practice itself is what causes them to appear. So a meditator shouldn't fear them but should focus exclusively on these feelings, noting them persistently, and they will gradually weaken and fade away.

The meditator may also see various kinds of images or visions. These can be as vivid as if you were actually seeing them with your eyes. You may see, for example, the radiant image of a graceful Buddha, a group of monks, or other noble people approaching you. You may feel as if you are actually in front of a Buddha statue, a pagoda, a panoramic vista of woods, hills, gardens, clouds, and so on. Or you may feel as if you are actually seeing a swollen corpse or skeleton lying nearby, or a huge building or giant person disintegrating. Or a meditator may see visions of his body swelling, bleeding, being torn into two or three pieces, or turning into a skeleton. You may see images of the internal parts of your body, such as the bones, flesh, sinews, intestines, liver, and so on. Visions of the hell realms and its victims, the hungry ghosts, or the celestial world with its devas and devīs may appear. It is only concentration that gives rise to these unusual kinds of conceptual images and visions. So you shouldn't be elated or frightened by them. Such images are just like dreams.

However, the mind consciousness that experiences these mental images is an ultimate reality, so you must note it. But you shouldn't note it if it is not very obvious. You should only note an object when it is obvious. Therefore focus your mind on whatever image you are seeing and note it as "seeing, seeing" until it disappears. You will find that the image or vision will undergo some changes and fade away or disintegrate. Initially, you will have to note three, four, or more times before it disappears. However, when your insight matures, you will find that it disappears after you note it just once or twice.

On the other hand, if you are curious about, afraid of, or attached to these images, they will tend to last for a long time. So take extra care not to think about any of these unusual objects. If a meditator finds herself thinking about them, she should immediately abandon that thought by closely noting it. Since some do not experience any of these unusual visions or feelings and only note the primary object, they grow lazy. Note this laziness as "lazy, lazy" until it disappears.

### *Seeing the Three Characteristics*

Regardless of whether or not you have any unusual experiences at this level of insight, you will clearly see the beginning, middle, and end of an object each time you note it. Prior to this stage, you will have had to note new objects that arose before previous objects had disappeared, so you will not have been able to clearly see objects disappear. At this level, you will be able to see one object disappear before noting a new one, and you will thus clearly see the beginning, middle, and end of an object. Clearly seeing each object instantly arise and immediately disappear with each noting, you will understand the impermanence of objects as described in Pāḷi texts and commentaries:

> Impermanent in the sense of destruction . . . impermanent in the sense of nonexistence after having come to be.[217]

You may reflect: "These objects are just disappearing! They are just vanishing. It is true that they are impermanent."

> Anything that is impermanent is unsatisfying. Because it is frightening, it is unsatisfactory. It is suffering to be constantly tormented by arising and passing away.[218]

You may reflect: "We enjoy our lives because of delusion. In truth, there is nothing to enjoy in our lives. It is really frightening that everything arises and passes away. It is constant torment. Everything is miserable and unsatisfying because it arises and immediately passes away. We can die at any time." When you encounter unpleasant feelings, you will tend to comprehend the misery and suffering in things as described in the Pāḷi texts and commentaries:

> . . . as suffering, as a disease, as a boil, as a dart, . . .[219]

Or you may reflect: "All mental and physical phenomena are unsatisfying, and no one can make them otherwise. They do not obey anyone's will. They pass away immediately after arising, so they lack a solid core, are insubstantial and useless. There is no self that has control and can keep them from arising or passing away. In truth they arise and pass away of their own accord." This realization is in accordance with the Pāḷi texts and commentaries:

> What is suffering is [not-self [220]].[221]
> . . . is not-self in the sense of having no core . . .[222]
> . . . and does not obey anyone's will.[223]

Immediately after you note these reflections, return to noting the primary object.

After seeing for yourself that every object that you directly note is impermanent, unsatisfying, and impersonal, you will reflect that all other phenomena you experience must also be impermanent, unsatisfying, and impersonal. This is called inferential knowledge (*anumānañāṇa*). Those who are less analytical or knowledgeable and those who give priority to continuous noting rather than to analyzing will experience less reflection on this inferential knowledge. Those who give precedence to it will tend to reflect a lot. Some meditators, though, continue to analyze this realization, interspersed with their noting, and their practice stagnates. Even without such analysis, however, your understanding will become clearer at higher levels of insight, so prioritize noting rather than analyzing. If you do analyze, note it without fail.

After you inferentially realize the arising and passing away of all phenomena, you will simply be aware of whatever arises without any further analysis. The five mental faculties—faith, energy, mindfulness, concentration, and wisdom—will then fall into harmony, and the noting mind will become quicker than ever before. Your object—that is, mental and physical phenomena—will also appear extremely quickly. Each time you breathe in, for example, you will clearly see that the rising movement of the abdomen consists of many segments. The same is true for other movements, such as the falling of the abdomen, bending, stretching, and so on. You will clearly experience subtle vibrations or sensations all over your body, which arise very quickly one after another. Some experience fine sensations of itchiness or prickling that arise very quickly and instantly one after another. Unpleasant sensations are rarely experienced during this period of practice.[224]

You will be unable to keep up with objects by trying to label or name each of them when they arise so quickly. A meditator should simply be aware of them from moment to moment, without naming them, so that she can follow them. If a meditator wants to name them, she does not try to name them all. When one object is labeled, she may become aware of four, five, or ten other objects. This isn't a problem. You may tire if you attempt to name all the objects that occur. What matters most is being precisely and accurately aware of each object. In this case, note any objects that come in through the six sense doors, without following the normal procedure. Of course, if noting in this way does not go smoothly, you can always revert to the normal procedure.

Mental and physical phenomena arise and pass away much faster than the twinkling of an eye or a flash of lightning. But when your insight knowledge matures, you will be able to clearly perceive each fleeting phenomena without missing a single one by simply being aware of them from moment to moment. Your mindfulness will become so strong it will seem as if it rushes into the object that arises; it will seem as if objects fall into the noting mind. The knowing mind, too, will clearly and distinctly know each and every single object that arises. You might even think: "Phenomena are arising and passing away instantaneously; their appearance and disappearance are very fast, like a machine running at full speed. Yet I am able to perceive them all from moment to moment. I don't think I am missing anything or that there's anything else that I should be aware of." This is the personally experienced insight knowledge that we cannot even dream of.

### *Distractions from the Path*

Due to the momentum of this insight knowledge you are likely to see a bright light or experience rapture as a result of being greatly delighted with both the noting mind and the noted objects. You may get goose bumps, feel a tear roll down your cheek, or find your body shaking. A meditator may experience a "springy" feeling, often mistaken for dizziness, or a light, comfortable feeling, as if swaying back and forth in a hammock, that creeps over his whole body. You may experience a peaceful calm that makes you feel comfortable whether sitting, reclining, standing, or in any other posture. Both the mind and body will become so light, supple, and flexible due to this quality of lightness that you will feel comfortable even during long periods of sitting or reclining, without any pain, heat, or stiffness.

At this point, the noting mind and the noted objects flow along concurrently and harmoniously. Your mental attitude becomes straightforward. Your mind avoids unwholesome activities and becomes extremely clear due to your strong faith and confidence. At times this mental clarity may last for a long period, even when there is no object to be noted. As your faith grows stronger, you may reflect: "It really is true that the Buddha knew everything," or, "There really is nothing other than impermanent, unsatisfying, and impersonal mental and physical phenomena." While noting, you will often see, extremely clearly, the arising and passing away of mental and physical phenomena, as well as impermanence and unsatisfactoriness, and you will probably think about encouraging others to practice. Without too much strain and free from laziness, balanced effort will manifest. It will seem as if objects are known of their own accord and so insight equanimity (*vipassanupekkhā*) dawns. A meditator is likely to experience an unusual degree of very strong delight or happiness and will be excited to tell others about it.

A meditator may like any of the pleasant experiences that occur—the bright light, good mindfulness, insight, rapture, and so on. This liking will cause him to think: "This practice is exceedingly enjoyable!" He may really enjoy the practice. But do not waste time enjoying the bright light and other pleasant experiences. Instead, whenever they arise, note them as "brightness, comfort, knowing, reflecting, venerating, happiness, liking, delight," and so on, according to whatever you experience.

If you notice brightness, note it as "bright, bright." If you think that you see it, note it as "seeing, seeing" until it disappears. You may often forget to note bright light and other pleasant experiences because you are so happy to experience them. Although you are noting, the light may not disappear very quickly because you are delighting in it. Only after experiencing it many times will you be able to note it skillfully enough that it disappears quickly. For some meditators, light is so powerful that even if they note it for a long time, it doesn't disappear; it remains. In this case, ignore the light completely and divert your attention to some other mental or physical object. Do not think about whether the light is still bright. If you do, you will find that it is. Any thoughts about the light should be noted so precisely that your awareness of them is very clear and firm.

Since your concentration will have become very powerful, other unusual objects besides bright light can arise if you incline your mind toward them. Do not let the mind incline in this way. If you do, quickly note it until it disappears. Some meditators see various kinds of faint shapes and forms arise one after another, like the linked carriages of a train. If this happens, note it as "seeing, seeing." With each noting, an object will disappear. If your insight weakens, the shapes and forms will tend to become more pronounced. But if you note them closely, each object will disappear on the spot as it is noted. Eventually they will stop coming.

To delight in bright light and other pleasant experiences is to be on the wrong path. The correct path of insight is to just continue noting. If you keep this in mind and carry on noting mental and physical phenomena that actually arise, your awareness will grow clearer and clearer. You will clearly see the sudden appearance and disappearance of phenomena. Every time you note, you will see each object arising and passing away on the spot. A meditator clearly sees that successive occurrences are distinct from one another, break up bit by bit, and cease. Thus every object you note helps you to realize impermanence, unsatisfactoriness, and not-self.

After practicing for quite a while, a meditator may feel satisfied with his practice and take a break every now and again, thinking: "It can't get any better than this. There can't be anything else special to experience." But you should not just relax whenever you want. Instead you should practice for longer and longer periods without taking a break.

### *Disappearance*

When insight knowledge develops to the next stage, you will no longer see objects arising, but only passing away. You will think that they are disappearing faster and faster. A meditator will also see that the noting objects and the noting mind disappear one after the other. When the rise of the abdomen is noted, for example, you will clearly see how the tiny movements of rising instantly disappear and how the noting mind, too, vanishes very quickly. So you see that moments of the rising movement and your awareness of it disappear one after the other. You will see this clearly for all other objects as well, such as the falling of the abdomen, sitting, bending, stretching, stiffness, and so on—each object and your awareness of it disappears moment by moment, one after the other. Some meditators even find that there are three things arising and passing away in sequence: a sense object, their awareness of it, and their knowledge of that very awareness. But it is sufficient to observe that objects and the mind that notes them disappear in pairs.

When noting becomes clear enough that you can see both sense objects and your awareness of them disappearing in pairs, you will lose the illusory sense of conceptual forms or shapes, such as the form of your body, head, arms, legs, and so on. You will experience only instantly disappearing phenomena. As a result, you may feel like your practice has become superficial, is not as good as it had been before, or that there are many gaps in your noting. But that is not the case. It's only that the mind naturally delights in concepts of solid form, and so it cannot feel comfortable when those concepts are absent.

In any case, this condition is an indication of progress in practice. When your meditation practice is immature, you first perceive concepts of solid form or shape when you note seeing, hearing, touching, and so on. But at this level of insight meditation, you perceive the instant disappearance of phenomena first. In other words, you experience insight knowledge of dissolution first; the sense of solid form will only return when you deliberately evoke it. Otherwise, due simply to uninterruptedly noting, your awareness will remain attuned to the ultimate reality of the dissolution of phenomena. Thus you verify that the saying from sages of old is true:

> When conventional reality emerges, absolute reality submerges. When absolute reality emerges, conventional reality submerges.

Although your awareness will have become extremely clear at this point, it may seem like there are gaps between successive moments of awareness. This is because you are starting to become aware of the life continuum that occurs between cognitive processes (*vīthi*). For example, when you note an intention to bend or stretch the arm, you may find that the movement of bending or stretching seems to be delayed for some time. This means that your awareness has become sharp and powerful. In this case, you should also note any distinct objects that arise at the six sense doors.

After your practice gains momentum due to noting the main objects, such as the rise and fall of the abdomen, sitting, and so on, you should note any obvious objects that arise, such as any sensations in other parts of the body, seeing, hearing, and so on. If your awareness becomes less precise or accurate while noting in this way, or if thoughts begin to interfere, or if you feel exhausted, return to just noting the primary objects of rising, falling, sitting, and so on. When, after a while, your practice again gains momentum, return to noting whatever arises. A meditator should let her practice proceed in this way some of the time.

Once you are able to extend, without strain, the range of objects that you note and observe, you will clearly see that whatever you see or hear instantly disappears and that two consecutive moments are not connected but are separate units. This is "understanding things as they really are." As a result, however, things may seem blurry or hazy when you look at them. A meditator is likely to worry: "I think something is wrong with my eyesight; it's getting dim." But nothing is actually wrong with your vision. It's just that your awareness is discerning each individual moment of seeing separately, which causes conceptual forms to blur.

At this point, as well, a meditator will continue to be aware of mental and physical phenomena even if she stops trying to practice. You may not even be able to fall asleep when trying to, but will instead feel alert and awake day and night. There is no need to worry about this, as it will not harm your health in any way. A meditator should simply continue practicing energetically. When your insight becomes powerful enough, it will seem as if your awareness pierces objects.

### *Disillusionment*

When you deeply understand that both objects and the mind that notes them instantly disappear, you will tend to reflect: "Nothing lasts for the twinkling of an eye or a flash of lightning. They are indeed impermanent. Previously I was simply ignorant of this fact. Everything that has happened in the past must have also disappeared in this way. Everything that happens in the future will disappear in this way, too." Note these reflections.

You may also occasionally reflect on how unstable and incessantly vanishing phenomena are, thinking: "Clearly, we are able to enjoy ourselves due to ignorance. To realize that phenomena instantly disappear is truly terrifying. Each time they disappear could be the moment of my death. To have come into existence and to have to continue existing endlessly is really horrible. How dreadful to make such great effort in order to be well off in a situation in which everything constantly vanishes. How appalling it is that these instantly disappearing phenomena continue to occur, now and in a new life. That we are all subject to aging, sickness, death, distress, worry, lamentation, and so on is truly frightening." Note this mental state of reflection without fail.

At this stage of practice, a meditator generally feels helpless, dejected, and languid, being frightened by mental and physical phenomena that disintegrate so quickly. You have no enthusiasm or joy, and you tend to feel sad. There is no need to worry. This indicates that your practice is improving according to the usual development of the meditation process. All you need do is remain equanimous by noting any reflections and other objects that arise. If you do so, you will soon overcome this stage. Otherwise, being long caught up in these reflections while feeling displeasure, a meditator might become so afraid that he cannot stand it. This kind of fear based on displeasure is not insight knowledge. Therefore note all these reflections without fail so that fear based on displeasure cannot arise.

In between instances of noting, you may have thoughts that find fault, such as: "These mental and physical phenomena are no good because they constantly vanish and do not last. It is depressing to see how they have continuously arisen since the beginning of this life without ever coming to an end, and that they create all kinds of forms and shapes although they do not exist. Striving hard to gain happiness and well-being feels so miserable. A new existence is undesirable. It is depressing to be subject to aging, sickness, death, distress, worry, grief, and lamentation. This is all suffering and devoid of peace." You should not forget to note these kinds of reflections.

Sometimes it will seem like every phenomenon that you note and the mind that notes it is terrible, harsh, useless, disgusting, rotten, decaying, and fragile. At such times, even though you note mental and physical phenomena as they arise, you will no longer feel pleased with them. You will clearly see them to be passing away every time they are noted, but you will not be as enthusiastic about this as before. Instead you will feel weary of phenomena. As a result, you will become lazy about noting. But you will not be able to help being aware. It is like being forced to travel on a filthy road, wherein every step arouses disgust and disillusionment.

Thus when you consider human life, you will understand that you cannot exist without these incessantly vanishing mental and physical phenomena. So you won't see anything delightful in becoming a man, a woman, a king, a rich person, or a celestial being. These instead will inspire disenchantment and disillusionment.

## *Looking for Relief*

Because you feel so weary of phenomena every time they are noted, it will seem as if the mind is struggling to escape from them. With the desire to be liberated from the conditioned phenomena, a meditator may think: "It would be so nice if there were no such thing as seeing, hearing, touching, thinking, sitting down, standing up, bending, stretching, and so on. I wish I could escape from those things or go somewhere where they don't exist." Do not fail to note such thoughts.

At other times, a meditator may wonder: "What can I do to escape from these phenomena? Continuing to note them seems like deliberately contemplating vile things. Everything I notice is disgusting. It would be nice not to have to notice them at all." Of course, you should note these mental states of wondering and thinking.

Based on such reflections, some meditators even try to avoid noting at this point and put off practice. But mental and physical phenomena such as seeing, hearing, knowing, the rise and fall of the abdomen, sitting, bending, stretching, thinking, and so on will not stop arising; they will continue to appear as always. They continue to be apparent to meditators as a result of their intensive insight practice. Awareness of phenomena simply continues of its own accord. A meditator will be encouraged by this, considering: "Even though I'm not trying to note, I keep noticing phenomena that arise anyway; my awareness of them just keeps going. So just avoiding practice won't help me get away from them. It's only when I note these phenomena, as they are, and realize their three characteristics that I won't worry about them and will be able to note with equanimity. That's what will lead me to the experience of nibbāna, where none of these exist. Only then can I realize liberation." Once you are able to appreciate your own experience in this way, you will carry on with your practice. Some meditators do not come to this conclusion by themselves. However, once their teachers explain their experience to them, they can carry on with their practice.

Some meditators will experience unbearable pain when their practice gains this kind of momentum. Do not despair. The true characteristics of unpleasant sensation are actually becoming obvious to you as pain (*dukkhato*), disease (*rogato*), an ulcer (*gaṇḍato*), a thorn (*sallato*), unprofitable (*aghato*), afflictions (*ābādhato*), and so on. Note the pain until you can overcome it.

Those who do not encounter severe pain may experience one of the forty qualities of impermanence, unsatisfactoriness, or not-self whenever they note. Even though their practice is going well and their thoughts do not wander, they will tend to think that their practice is no good or feel that objects and the mind that notes them are not concurrent. Actually it is simply that you are so eager to realize the impermanent, unsatisfactory, and not-self nature of mental and physical phenomena that you cannot feel satisfied with your practice. As a result, you may often change your posture. For example, when you are sitting you feel like you want to walk; when you are walking you want to sit down again. You feel agitated and want to rearrange your arms and legs, move to another place, or lie down. You cannot manage to stay in your place or posture for very long and keep changing. Do not feel frustrated!

A meditator lacks satisfaction because he rightly understands that there are no pleasurable conditioned mental and physical phenomena. At this point, you think that your noting is no good. You will not yet be able to note with equanimity, as you will be when you attain the next insight knowledge, knowledge of equanimity toward phenomena. Try your best to practice without constantly changing your posture and to remain in one posture for a long time. After a while, you will be able to practice calmly again. If you practice with patience and persistence, your mind will grow clearer and clearer until all the agitation and dissatisfaction disappear.

## *Equanimity*

Eventually, your insight meditation will strengthen enough that you will be effortlessly equanimous with respect to conditioned mental and physical phenomena. The noting mind will become so clear and subtle that your awareness will seem to easily flow by itself. The meditator will even be able to perceive very subtle mental and physical activities without any effort, and will see their impermanence, unsatisfactoriness, and not-self natures without reflecting about it.

If a meditator notes touch points at different places on the body, she will be aware of just one sensation of touch after another, but not of any physical form or shape, and the sensations of touch will feel very subtle, like the touch of a cotton ball. Sometimes you may feel so many different sensations in the body that your awareness moves very quickly all around the body. Sometimes it will feel as if both the body and the mind are moving upward. At other times, only a few regular objects will be obvious and you will be able to calmly and steadily note them.

Sometimes the rising, falling, touching, hearing, and so on, together with the whole body, may disappear, and you will only be aware of the mind arising and passing away. You may experience a rapture that feels like being bathed in a cool, soothing shower, a tranquility, or a crystal-clear light like a bright sky. Although the meditator may not take such extreme delight in such pleasant experiences as she would have before, she may still become attached to them. Note any attachment that arises, in addition to noting the rapture, tranquility, or clear light. If these experiences persist, ignore them and note other objects instead.

At this level of insight meditation, the meditator will clearly comprehend every object and the mind that notes them. You will know: "These phenomena are not me or mine, and they are also not anyone else or anyone else's. They are only conditioned mental and physical phenomena. Conditioned phenomena are noting conditioned phenomena." Observing objects becomes very pleasant at this point, like tasting a delicious flavor. No matter how long you practice, you will not be gratified and will not feel any unpleasant sensations, such as stiffness, numbness, pain, or itching. Thus your meditation postures will become very stable. You will be able to easily maintain the positions of your head, body, arms, and legs, and to practice for two or three hours in a single posture, whether sitting or reclining, without getting tired or feeling stiff. Time will pass so quickly that two or three hours of practice will seem like just a few moments.

Sometimes the noting mind will become very swift and your noting will be especially good. If you begin to feel anxious about what is happening, note it as "anxious, anxious." If you begin to think that your practice is improving, note it as "evaluating, evaluating." And if you begin to anticipate further progress in insight knowledge, note it as "anticipating, anticipating." Afterward, return to steadily noting the usual objects.

You should neither increase nor decrease your energy at this stage. Because some meditators fail to note mental states such as anxiety, excitement, attachment, or anticipation, their awareness gets dispersed and decreases. Some meditators feel excited and increase their energy. Ironically, this leads to a decline in practice because the wandering minds of anxiety, excitement, attachment, or anticipation take them far away from insight. This is why, when your awareness becomes swift and your noting becomes especially good, you should keep your practice steady, without increasing or decreasing your energy. Using this approach, your practice will lead directly to nibbāna, where all conditioned phenomena cease.

Nonetheless, the meditator may experience many fluctuations in his practice at this level of insight meditation. Do not be disappointed; be persistent. Priority should be given to noting any objects that arise at the six sense doors as they present themselves and to widening your awareness to note whatever arises in any part of the body. But it is impossible to note this way once your practice becomes very subtle and continuous. So once your practice gains momentum, before it becomes too subtle, note objects without setting any limits. If the meditator notes objects carefully, whether it is "rising," "falling," "sitting," or other mental and physical activities, his practice will gain momentum before long. Then awareness will flow smoothly, as if by itself, without much effort. The meditator clearly and calmly perceives conditioned phenomena that instantaneously disappear.

At this point your mind will no longer be vulnerable to any kind of temptation or disturbance. However alluring an object might be, it will not be able to captivate your mind. Likewise, however disgusting an object might be, it will not affect your mind either. A meditator simply perceives seeing as seeing, hearing as hearing, smelling as smelling, tasting as tasting, touching as touching, and knowing as knowing. Thus "sixfold equanimity" or equanimity regarding the six senses will appear every time you note. Even thoughts or reflections like, "How long have I been sitting? What time is it?" will no longer arise. These thoughts, along with the previous kinds of reflections, will have ceased.

However, if your insight knowledge is not yet mature enough to produce noble path knowledge, after one, two, or three hours your concentration will weaken and the mind will begin to wander. Then your noting mind may slacken and have gaps in between. On the other hand, if your noting becomes swift and especially good, you may become excited and anticipate progress. This, too, can lead to slackening. If you note these mental states of evaluation, anticipation, or excitement without fail, then your practice will regain strength.

But if your insight knowledge is still not mature enough, your practice will eventually decline again. Thus there can be a great deal of fluctuation in practice at this time. Those who know or have heard about the stages of insight knowledge may encounter even more fluctuations. This is why it is better not to learn how the insight knowledges progress in advance. In any event, do not be disappointed. These fluctuations indicate that your insight is coming very close to path knowledge and fruition knowledge. You could realize path, fruition, and nibbāna at any time, once the mental faculties of faith, energy, mindfulness, concentration, and wisdom fall in harmony.

## The Experience of Nibbāna

These fluctuations in insight knowledge are like the flights of a bird sent out from a ship at sea: In the old days when sailors didn't know where the nearest land was, they would send out a crow that they had brought along on the voyage. The bird would fly in every direction, looking for the nearest shore. As long as it couldn't find any nearby land, the bird would keep returning to the ship. But once it spied land, it would fly directly to it. In the same way, as long as your insight is not strong enough to realize nibbāna by attaining path knowledge, it keeps drawing back—that is, there will be gaps in your noting. But once your insight knowledge is mature enough and the five mental faculties are in harmony, for at least three or four moments you will see mental and physical phenomena arising and passing away with increasing swiftness and clarity. Then, immediately after noting an obvious object from among the six kinds of conditioned mental and physical phenomena,[225] you will attain path and fruition while experiencing nibbāna as the cessation of both noted objects and the mind that notes them.

Those who reach that spiritual state clearly experience their awareness accelerating prior to their attainment. They also clearly experience how all conditioned objects are abandoned after a final moment of noting and how the mind takes nibbāna, the cessation of all those conditioned phenomena, as its object. These are some of the ways meditators describe the experience:

> "Both the objects and the noting mind were abruptly cut off and stopped."
>
> "The objects and the noting mind were cut off, like a creeping vine being hewn down."
>
> "I saw the objects and the noting mind drop away, like a heavy burden being dumped."
>
> "Objects and the mind noting them seemed to fall away, as if I had lost my hold on them."
>
> "I got away from objects and the mind that notes them, as if suddenly escaping from confinement in prison."
>
> "Objects and the mind that notes them suddenly disappeared, like the light of a candle being blown out."
>
> "I escaped from objects and the mind that notes them, as if suddenly emerging from darkness into light."
>
> "I emerged from objects and the mind that notes them, as if suddenly emerging from a mess into a clear space."
>
> "I found that both objects and the mind that notes them submerged, as if sinking into water."
>
> "Both objects and the mind that notes them suddenly stopped, like a running person thwarted by a blocked passage."

The experience of the cessation of conditioned mental and physical phenomena does not last very long. It's as brief as a single moment of noting. Afterward one has a recollection of the event, such as: "The cessation of objects and the mind that notes them that I've just experienced must have been either something special or path, fruition, and nibbāna." Those with scriptural knowledge might reflect: "The cessation of conditioned mental and physical phenomena is nibbāna. What I have realized while experiencing the cessation is path knowledge and fruition knowledge. I have realized nibbāna, and I have attained the path and fruition of the first stage of enlightenment." These kinds of reflections tend to arise in a systematic and thorough way for those who have heard how it is to experience the cessation of conditioned mental and physical phenomena. Such people also tend to reflect on which mental defilements have been eliminated and which have not.

After these recollections they return to noting mental and physical phenomena as usual. At that time the arising and disappearance of phenomena is quite coarse and so is obvious. They are clearly aware of the beginning and end, or of the arising and passing away, of phenomena. Thus they may think that there must be gaps in their noting again or that their practice must have declined. This is actually true. They have returned to insight knowledge of arising and passing away. Accordingly, they may again experience bright light and images, as is usual at this stage. Some meditators may find that their noting mind is suddenly not concurrent with the objects it notes, as it was in the beginning stages of practice, or they encounter moments of various kinds of unpleasant sensation.

For the most part, however, their minds remain clear from moment to moment. At this stage they will feel very peaceful, as if their minds were floating alone in space. But they will not be able to note that mental state. Even if they try to note it, they will not be able to be effectively aware of it. They will not want to contemplate anything else and will not be able to note other objects. Their minds are simply clear and peaceful. Gradually this clear mental state will grow weaker and weaker. Then if they continue noting, they will be able to clearly see arising and passing away again. After some time they will return to a state of very subtle noting, and if their insight is strong enough, they may fall into the cessation of phenomena again, as they did before. They might experience this repeatedly, depending on the strength of their concentration and insight knowledge. Nowadays many repeatedly attain the first fruition knowledge that they have already experienced, because their main aim is only to attain the first path and fruition. This is how the fruition of the first stage of enlightenment is attained through successive insights.

The mental attitude of those who have achieved path and fruition is not the same as it was before; it is so special that they feel as if they have been reborn. Their faith becomes extremely strong and, as a result, they experience very powerful rapture and tranquility. Happiness also often spontaneously arises. Sometimes the mental factors of faith, rapture, tranquility, and happiness may be so strong that immediately after having attained path and fruition objects cannot be distinguished very well, even though meditators note them. However, after a few hours or days, those mental factors will weaken, and they will be able to distinguish objects again, so the practice will improve once more.

Some meditators feel relieved, reluctant to note, or satisfied immediately after attaining the path and fruition. Such contentment probably arises because their initial motivation was only to achieve that path knowledge and fruition knowledge. If they wish to realize and experience the peace of nibbāna again by means of the fruition that they have already attained, they should note present phenomena as usual.

## *Entering Fruition*

The first insight knowledge that ordinary meditators encounter in the course of insight meditation is the insight knowledge that discerns mental and physical phenomena. But for meditators with path knowledge and fruition knowledge it will be the insight knowledge of arising and passing away. So if the insight knowledge of arising and passing away is the first to occur while you are noting phenomena, it will soon be followed by successively higher insight knowledges, up through equanimity toward phenomena, which is the most subtle and best knowledge. When that knowledge is strong enough, the mind will shift its attention to nibbāna, the cessation of all conditioned phenomena, just as before, and the mental process of fruition will appear.

If you do not determine the period for this fruition absorption in advance, it may last for only a few moments or for quite a long time—5, 10, or 15 minutes, half an hour, or an hour. The commentaries say that it can even last for a whole day and night, or for whatever period you have predetermined. These days, too, we can find meditators with strong concentration and sharp insight who are able to become absorbed in fruition for long periods of time, such as one, two, or three hours, or a period that they have predetermined, as described in the commentaries. Even when there is no need to do so, if you predetermine that the fruition absorption should end, you will easily emerge. In the case of such long periods of absorption, however, there may be intervals of reflection. If you note such reflection four or five times, you will become absorbed in fruition again. In this way, you may experience fruition absorption for hours.

During fruition absorption, the mind is fully absorbed in its object, nibbāna, the cessation of all conditioned phenomena. It does not perceive anything else. Nibbāna is completely different from the conditioned mental and physical phenomena and conceptual objects that belong to this world or any other. So you cannot perceive or remember this world (i.e., your own body) or any other during fruition absorption, and you are free from all thoughts. Even if there are obvious objects around to see, hear, smell, touch, and so on, you will not be aware of any of them. Your bodily posture will also be firm and stable while you are absorbed, even if for long periods. For example, if you are sitting when you become absorbed in fruition, you will maintain that sitting posture without swaying, slouching, or changing it in any way. As the Pāḷi passage says:

> The [impulsions] of absorption also uphold the bodily postures.[226]

When the mental process of fruition ends, the first object that you experience might be the recollection of cessation or of absorption in that cessation, some kind of visual image, or simply a thought. Then the normal noting process, brightness, or reflections will accordingly appear. Initially you will be only intermittently able to be aware of obvious objects after you emerge from absorption in fruition. However, there may also be times when you will be continuously able to be aware of subtle objects immediately after the fruition process if your insight is strong. Remember that the determination to enter fruition quickly or to be absorbed for a long time should be made before beginning to note. While you are noting, you should not think about it.

When your insight is not yet strong enough for you to become absorbed in fruition, you may experience goose bumps, yawning, shaking, and deep breaths, followed by intermittent noting. At other times, when your noting is improving, you may become excited, thinking that nibbāna is near. But, as a result, your noting will then become discontinuous. So you should not entertain such thoughts. If they arise, note them precisely and accurately. Some meditators encounter these kinds of fluctuations many times before they are able to enter fruition absorption. Even then, if your concentration and insight knowledge are still weak, it may take some time to reach the state of fruition, or you may not be able to remain there for very long.

## *Clarifying the Insight Knowledges*

Sometimes the insight knowledges of fear, danger, disenchantment, and desire for deliverance are not clear because you have not experienced them for a long time. If you want to experience them clearly and distinctly, you should determine a time period for the experience of each insight knowledge. For example, if you set a time limit when you practice by resolving, "May the knowledge of arising and passing away last for half an hour," then that insight knowledge will occur within that time period but not beyond. Afterward, the subsequent insight knowledge of dissolution will occur spontaneously, since you see only phenomena passing away. But if that knowledge does not occur spontaneously, you should resolve that it will arise. Then it will be present for that period of time, and the next higher insight knowledge will spontaneously follow it. Proceed in this way, in order, for all of the knowledges.

If your practice does not automatically move to the next higher insight knowledge after achieving mastery of the current level of knowledge, resolve that it will arise. So after attaining insight knowledge of dissolution, resolve: "May insight knowledge of fear arise." That knowledge will then occur. When you are satisfied with it, resolve: "May insight knowledge of danger arise." Then you will realize that knowledge by seeing the dangers of phenomena every time you note them. When you are satisfied with that knowledge, resolve to attain insight knowledge of disenchantment. That knowledge will then occur, causing you to become weary and disenchanted. When you are satisfied with that knowledge, resolve: "May insight knowledge of desire for deliverance arise." Then that knowledge will arise, causing you to wish to escape from phenomena every time you note them. Then resolve to attain insight knowledge of reobservation. That knowledge will then occur, accompanied by unpleasant sensations, discontentment, and the desire to change posture. Finally, resolve to attain insight knowledge of equanimity toward phenomena. Then that very subtle knowledge will arise, during which the momentum of noting will flow as if by itself.

Thus you will find that you can reach a particular level of insight knowledge within a specified time limit, according to your resolve. You will also find that your knowledge shifts, in due time, like the needle of a compass, to the next higher level of knowledge once you are satisfied with the current level. If you have not yet experienced all of the insight knowledges distinctly, repeatedly practice in this way. On the other hand, people with strong concentration and sharp insight may reach insight knowledge of equanimity within a short time—that is, within about four, five, or ten notings, when they note without resolve. They can often experience fruition too. If you become very proficient at the practice, you can even experience fruition while walking, eating, and so on.

### *Practicing for Higher Paths and Fruitions*

When you are skilled enough in the practice that you can very quickly enter the fruition that you have attained and remain in it for a long time, you should practice with the purpose of attaining higher paths and fruitions. To do this, you should first determine how many days you are going to practice, and then resolve: "May the fruition that I have already attained no longer arise during this period of time; may the next higher path knowledge and fruition knowledge arise instead." After this, simply note present phenomena as usual.

The reason for making a resolution is so that your insight knowledge, if strong enough, can lead directly to a higher path and fruition within the specified time period rather than returning to the previous one. Otherwise you will often return to the fruition that you have already attained. The benefit of making a resolution in the form stated above is that if the higher path knowledge and fruition knowledge do not arise, the previous fruition knowledge may be realized again after your period of practice. Otherwise if you resolve, "From now on, may the next higher path knowledge and fruition knowledge arise," you may find it difficult to return to the previous fruition. Then the meditator may feel upset if he can neither gain a higher path knowledge and fruition knowledge nor return to one previously attained.

After determining a time period and wishing not to return to the previous fruition before the period ends, simply note phenomena as usual. Then the insight knowledges will arise in order, beginning with insight knowledge of arising and passing away, and insights will develop in a manner similar to that which led to the first path rather than that which led to the first fruition. Before the insight knowledge of arising and passing away matures, you may experience bright lights, images, and unpleasant sensations. The arising and passing away of mental and physical phenomena tends to be not very refined or distinct. Even if, when you practice to reach fruition, it usually only takes a few moments to return to knowledge of equanimity toward phenomena and the absorption of fruition, you may now spend a long time at lower levels of insight knowledge. But you will not experience as much difficulty or delay in attaining knowledge of equanimity toward phenomena as you experienced in the immature stages of practice. You will be able to progress through the successive stages of insight knowledge to return to knowledge of equanimity toward phenomena within a single day.

Your awareness will be much better than it was during the first stages of practice. It will be more precise and accurate. Your understanding will be broader and clearer. Sensual, worldly objects and the cycle of suffering will be more frightening, dangerous, and wearying to the meditator, and the desire to escape will be stronger than before. Even if you were formerly able to enter fruition three or four times an hour, your insight knowledge may now stagnate at the level of equanimity toward phenomena, because it is not strong enough to progress to the next higher path knowledge. You may remain in that condition for a long time, anywhere from one or two days to months or years.

When your insight knowledge eventually grows strong enough, your noting mind will become extremely clear and swift. Following this acceleration, your mind will shift its focus and take nibbāna, the cessation of all conditioned phenomena, as its object. Thus will you attain the second stage of path knowledge and fruition knowledge, followed by recollection of this new path and fruition, and a review of remaining mental defilements. Afterward, as you note as usual, knowledge of arising and passing away will arise together with an extremely clear mind. This is how you should practice for and experience the second stage of path knowledge and fruition knowledge, and become a once returner.

If you want to attain the path knowledge and fruition knowledge of the third stage of enlightenment, you should determine a period of time to practice and stop wishing for the absorption of the fruition that you have already attained. Resolve: "May the fruition already realized no longer arise during this period of time." Then note mental and physical phenomena in the usual way. Beginning with insight knowledge of arising and passing away, the insight knowledges will progress in sequence until, before long, you reach knowledge of equanimity toward phenomena. If your insight knowledge is not yet mature, it will stagnate at that level for some time. As it did previously, when it is powerful enough, it will shift its focus and take nibbāna, the cessation of conditioned phenomena, as its object. Thus will the path knowledge and fruition knowledge of the third stage of enlightenment arise, followed by the usual process of recollection. This is how you should practice for and experience the third path knowledge and fruition knowledge and become a nonreturner.

To attain the path knowledge and fruition knowledge of the fourth and final stage of enlightenment, simply follow the same procedure: after determining a time period, setting aside your desire for the current fruition absorption, and resolving to experience the peak of enlightenment, note present mental and physical phenomena. There is no other way to practice. This is why the *Satipaṭṭhāna Sutta* uses the term "the only way." Beginning with insight knowledge of arising and passing away, the knowledges will progress in sequence until, before long, you will reach insight knowledge of equanimity toward phenomena. If this knowledge is not yet powerful enough, you will stop and remain at this stage. When it is powerful enough, it will shift its focus and take nibbāna, the cessation of conditioned phenomena, as its object, just as it did previously. Thus will the path knowledge and fruition knowledge of the fourth stage of enlightenment arise.

Immediately after you have attained the path and fruition knowledge of arahantship, you will recollect the path, fruition, and nibbāna that you have clearly comprehended. You might reflect: "All mental defilements have been eradicated; they will no longer arise. I have accomplished everything that needed to be done." This is how you should practice for and experience the attainment of arahantship.

### *A Note on Pāramī*

The phrase "Thus will such-and-such path knowledge and fruition knowledge arise" is only intended for those whose *pāramīs* are mature. If your *pāramī* is not yet mature enough, your insight will not move beyond insight knowledge of equanimity toward phenomena.

In addition, it is relatively easy to attain the second path knowledge and fruition knowledge fairly soon after attaining the first, but it will probably take a long time to attain the third path knowledge and fruition knowledge after the second. The reason is that only training in morality need be completely fulfilled in order to attain both the first and second path knowledge and fruition knowledge, whereas you must also completely fulfill training in concentration (*samādhisikkhā*) in order to attain the third path knowledge and fruition knowledge. Therefore someone who has already attained the first path knowledge and fruition knowledge can easily attain the second, but it is not so easy to then attain the third.

In any event, it is not possible to know in advance whether your *pāramīs* are mature enough to reach a particular level of path knowledge and fruition knowledge. Moreover, different people may need days, months, or years to attain enlightenment. If you have just been practicing for a few days or months without attaining path knowledge and fruition knowledge, you cannot yet decide that your *pāramīs* are not mature. Besides, your current practice itself naturally helps your *pāramīs* to mature, so you should not evaluate whether or not your *pāramīs* are mature.

One should never give up, but continue practicing with full energy, keeping this point in mind: "If I don't practice, then there is no way that my *pāramīs* can develop. And even if my *pāramīs* were mature, I cannot attain path and fruition in this life without practice. On the other hand, if my *pāramīs* are mature and I also practice, then I can easily and quickly attain path and fruition. And if my *pāramīs* are fairly mature, then my current practice will help it to mature enough to attain path and fruition in this very life. At the very least, my current practice certainly develops my *pāramīs* and my potential to attain path and fruition in the life to come."

## A Word of Advice

> During this, the era of Gotama Buddha, those who aspire to know the truly enjoyable taste of insight should practice mindfulness that penetrates the phenomena of the body, feelings, mind, and mental objects.[227]

The explanations of how to practice insight that I have given in this book are perfectly sufficient for those of fair intelligence. If they read this book and properly and systematically practice, with strong faith, aspiration, and energy, they can surely attain the different insight knowledges as well as path knowledge and fruition knowledge. However, it is impossible to mention here all of the different experiences that meditators may have, and there are many that I have not included. A meditator will not experience everything that is mentioned here either. The experience particular to one may be quite different from another's, depending on the maturity of her *pāramīs* and the accuracy, precision, and continuity of her awareness.

Moreover, it is impossible for a meditator's faith, aspiration, and energy to remain strong all the time. If a person practices by following teachings based on intellectual knowledge and without a teacher, he may have doubts and feel uncertain, just like a person traveling alone in an unfamiliar place. So it is not easy for an ordinary person to attain the insight knowledges, as well as path knowledge and fruition knowledge, if he practices without a teacher who can give careful guidance. That is why the Saṃyutta Nikāya says:

> One . . . should search for a teacher in order to know this as it really is.[228]

So I would like to advise you to practice under the close guidance of an experienced teacher who can clearly explain the stages of insight knowledge up through path knowledge and fruition knowledge, reviewing knowledge, and fruition absorptions. Please be humble. Remember the story of Venerable Potthila, and do not proudly think, "I am special and don't need anyone's guidance!" When you practice, do so sincerely and keep in mind the following advice given by the Buddha:

> Not by means of slack endeavor,
> not by means of feeble effort,
> is this nibbāna to be achieved,
> release from all suffering.[229]

This means that with great effort and a firm practice, you can attain nibbāna.

Here ends the chapter regarding practical instructions.

# Appendixes

# Appendix 1: Spiritual Faculties

| Cetasika (mental state) | Spiritual Faculty | Characteristic (salient quality) | Function (task or goal achievement) | Manifestation (the way it presents itself) | Proximate Cause (condition it depends on) |
|---|---|---|---|---|---|
| saddha | faith/confidence, trusting | placing of faith, trusting | clarifying, setting forth | nonfogginess, resolve | something to place faith in |
| viriya | energy/perservering | supporting, exertion, marshalling | supporting associated mental states | noncollapse | samvega: spiritual urgency, ground for arousing energy |
| sati | mindfulness/remembering, observing | not wobbling, not floating away, no “spin” | remembering, nonforgetfulness, absence of confusion | guardianship, confronting an objective field, observing | strong perception, four foundations of mindfulness |
| ekaggatā (samādhi) | one-pointedness/stabilizing mind, concentration | nonwandering, nondistraction, nonrestlessness | consolidating associated mental states | peace | happiness, sukha: happy comfort of body and mind |
| pañña | wisdom/understanding | penetrating intrinsic nature of things | illuminating the objective field | nonbewilderment | wise attention |
| sañña | perception | recognizing qualities of the object | making a sign, recognizing previous perception | interpreting the object | the object |
| manasikara | attention | conducting associated mental states toward object | yoking associated mental states with object | confronting the object | the object |

1. Faith arouses energy to be mindful. The continuity of mindfulness strengthens stability of mind. A stable, collected mind sees things more clearly in more detail, from which wise understanding arises.
2. The function of faith is to clarify one's spiritual object and to set forth confidently.
3. Faith needs a sense of urgency (samvega) to arouse energy/effort.
4. Energy manifests as noncollapse in the face of difficulties, challenges—that is, perserverance.
5. The function of mindfulness is to remember to recognize the present-moment experience—that is, awareness and the object.
6. To recognize the unique nature of the object (sabhāva) is the function of perception.
7. Perception is characterized by recognizing the unique qualities of the object, thereby recognizing something as familiar or marking its distinctive qualities with a name.
8. Labeling your experience or the object of awareness is a technique for strengthening perception.
9. Strong perception is the proximate cause for the arising of mindfulness.
10. Mindfulness is characterized by not floating away on thoughts about the object or experience but sticking to it.
11. Mindfulness manifests as confronting or observing the object.
12. The proximate cause for stability of mind is sukha: happy comfort of body and mind—that is, be comfortable.
13. Stability of mind is nonrestlessness—that is, the mind is not thinking aimlessly without awarenesss.
14. Wisdom functions to illuminate the object or awareness and is characterized by understanding their unique natures.
15. Wisdom arises due to wisely confronting the object.
16. Wisdom manifests as nonbewilderment—that is, nondelusion.
17. Insight wisdom is greater than knowledge or inspired feeling to place one's faith in, which in turn supports greater energy, manifesting as more momentum or continuity of mindfulness, which is the very definition of stability of mind. This in turn results in even greater wisdom. In this way, the five faculties grow cyclically through their cause-effect relationship, incrementally to balanced maturity.
18. Excessive energy and excessive concentration need to be kept in balance to prevent agitation and/or sinking mind.
19. Excessive or blind faith and excessive book knowledge/wisdom need to be kept in balance to prevent unwise faith and/or overintellectualization.
20. Sati balances the other faculties by observing them with an absence of confusion or reactivity.

# Appendix 2: Stream of Consciousness

| | ... | ... | V1 | V2 | V3 | V4 | V5 | V6 | V7 | V8 | V9 | V10 | V11 |
|---|---|---|---|---|---|---|---|---|---|---|---|---|---|
| H1 | ... | LC | LC | LC | LC | LC | LC | LC | LC | LC | LC | LC | LC |
| H2 | ... | LC | Plc | Vlc | Alc | 5A | eye | Rc | I | D | **J** | **J** | **J** |
| H3 | ... | LC | Plc | Plc | Vlc | Alc | 5A | ear | Rc | I | D | **J** | **J** |
| H4 | ... | LC | Plc | Plc | Plc | Plc | Vlc | Alc | 5A | nose | Rc | I | D |
| H5 | ... | LC | Plc | Plc | Plc | Plc | Plc | Plc | Plc | Plc | Plc | Plc | Plc |
| H6 | ... | LC | Plc | Vlc | Alc | M | **J** | **J** | **J** | **J** | **J** | **J** | **J** |
| H7 | ... | LC | Plc | Vlc | Alc | M | **J** | **J** | **J** | **J** | **J** | **J** | **J** |
| H8 | ... | LC | Vlc | Vlc | M | M | M | LC | LC | LC | LC | LC | LC |
| H9 | ... | LC | Vlc | Vlc | M | **J** | **J** | **J** | **J** | **J** | **J** | **J** | R |
| H10 | ... | LC | Plc | Vlc | Alc | 5A | eye | Rc | I | D | **J** | **J** | **J** |
| H11 | ... | LC | Plc | Vlc | Alc | M | **J** | **J** | **J** | **J** | **J** | **J** | **J** |
| H12 | ... | LC | Plc | Vlc | Alc | M | **J** | **J** | **J** | **J** | **J** | **J** | **J** |
| H12A | ... | LC | Plc | Vlc | Alc | M | M | M | LC | LC | LC | LC | LC |
| H13 | ... | LC | Vlc | Alc | M | **Prp** | **Ac** | **Ad** | **Chg** | **Jh** | LC | LC | LC |
| H14 | ... | LC | Vlc | Alc | M | **Prp** | **Ac** | **Ad** | **Chg** | **any # *jhāna* consciousness** | | | |
| H15 | ... | LC | Plc | Vlc | Vlc | M | **J** | **J** | **J** | **J** | **J** | **J** | **J** |
| H16 | ... | LC | Plc | Vlc | Vlc | M | **J** | **J** | **J** | **J** | **J** | **J** | **J** |
| H17 | ... | LC | Plc | Vlc | Vlc | M | **J** | **J** | **J** | **J** | **J** | **J** | **J** |
| H18 | ... | LC | Vlc | Alc | M | **Prp** | **Ac** | **Ad** | **Chg** | **Path** | **F** | **F** | LC |
| H19 | ... | LC | Vlc | Alc | M | **Prp** | **Ac** | **Ad** | **Pr** | **Path** | **F** | **F** | LC |
| H20 | ... | LC | Vlc | Alc | M | **Ad** | **Ad** | **Ad** | **Ad** | **any # fruition consciousness** | | | |
| H21 | ... | LC | Vlc | Alc | M | **Prp** | **Ac** | **Ad** | **Chg** | **Jh** | **Jh** | (cessation...) | |
| H22 | ... | LC | Vlc | Alc | M | **J** | **J** | **J** | **J** | **J** | R | R | Dth |
| | | LC | LC | LC | LC | LC | LC | LC | LC | LC | LC | M | **J** |
| H23 | ... | LC | Vlc | Alc | M | **J** | **J** | **J** | **J** | **J** | Dth | X | X |
| H24 | ... | LC | Vlc | Alc | M | **Prp** | **Px** | **Ad** | **Chg** | **any # *jhāna* consciousness** | | | |
| H25 | ... | LC | Vlc | Alc | M | **Prp** | **Px** | **Ad** | **Pr** | **Path** | **F** | **F** | LC |
| | | **J** | **J** | **J** | **J** | **J** | **J** | LC | LC | LC | Vlc | Alc | M |

| V12 | V13 | V14 | V15 | V16 | V17 | … | … | Number of thought moments |
|---|---|---|---|---|---|---|---|---|
| LC | LC | LC | LC | LC | LC | LC | … | Deep, dreamless sleep |
| J | J | J | J | R | R | LC | … | Eye door stream, very great object |
| J | J | J | J | J | LC | LC | … | Ear door stream, great object |
| D | D | LC | LC | LC | LC | LC | … | Nose door stream, slight object |
| Plc | Plc | Plc | Plc | Vlc | Vlc | LC | … | Body door stream, very slight object |
| R | R | LC | LC | LC | LC | LC | … | Mind door stream, clear object |
| LC | LC | LC | LC | LC | LC | LC | … | Mind door stream, obscure object |
| LC | LC | LC | LC | LC | LC | LC | … | Dreaming, not knowing |
| R | LC | LC | LC | LC | LC | LC | … | Dreaming, knowing |
| J | J | J | J | R | R | LC | … | 1st mental process sees visible form |
| R | R | LC | LC | LC | LC | LC | … | 2nd perceives preceding form |
| R | R | LC | LC | LC | LC | LC | … | 3rd interprets the form, e.g., person, etc. |
| LC | LC | LC | LC | LC | LC | LC | … | Developed insight stops sequence at M/D. |
| LC | LC | LC | LC | LC | LC | LC | … | First time attaining *jhāna* |
| | | | LC | LC | LC | LC | … | Developed *jhāna* |
| LC | LC | LC | LC | LC | LC | LC | … | Peak-reaching equanimity insight knowledge adverting to some aspect of *anicca, dukkha,* or *anattā* leading to emergence occurs 2–3 times. |
| LC | LC | LC | LC | LC | LC | LC | … | |
| LC | LC | LC | LC | LC | LC | LC | … | |
| LC | LC | LC | LC | LC | LC | LC | … | Stream at first stage enlightenment |
| LC | LC | LC | LC | LC | LC | LC | … | Stream at higher stage enlightenment |
| | | | LC | LC | LC | LC | … | Developed fruition |
| | | F | LC | LC | LC | LC | … | *Nirodhasamapatti* stream |
| R-L | LC | LC | LC | LC | LC | LC | | Stream at death of ordinary unenlightened being |
| J | J | J | J | J | J | LC | … | |
| X | X | X | X | X | X | X | X | Usual stream at death of *arahat* |
| | | | | Dth | X | X | X | Death of *arahat* after *jhāna* |
| LC | LC | LC | Vlc | Alc | M | J | | Attaining full enlightenment at death |
| J | J | J | J | J | Dth | X | X | |

## Legend to Appendix 2

| | |
|---|---|
| **Ac** | Access, proximate to higher cons. |
| **Ad** | Adaptation/conformity |
| Alc | Arresting life continuum |
| **Chg** | Change of lineage |
| D | Determining |
| Dth | Death |
| ear | Ear consciousness |
| eye | Eye consciousness |
| **F** | Fruition |
| I | Investigating |
| **J** | *Javana* impulsion |
| **Jh** | *Jhāna*, ecstatic concentration |
| LC | Life continuum/*bhavaṅga* |
| M | Mind-door-adverting cons. |
| nose | Nose consciousness |
| **Path** | Enlightenment |
| Plc | Passed life continuum |
| **Pr** | Purification, prior to higher enlight. |
| **Prp** | Preparation for higher cons. |
| R | Retention/registration |
| Rc | Receiving consciousness |
| R-L | Re-linking, rebirth cons. |
| Vlc | Vibrating life continuum |
| X | Nothing arising onward |
| 5A | Five-sense-door-adverting cons. |
| ( ) | An indefinite amount |

## APPENDIX 3A: MENTAL STATES

| | | | |
|---|---|---|---|
| 1 | Contact | UNIVERSALS | COMMON TO EACH OTHER |
| 2 | Feeling | | |
| 3 | Perception | | |
| 4 | Volition | | |
| 5 | One-pointedness | | |
| 6 | Psychic life | | |
| 7 | Attention | | |
| 8 | Initial application/connecting | PARTICULARS | |
| 9 | Sustained application | | |
| 10 | Decision/resolution | | |
| 11 | Energy | | |
| 12 | Joy | | |
| 13 | Conation/wish to do | | |
| 14 | Delusion | UNWHOLESOME | |
| 15 | Moral shamelessness | | |
| 16 | Remorselessness | | |
| 17 | Restlessness | | |
| 18 | Greed/attachment | | |
| 19 | Wrong belief | | |
| 20 | Conceit | | |
| 21 | Aversion | | |
| 22 | Envy | | |
| 23 | Avarice | | |
| 24 | Worry | | |
| 25 | Sloth | | |
| 26 | Torpor | | |
| 27 | Doubt | | |

*Continued on next page*

## Appendix 3a: Mental States

| | | | |
|---|---|---|---|
| 28 | Confidence | BEAUTIFUL | BEAUTIFUL |
| 29 | Mindfulness | | |
| 30 | Modesty | | |
| 31 | Conscience | | |
| 32 | Nonattachment | | |
| 33 | Lovingkindness | | |
| 34 | Equanimity | | |
| 35 | Tranquility of mental states | | |
| 36 | Tranquility of mind | | |
| 37 | Lightness of mental states | | |
| 38 | Lightness of mind | | |
| 39 | Pliancy of mental states | | |
| 40 | Pliancy of mind | | |
| 41 | Adaptability of mental states | | |
| 42 | Adaptability of mind | | |
| 43 | Proficiency of mental states | | |
| 44 | Proficiency of mind | | |
| 45 | Rectitude of mental states | | |
| 46 | Rectitude of mind | | |
| 47 | Right speech | ABSTINENCES | |
| 48 | Right action | | |
| 49 | Right livelihood | | |
| 50 | Compassion | ILLIMITABLES | |
| 51 | Sympathetic joy | | |
| 52 | Wisdom | | |

## APPENDIX 3B: MENTAL FACTORS

| | | | | 6 - HINDRANCES | 10- DEFILEMENTS | 5 - JHANIC FACTORS | 5 - FACULTIES/POWERS | 7 - ENLIGHTENMENT FACT. | 4 - DIVINE ABODES | 8 - PATH FACTORS |
|---|---|---|---|---|---|---|---|---|---|---|
| | | 1 | Contact | | | | | | | |
| | | 2 | Feeling | | | X | | | | |
| | | 3 | Perception | | | | | | | |
| | 7 UNIVERSALS | 4 | Volition | | | | | | | |
| | | 5 | One-pointedness/unification of mind | | | X | X | X | | X |
| | | 6 | Psychic life | | | | | | | |
| 13 ETHICALLY VARIABLE | | 7 | Attention | | | | | | | |
| | | 8 | Initial application of mind/connecting | | | X | | | | X |
| | | 9 | Sustained application of mind | | | X | | | | |
| | | 10 | Decision/resolution | | | | | | | |
| | 6 OCCASIONALS | 11 | Energy | | | | X | X | | X |
| | | 12 | Joy | | | X | | X | | |
| | | 13 | Conation/wish to do | | | | | | | |
| | | 14 | Delusion/ignorance | X | X | | | | | |
| | | 15 | Lack of self-respect | | X | | | | | |
| | | 16 | Lack of respect for others | | X | | | | | |
| | | 17 | Restlessness | X | X | | | | | |
| | | 18 | Greed/attachment | X | X | | | | | |
| | | 19 | Wrong belief | | X | | | | | |
| | | 20 | Conceit | | X | | | | | |
| 14 UNWHOLESOME | | 21 | Aversion | X | X | | | | | |
| | | 22 | Envy | | | | | | | |
| | | 23 | Avarice/stinginess | | | | | | | |
| | | 24 | Worry | | | | | | | |
| | | 25 | Sloth | X | X | | | | | |
| | | 26 | Torpor | | | | | | | |
| | | 27 | Doubt | X | X | | | | | |
| | | 28 | Confidence/faith | | | | X | | | |

*Continued on next page*

# Appendix 3B: Mental Factors

| | | | | 6 - HINDRANCES | 10- DEFILEMENTS | 5 - JHANIC FACTORS | 5 - FACULTIES/POWERS | 7 - ENLIGHTENMENT FACT. | 4 - DIVINE ABODES | 8 - PATH FACTORS |
|---|---|---|---|---|---|---|---|---|---|---|
| 25 BEAUTIFUL | 19 BEAUTIFUL | 29 | Mindfulness/awareness | | | | X | X | | X |
| | | 30 | Modesty/shame to act wrongly | | | | | | | |
| | | 31 | Conscience/fear of acting wrongly | | | | | | | |
| | | 32 | Nonattachment/generosity | | | | | | | |
| | | 33 | Nonaversion/loving-kindness | | | | | | X | |
| | | 34 | Equanimity | | | | | X | X | |
| | | 35 | Tranquility of mental states | | | | | X | | |
| | | 36 | Tranquility of mind | | | | | | | |
| | | 37 | Lightness of mental states | | | | | | | |
| | | 38 | Lightness of mind | | | | | | | |
| | | 39 | Pliancy of mental states/malleability | | | | | | | |
| | | 40 | Pliancy of mind/malleability | | | | | | | |
| | | 41 | Adaptability of mental state/wieldiness | | | | | | | |
| | | 42 | Adaptability of mind/wieldiness | | | | | | | |
| | | 43 | Proficiency of mental states | | | | | | | |
| | | 44 | Proficiency of mind | | | | | | | |
| | | 45 | Rectitude of mental states/straightness | | | | | | | |
| | | 46 | Rectitude of mind/straightness | | | | | | | |
| | 3 ABSTINENCES | 47 | Right speech | | | | | | | X |
| | | 48 | Right action | | | | | | | X |
| | | 49 | Right livelihood | | | | | | | X |
| | 2 ILLIMITABLES | 50 | Compassion | | | | | | X | |
| | | 51 | Sympathetic joy | | | | | | X | |
| | 1 WISDOM | 52 | Nondelusion/wisdom | | | | X | X | | X |

## APPENDIX 4: THE PROGRESS OF INSIGHT KNOWLEDGE THROUGH THE STAGES OF PURIFICATION

| |
|---|
| Purification of Conduct (*Sīla*) |
| Purification of Mind (*Samādhi*) |
| Purification of View |
|     1. Knowledge that discerns mental and physical phenomena |
| Purification by Overcoming Doubt |
|     2. Knowledge that discerns conditionality |
|     3. Insight knowledge by comprehension |
|         immature: first "rolling-up-the-mat" stage |
|         mature: first *vipassanā jhāna* |
|     4. Insight knowledge of arising and passing away |
|         immature: second *vipassanā jhāna* |
|         ten corruptions of insight—e.g., pseudo-*nibbāna*, "spiritual goodies" |
|             brilliant light |
|             rapture: joy, ecstasy |
|             tranquility |
|             resolution |
|             energy |
|             happiness of body and mind |
|             insight knowledge |
|             mindfulness |
|             equanimity |
|             delight |
| Purification by Knowledge and Vision of What Is Path and Not Path |

*Continued on next page*

## APPENDIX 4: THE PROGRESS OF INSIGHT KNOWLEDGE THROUGH THE STAGES OF PURIFICATION

| |
|---|
| Purification by Knowledge and Vision of the Way |
| mature arising and passing: third *vipassanā jhāna* |
| 5. Insight knowledge of dissolution |
| insight knowledges of *dukkha*, second "rolling-up-the-mat" stage |
| *suññata*, emptiness |
| 6. Insight knowledge of fear |
| 7. Insight knowledge of danger |
| 8. Insight knowledge of disenchantment |
| 9. Insight knowledge of desire for deliverance |
| 10. Insight knowledge derived from reobservation |
| third "rolling-up-the-mat" stage |
| 11. Insight knowledge of equanimity toward phenomena: fourth *vipassanā jhāna* |
| 12. Insight knowledge leading to emergence |
| 13. Insight knowledge of adaptation |
| 14. Knowledge of change of lineage |
| Purification by Knowledge and Vision |
| 15. Knowledge of path: first stage of enlightenment with realization of *nibbāna* |
| 16. Knowledge of fruit |
| 17. Knowledge of reviewing |
| 18. Attainment of fruition |
| 19. The higher paths and fruitions (second, third, and fourth stages of enlightenment) |

# Abbreviations

## Pali Texts

| | |
|---|---|
| Abhidhamma-mūlaṭīkā | Abhidh-mlṭ |
| Abhidhammattha Saṅgaha | Abhidh-s |
| Abhidhammatthasaṅgaha-aṭṭhakathā | Abhidh-s-a |
| Abhidhammatthavibhāvinī-ṭīkā | Abhidh-vibh-ṭ |
| Aṅguttara Nikāya | AN |
| Aṭṭhasālinī | As |
| Cullaniddesa | Nidd II |
| Dhammapada | Dhp |
| Dhammapada-aṭṭhakathā | Dhp-a |
| Dhammasaṅgaṇi | Dhs |
| Dhammasaṅgaṇi-aṭṭhakathā | Dhs-a |
| Dhammasaṅgaṇi-mūlaṭīkā | Dhs-mlṭ |
| Dhīga Nikāya | DN |
| Dīgha Nikāya Aṭṭhakathā ṭīkā | DNĀṭ |
| Dhīga-nikāya-ṭīkā | DN-ṭ |
| Itivuttaka-aṭṭhakathā | It-a |
| Kathāvatthu | Kvg |
| Mahāniddesa | Nidd I |
| Majjhima Nikāya | MN |
| Majjhima-nikāya-ṭīkā | MN-ṭ |
| Manorathapūraṇī (Aṅguttara-nikāya-aṭṭhakathā) | Mp |
| Milindapañha | Mil |
| Nettippakaraṇa | Nett |
| Nettippakaraṇa-aṭṭhakathā | Nett-a |
| Pañcapakaraṇaṭṭhakathā | Ppk-a |
| Papañcasūdanī (Majjhima-nikāya-aṭṭhakathā) | Ps |
| Paṭisambhidāmagga | Paṭis |

| | |
|---|---|
| Paṭṭhāna (Mahāpakaraṇa) | Paṭṭh |
| Puggalapaññatti | Pp |
| Saṃyutta Nikāya | SN |
| Sāratthappakāsinī (Saṃyutta-nikāya-aṭṭhakathā) | Spk |
| Sumaṅgalavilāsinī (Dhīga-nikāya-aṭṭhakathā) | Svg |
| Udāna-aṭṭhakathā | Ud-a |
| Vibhaṅga | Vibh |
| Vibhaṅga-aṭṭhakathā (Sammohavinodanī) | Vibh-a |
| Vinaya Piṭaka | Vin |
| Visuddhimagga | Vism |
| Visuddhimagga-mahāṭīkā (the *Mahāṭīkā*) | Vism-mhṭ |
| Yamaka | Yam |

## Other Abbreviations

| | |
|---|---|
| Mahāsi Sayadaw | MS |
| Vipassanā Research Institute | VRI |

# Notes

1 Homage to the Blessed One, the Perfect One, the Fully Enlightened One!

2 The Blessed One (*bhagavā*) is (1) accomplished (*arahaṃ*), (2) fully enlightened (*sammāsambuddho*), (3) perfect in true knowledge and conduct (*vijjācaraṇasampanno*), (4) sublime (*sugato*), (5) knower of worlds (*lokavidū*), (6) incomparable leader of persons to be tamed (*anuttaro purisadammasārathi*), (7) teacher of gods and humans (*satthā devamanussānaṃ*), (8) enlightened (*buddho*), and (9) blessed (*bhagavā*).

3 The Dhamma is (1) well proclaimed by the Blessed One (*svākkhātobhagavatā dhammo*), (2) visible here and now (*sandiṭṭhiko*), (3) immediately effective (*akāliko*), (4) inviting inspection (*ehipassiko*), (5) onward leading (*opanayyiko*), and (6) to be experienced by the wise for themselves (*paccattaṃ veditabbo viññūhī*).

4 The Saṅgha of the Blessed One's disciples (1) practices the good way (*supaṭipannobhagavato sāvakasaṅgho*), (2) practices the straight way (*ujupaṭipanno*), (3) practices the true way (*ñāyapaṭipanno*), (4) practices the proper way (*sāmīcipaṭipanno*), are the four pairs of persons (*cattāri purisayugāni*) and eight types of individuals (*aṭṭha purisapuggalā*) who are (5) worthy of gifts (*āhuṇeyyo*), (6) worthy of hospitality (*pāhuṇeyyo*), (7) worthy of offerings (*dakkhiṇeyyo*), (8) worthy of reverential salutation (*añjalikaraṇīyo*), and are (9) the unsurpassed field of merit for the world (*anuttaraṃ puññakkhettaṃ lokassā*).

5 *The Dhammapada: A New Translation of the Buddhist Classic with Annotations*, trans. Gil Fronsdal (Boston: Shambhala, 2005), 43.

> *Yo sāsanaṃ arahataṃ, ariyānaṃ dhammajīvinaṃ;*
> *paṭikkosati dummedho, diṭṭhiṃ nissāya papikaṃ;*
> *phalāni kaṭṭhakasseva, atthaghātāya phallati.* (Dhp 164)

6 *The Middle Length Discourses of the Buddha: A New Translation of the Majjhima Nikāya*, trans. Bhikkhu Bodhi (Boston: Wisdom Publications, 1995), 1039 (MN 131.3).

7 Ibid., 210 (MN 19.27).

8 Joseph Goldstein, foreword to *Manual of Insight: Mahāsi Sayadaw*, trans. and ed. Vipassanā Mettā Foundation Translation Committee (Somerville, MA: Wisdom Publications, 2016), xvii. Unless otherwise noted, all quotes and excerpts in the introduction are from *Manual of Insight*, page numbers omitted.

9 Thanissaro Bhikkhu, "Lost in Quotation," in *Access to Insight* (BCBS edition), August 29, 2012, http://www.accesstoinsight.org/lib/authors/thanissaro/lostinquotation.html.

10 The Pāḷi word *pāramī* is usually translated as "perfection." However, its literal meaning is "deeds of a noble person" (*paramānaṃ uttamapurisanaṃ bhāvo kammaṃ*). The word specifically refers to the qualities of generosity, morality, renunciation, wisdom, effort, patience, honesty, determination, loving-kindness, and equanimity. The potential for these qualities lies dormant in one's mental processes throughout the life cycle.

11 That is, should one observe ultimately real phenomena by using accurate names?

12 *Nanu ca tajjā paññattivasena sabhāvadhammo gayhatīti? Saccaṃ gayhati pubbabhāge, bhāvanāya pana vaddhamānāya paññattiṃ samatikkamitvā sabhāveyeva cittaṃ tiṭṭhāti.* (Vism-mhṭ)

13 For example, knowledge that discerns mental and physical phenomena (*nāmarūpaparicchedañāṇa*).

14 *Visuddhimagga-mahāṭīkā.* (Vism-mhṭ)

15 Specifically, the *Mahāṭīkā* and *Abhidhammatthavibhāvinī*.

16 *Kasmā panettha ubhayaggahaṇaṃ? Puggalajjhāsayato. Ekaccassa hi dhātuyo manasi karontassa tā sabhāvato gahetabbataṃ gacchanti, ekaccassa sakiccakaraṇato. Yo rasoti vuccati.*

17 This phrase refers to passages in the *Satipaṭṭhāna* (MN 10.40) and *Mahāsatipaṭṭhāna Suttas* (DN 22.15). Our translation follows Bodhi's *Middle Length Discourses*, 153.

18 *Cakkhupasādaṃ . . . rūpañca yathāvasarasalakkhanavasena.* (Sv)

19 *Upekkhā pana akusalavipākabhūtā aniṭṭhattā dukkhe avarodetabbā, itarā iṭṭhattā sukheti.* (Abhidh-mlṭ)

20 The exact passage as quoted by Mahāsi Sayadaw occurs only in the *Paṭisambhidāmagga* and the *Visuddhimagga*. A series of suttas in the Saṃyutta Nikāya, however, convey the same meaning, each with a slightly different emphasis. See *The Connected Discourses of the Buddha: A New Translation of the Saṃyutta Nikāya*, trans. Bhikkhu Bodhi (Boston: Wisdom Publications, 1999), 1141–43 (SN 35:25–27).

21 [*Cakkhuṃ*[MS]][*Cakkhu*[VRI]] *bhikkhave abhiññeyyaṃ. Rūpā abhiññeyyā, cakkhuviññāṇaṃ abhiññeyyaṃ, cakkhusamphasso abhiññeyyo, yampidaṃ cakkhusamphassapaccayā upajjati vedayitaṃ sukhaṃ vā dukkhaṃ vā adukkhamasukhaṃ vā. Tampi abhiññeyyaṃ.* (Paṭis; Vism)

22 *Sabhāvadhammānaṃ lakkhanasallakkhaṇato ñeyya-abhimukhā paññā abhiññāpaññā.* (Vism-mhṭ)

23 *Apica sutamayāya, cintāmayāya, ekaccabhāvanāmayāya ca abhivisitthāyapaññāya ñātā abhiññātā.* (Vism-mhṭ)

24 See *The Connected Discourses*, 1147 (SN 35:46).

25 See *The Connected Discourses*, 1856–57 (SN 56:29).

26 *The Connected Discourses*, 1175. "*Taṃ kiṃ maññasi mālukyaputta, ye te cakkhuviññeyyā rūpā adiṭṭhā adiṭṭhapubbā, na ca passati, na ca te hoti passeyyanti? Atthi te tattha chando vā rāgo vā pemaṃ vā"ti?" "No hetaṃ bhante.*" (SN 35:95)

27 Ibid., 1175–76. "*Ettha ca te Mālukyaputta diṭṭhasutamutaviññātesu dhammesu diṭṭhe diṭṭhamattaṃ bhavissati, sute sutamattaṃ bhavissati, mute mutamattaṃ bhavissati, viññāte viññānamattaṃ bhavissati. Yato kho te Mālukyaputta*

*diṭṭhasutamutaviññātabesu dhammesu diṭṭhe diṭṭhamattaṃ bhavissati, sute sutamattaṃ bhavissati, mute mutamattaṃ bhavissati, viññāte viññānamattaṃ bhavissati; tato tvaṃ Mālukyaputta, na tena. Yato tvaṃ Mālukyaputta, na tena; tato tvaṃ mālukyaputta, na tattha; yato tvaṃ Mālukyaputta na tattha; tato tvaṃ Mālukyaputta, nevidha, na huraṃ, na ubhayamantarena. Esevanto dukkhassati."* (SN 35:95)

28 Udāna-aṭṭhākathā: Bāhiyasuttavaṇṇanā.

29 *"Vipassanāya visayaṃ diṭṭhādīhi catūhi koṭṭhāsehi vibhajitvā tatthassa ñātatīraṇapariññaṃ dasseti."*

30 Attachment, pride, and wrong view constitute the three proliferating tendencies of mind (*papañca*).

31 *The Connected Discourses*, 1176. *Rūpaṃ disvā sati muṭṭhā, piyaṃ nimittam manasikaroto; Sārattacitto vedeti, tañca ajjhosa tiṭṭhati. Tassa vuḍḍhanti vedanā, anekā rūpasambhavā. Abhijjhā ca vihesā ca, cittamassupahaññati; Evaṃ ācinato dukkhaṃ, ārā nibbānavuccati.* (SN 35:95)

32 *The Connected Discourses*, 1176–77. *Na so rajjati rūpesu, rūpaṃ disvā paṭissato; Virattacitto vedeti, tañca najjhosa tiṭṭhati. Yathāssa passato rūpaṃ, sevato cāpi vedanaṃ; Khīyati nopacīyati, evaṃ so carati sato; Evaṃ apacinato dukkhaṃ, santike nibbāna vuccati.* (SN 35:95)

33 See *The Connected Discourses*, 1175–78 (SN 35:95), or Saḷāyatanavaggapāḷi, PTS 4.74.

34 See *The Connected Discourses*, 959–61 (SN 22.101).

35 See *The Connected Discourses*, 1250 (SN 35.244).

36 See Appendix 2: Stream of Consciousness, line H10-12/12A. Line H12A ending at investigation or determining without any impulsion is seen by the subsequent insight knowledge stream.

37 *Dandho bhikkhave satuppādoti satiyā uppādoyeva dandho uppannamattāya pana tāya kāci kilesā niggahitāva honti, na saṇṭhātuṃ sakkonti. Cakkhudvārasmiñhi rāgādīsu uppannesu dutiya . . . javanaṃyeva javati. Anacchariyañcetaṃ, yaṃ vipassako tatiyajavanavāre kilese niggaṇheyya. Cakkhudvāre pana iṭṭhārammaṇe āpāthagate bhavaṅgaṃ āveṭṭetvā āvajjanādīsu uppannesu voṭṭhabbanānantaraṃ sampattakilesajavanavāraṃ nivattetvā kusalameva uppādeti. Āraddhavipassakānañhi ayamānisaṃso bhāvanāpaṭisaṅkhāne patiṭṭhitabhāvassa.* (Spk)

38 *Balavavipassakassa sacepi cakkhudvārādīsu ārammaṇe āpāthagate ayoniso āvajjanaṃ upajjati, voṭṭhabbanaṃ patvā ekaṃ dve vāre āsevanaṃ labhitvā cittaṃ bhavaṅgameva otarati, na rāgādivasena uppajjati, ayaṃ koṭipatto tikkhavipassako. Aparassa rāgādivasena ekaṃ vāraṃ javanaṃ javati, javanapariyosāne panarāgādivasena evaṃ me javanaṃ javitanti āvajjato ārammaṇaṃ pariggahitameva hoti, puna vāraṃ tathā na javati. Aparassa ekavāraṃ evaṃ āvajjato puna dutiyavāraṃ rāgādivasena javanaṃ javatiyeva, dutiyavāravasane pana evaṃ me javanaṃ javitanti āvajjato ārammaṇaṃ pariggahitameva hoti, tatiyavāre tathā na uppajjati.* (Ps)

39 *The Numerical Discourses of the Buddha: A New Translation of the Aṅguttara Nikāya*, trans. Bhikkhu Bodhi (Boston: Wisdom Publications, 2012), 761. *Sādhu bhikkhave bhikkhu kālena kālaṃ patikūlañca appaṭikūlañca tadubhayaṃ abhinivejjetvā upekkhako vihareyya sato sampajāno.* (AN 5:144)

40 *Chaḷaṅgupekkhāvasena pañcamo. Chaḷaṅgupekkhā cesā khīṇāsavassa upekkhāsadisā, na pana khīṇāsavupekkhā . . . imasmim sutte pañcasu ṭhānesu vipassanāva kathitā. Taṃ āraddhavipassako . . . kātum sakkoti . . .* (Mp)

41 See *The Middle Length Discourses*, 278–85 (MN 28).

42 *Upekkhā kusalanissitā santhātīti idha chaḷaṅgupekkhā, sā panesā kiñcāpi khīnāsavassa iṭṭhāniṭṭhesu . . . arajjanādivasena pavattati, ayaṃ pana bhikkhu vīriyabalena bhāvanāsiddhiyā attano vipassanaṃ khīṇāsavassa chaḷaṇgupekkhāthāne thapetīti vipassanāva chaḷaṅgupekkhā nāma jātā.* (Ps)

43 Mahāsi Sayadaw suggested "Good-for-nothing Potthila," "Useless Potthila," "Futile Potthila" as other renderings.

44 1 yojana = approx. 8 miles.

45 *The Middle Length Discourses*, 1147. *Evaṃ sante kho, Uttara, andho bhāvitindriyo bhavissati, badhiro bhāvitindriyo bhavissati, yathā pārāsiviyassa brāhmanassa vacanaṃ. Andho hi, Uttara, cakkhunā rūpaṃ na passati, badhiro sotena saddaṃ na sunāti.* (MN 152.2)

46 *The Numerical Discourses*, 857. *Cakkhunā rūpaṃ disvā neva sumano hoti na dummano, upekkhako viharati sato sampajāno.* (AN 6:1)

47 *The Dhammapada*, 73. *Yogā ve jāyatī bhūrī, ayogā bhūrisaṅkhayo; etaṃ dvedhāpathaṃ ñatvā, bhavāya vibhavāya ca; tathāttānaṃ niveseyya, yathā bhūrī pavaḍḍhati.* (Dhp 282)

48 See also *The Path of Purification: Visuddhimagga*, trans. Bhikkhu Ñāṇamoli (Onalaska: BPS Pariyatti Editions, 1991), 610. *Evaṃ suvisuddharūpapariggahassa panassa arūpadhammā tīhākārehi upaṭṭhahanti phassavasena vā, vedanāvasena vā, viññāṇavasena vā.* (Vism 18.18)

49 *Tenassa phusanākārena supākaṭabhāvena upaṭṭhānaṃ dasseti. Phasse pana upaṭṭite yasmiṃ ārammaṇe so phasso, tassa anubhavanalakkhaṇā vedanā, sañjānanalakkhaṇā saññā, āyūhanalakkhaṇā cetanā, paṭivijānanalakkhaṇaṃ viññāṇanti imepi pākaṭā honti.* (Vism-mhṭ)

50 See *The Long Discourses of the Buddha: A New Translation of the Dīgha Nikāya*, trans. Maurice Walshe (Boston: Wisdom Publications, 1995), 321–34 (DN 21).

51 See *The Middle Length Discourses*, 145–55 (MN 10).

52 *Yassa phasso pākaṭo hoti, sopi "na kevalaṃ phassova uppajjati, tena saddhiṃ tadeva ārammaṇaṃ anubhavanāmānā vedanāpi uppajjati, sañjānamānā saññāpi, cetayamānā cetanāpi, vijānanamānaṃ viññāṇampi uppajjatī"ti phassapañcamakeyeva parigganhāti.* (Vibh-a)

53 *Idha pana cakkhuviññāṇasampayuttā tayo khandhā. Te hi cakkhuviññāṇena saha viññātabbattā "cakkhuviññāṇaviññātabbā"ti vuttā.* (Spk)

54 *Phassāhāre tīhi pariññāhi pariññāte tisso vedanā pariññātāva honti tammūlakattā tamsampayuttattā ca.* (Spk)

55 That is, seeing phenomena as they really are.

56 That is, seeing phenomena in terms of impermanence and so on.

57 That is, seeing phenomena without attachment.

58 *Viññāṇasmiñhi pariññāte taṃ pariññātameva hoti tammūlakattā, sahuppannattā ca.* (Spk)

59 See *The Middle Length Discourses*, 925–30 (MN 115).

60 *The Middle Length Discourses*, 926. *Chayimā, Ānanda dhātuyo—pathavīdhātu, āpodhātu, tejodhātu, vāyodhātu, akāsadhātu, viññānadhātu. Imā kho ānanda cha dhātuyo yato jānāti passati—ettāvatāpi kho, Ānanda "dhātukusalo bhikkhūti alaṃ vacanāyā"ti.* (MN 115.5)

61 This does not refer to theoretical knowledge (*sutamayañāṇa*) or analytical knowledge (*cintāmayañāṇa*) but to empirical knowledge (*bhāvanāmayañāṇa*), the understanding gained through insight and path.

62 *Jānāti passatīti saha vipassanāya maggo vutto. Pathvīdhātu-ādayo saviññāṇakakāyaṃ suññato nissattato dassetuṃ vuttā. Tāpi purimāhi aṭṭharasahi dhātūhi pūretabbā. Pūrentena viññāṇadhātuto nīharitvā pūretabbā. Viññāṇadhātu hesā cakkhuviññāṇādivasena chabbidhā hoti. Tattha cakkhuviññāṇadhātuyā pariggahitāya tassā vatthu cakkhudhātu, ārammaṇaṃ rūpadhātūti dve dhātuyo pariggahitāva honti. Esa nayo sabbattha. Manoviññāṇadhātuyā pana pariggahitāya tassā purimapacchimavasena manodhātu, ārammaṇavasena dhammadhātūti dve dhātuyo pariggahitāva honti. Iti* [. . . [MS]] *idampi ekassa bhikkhuno niggamanaṃ matthakaṃ pāpetvā kathitaṃ hoti.* (Ps)

63 See *The Middle Length Discourses*, 145–55 (MN 10).

64 *Ettha ca "kakkhaḷaṃ mudukaṃ saṇhaṃ pharusaṃ garukaṃ lahukan"ti padehi pathvīdhātu eva bhājitā.* [. . . [MS]] *"Sukhasamphassaṃ dukkhasamphassan"ti padadvayena pana tīnīpi mahābhūtāni bhājitāni.* (As)

65 See *The Path of Purification*, 463. *Aniṭṭhaphoṭṭhabbānubhavanalakkhaṇaṃ dukkhaṃ.* (Vism 14.127)

66 Ibid. *Sampayuttānaṃ milāpanarasaṃ.* (Vism 14.127)

67 Ibid. *Kāyikābādhapaccupaṭṭhānaṃ.* (Vism 14.127)

68 Ibid. *Kāyindriyapadaṭṭhanaṃ, "Phassapadaṭṭhāna vedanā."* (Vism 14.127)

69 *The Middle Length Discourses*, 145–46: . . . *satova assasati, satova passasati.* (MN 10.4; DN 22.2)

70 Ibid., 146: . . . *samudayadhammānupassī vā kāyasmiṃ viharati* . . . (MN 10; DN 22)

71 Ibid., 146: . . . *vayadhammānupassī vā* [*kayasmi*[VRI]] *viharati* . . . (MN 10; DN 22)

72 Ibid., 146: *Atthi kāyo"ti vā panassa sati paccupatthitāhoti* . . . (MN 10; DN 22)

73 Ibid., 146: . . . *Yathā yathā vā panassa kāyo panihito hoti, tathā tathā naṃ pajānāti.* (MN 10; DN 22)

74 The twenty parts that are dominated by the earth element are: (1) head hair, (2) body hair, (3) nails, (4) teeth, (5) skin, (6) flesh, (7) sinews, (8) bones, (9) bone marrow, (10) kidneys, (11) heart, (12) liver, (13) diaphragm, (14) spleen, (15) lungs, (16) large intestines, (17) small intestines, (18) contents of the stomach, (19) feces, and (20) brain.

75 The twelve dominated by the water element are: (1) bile, (2) phlegm, (3) pus, (4) blood, (5) sweat, (6) fat, (7) tears, (8) grease, (9) spittle, (10) snot, (11) oil of the joints, and (12) urine.

76 The four dominated by the fire element are that by which one is warmed, ages, and is consumed, and that by which what is eaten, drunk, consumed, and tasted gets completely digested.

77 The six dominated by the air element are: (1) up-going winds, (2) down-going winds, (3) winds in the belly, (4) winds in the bowels, (5) winds that

course through the limbs, and (6) the in breath and out breath.

78 *The Middle Length Discourses*, 148. *Imameva kāyaṃ yathāṭhitaṃ yathāpaṇihitaṃ dhātuso paccavekkhati "atthi imasmiṃ kāye pathavīdhātu āpodhātu, tejodhātu vāyodhātu"ti.* (MN 10; DN 22)

79 *The Middle Length Discourses*, 146. *Gacchanto vā "gacchāmī"ti pajānāti.* (MN 10; DN 22)

80 *Esa evaṃ pajānāti—"gacchāmī"ti cittaṃ uppajjati, taṃ vāyaṃ janeti, vāyo viññattiṃ janeti, cittakiriyavāyodhātuvipphārena sakalakāyassa purato abhinīhāro gamananti vuccati.* (Sv)

81 *Imassa pana bhikkhuno jānanaṃ sattūpaladdhiṃ pajahati. Attasaññaṃ ugghāṭeti kammaṭṭhānañceva satipaṭṭhānabhāvanā ca hoti.*

82 *The Middle Length Discourses*, 147: . . . *abhikkante paṭikkante sampajānakārī hoti.* (MN 10; DN 22)

83 Referring to a Pāḷi word that means "a collection (or mass) of bones," Mahāsi Sayadaw inserted the following comment at this point into the original Pāḷi quote: "*rūpasanghāṭo* is preferred to *aṭṭhisaṅghāto*"; we have applied his preferred usage in the English translation.

84 *Abhikkamādīsu pana asammuyhanaṃ asammohasampajaññaṃ. Taṃ evaṃ veditabbaṃ—idha bikkhu abhikkamanto vā paṭikkamanto vā yathā andhbalāputhujjanāabhikkamādīsu "attā abhikkamati, attanā abhikkamo nibbattito"ti vā, "ahaṃ abhikkamāmi, mayā abhikkamo nibbattito"ti vā sammuyhanti tathā asammuyhanto "abhikkamāmī"ti citte uppajjamāne teneva cittena saddhiṃ cittasamuṭṭhānā vāyodhātu viññattiṃ janatamānā uppajjati. Iti cittakiriyavāyodhātuvipphāravasena ayaṃ kāyasammato aṭṭhisaṅghāto abhikkamati. Tassevaṃ abhikkamato ekekapāduddharaṇe pathvīdhātu āpodhātūti dve dhātuyo omattā honti mandā, itarā dve adhimattā honti balavatiyo; tathā atiharaṇavītiharaṇesu.* [*Vosajjane tejovāyodhātuyo omattā honti mandā, itarā dve adhimattā* [*honti*[MS]] *balavtiyo; tathā sannikkhepanasannirumbhanesu*[MS, MNCom'y]]. [*Vosajjane tejodhātu vāyodhātuti dve dhātuyo omattā honti mandā, itarā dve adhimattā balavtiyo; tathā sannikkhepanasannirujjhanesu*[DNCom'y]]. (Ps; Sv)

85 Literally: "The old mind vanishes and the new mind appears."

86 *Tattha uddharaṇe pavattā rūpārūpadhammā atiharaṇaṃ na pāpuṇanti, tathā atiharaṇe pavattā vītiharaṇaṃ vītiharaṇe pavattā vosajjanaṃ, vosajjane pavattā sannikkhepanaṃ, sannikkhepane pavattā sannirujjhanaṃ* [*sannirumbhanaṃ*] *na pāpuṇanti. Tattha tattheva pabbaṃ pabbaṃ sandhi sandhi odhi odhi hutvā tattakapāle pakkhittatilāni viya paṭapaṭāyantā bhijjanti. Tattha ko eko abhikkamati, kassa vā ekassa abhikkamanaṃ? Paramatthato hi dhātūnaṃyeva gamanaṃ, dhātūnaṃ ṭhānaṃ, dhātūnaṃ nisajjānaṃ, dhātūnaṃ sayanaṃ. Tasmiṃ tasmiṃ* [*hi*[MS]] [*kaṭṭhāse*[MS]] [*koṭṭhāse*[VRI]] *saddhiṃ rūpena.*

> *Aññaṃ upajjate cittaṃ, aññaṃ cittaṃ nirujjhati;*
> *avīcimanusambandho, nadīsotova vattatīti.*

*Evaṃ abhikkamādīsu asammuyhaṃ asammohasampajaññaṃ nāmati.* (Ps; Sv)

87 Mahāsi Sayadaw cites as an example: ". . . when standing, he understands: 'I am standing'" (*Ṭhitovāṭhitomhī'ti pajānāti*). (MN 10; DN 22)

88 *Eko hi bhikkhu gacchanto aññaṃ cintento aññaṃ vitakkento gacchati, eko kammaṭṭhānaṃ avisajjetvāva gacchati, tathā eko tiṭṭhanto, nisīdanto, sayanto, aññaṃ cintento aññaṃ vittakkento sayati, eko kammaṭṭhānaṃ avisajjetvāva sayati.* (Vibh-a)

89 *The Middle Length Discourses*, 147. *Ālokite vilokite sampajānakārī hoti.* (MN 10; DN 22)

90 *Kammaṭṭhānassa pana avijahanameva gocarasampajaññaṃ. Tasmā [ettha*[DNCom'y]*] khandhadhātuāyatanakammaṭṭhānikehi attano kammaṭṭhānavaseneva, kasiṇādikammaṭṭhānikehi vā pana kammaṭṭhānasīseneva ālokanavilokanaṃ*[MNCom'y, SNCom'y, ACom'y]*][ālokanaṃ vilokanaṃ*[DNCom'y]*] kātabbaṃ.* (Ps; Sv)

91 *The Middle Length Discourses*, 147. *Samiñjite pasārite sampajānakārī . . .* (MN 10; DN 22)

92 Ibid. *Saṅghāṭipattacīvaradhāraṇe sampajānakārī . . .*

93 Ibid. *Asite pīte khāyite sāyite sampajānakārī . . .*

94 Ibid. *Uccārapassāvakamme sampajānakārī . . .*

95 Ibid. *Gate ṭhite nisinne sutte jāgarite bhāsite tuṇhībhāve sampajānakārī hoti.*

96 In Burma strangers are addressed depending on their age. A woman who is about the same age as one's mother is addressed as "auntie," a man who is about the same age as one's grandfather is addressed as "grandfather," a child who is about the same age as one's child is addressed as "niece or nephew," a person who is about the same age as oneself is addressed as "sister" or "brother," and so on.

97 Ibid. *Bahiddhā vā kāye kāyānupassī viharati . . .*

98 Ibid. *Ajjhattabahiddhā vā kāye kāyānupassī viharati . . .*

99 Ibid. *Samudayadhammānupassī vā . . . vayadhammānupassī vā kāyasmiṃ viharati . . .*

100 Ibid. *Yathā yathā vā panassa kāyo panihito hoti, tathā tathā naṃ pajānāti . . .*

101 Ibid., 149. *Sukhaṃ vā vedanaṃ vedayamāno "sukhaṃ vedanaṃ vedayāmī"ti pajānāti . . .*

102 *Vatthuṃ ārammaṇaṃ katvā vedanāva vedayatīti sallakkhento esa "sukhaṃ vedanaṃ vedayāmīti pajānātī"ti veditabbo . . .* (Sv)

103 See *The Middle Length Discourses*, 396–403 (MN 44).

104 See *The Long Discourses*, 479–510 (DN 33).

105 MN 115. See *The Middle Length Discourses*, 925–30.

106 See *The Long Discourses*, 321–34 (DN 21).

107 See *The Middle Length Discourses*, 145–55 (MN 10).

108 *Adukkhamasukhā pana duddīpanā [andhakārāva*[MNCom'y]*][andhakarena viya*[DNCom'y]*] [andhakārā*[KN, ACom'y]*] avibhūtā. Sā sukhadukkhānaṃ apagame sātāsātapaṭipakkhepavasena majjhattākārabhūtā adukkhamasukhā vedanāti nayato ganhantassa pākaṭā hoti.* (Ps; Sv)

109 *Duddīpanāti ñānena dīpetum asakkuneyyā, dubbiññeyyāti attho. Tenāha andhakārāva avibhūtāti.* (DN-ṭ)

110 *Sāmisaṃ vā sukhaṃ vedanaṃ vedayamāno sāmisaṃ sukhaṃ vedanaṃ vedayāmīti pajānāti . . .* (Ps; Sv)

111 *The Middle Length Discourses*, 1068. *Rūpānaṃ tveva aniccataṃ viditvā viparināmavirāganirodhaṃ, "pubbe ceva rūpā tarahi ca sabbe te rūpā aniccā dukkhā vipariṇāmadhammā"ti evamevaṃ yathābhūtaṃ ammappaññāya passato*

*uppajjati somanassaṃ. Yaṃ evarūpaṃ somanassaṃ idaṃ vuccati nekkhammasitaṃ somanassaṃ.* (MN 137.11)

112 Ibid., 149. *Nirāmisaṃ vā sukhaṃ vedanaṃ vedayamāno "nirāmisaṃ sukhaṃ vedanaṃ vedayāmī"ti pajānāti.* (MN 10; DN 22)

113 Ibid., 150. *Sāmisaṃ vā dukhaṃ vedanaṃ vedayamāno "sāmisaṃ sukhaṃ vedanaṃ vedayāmī"ti pajānāti.*

114 Ibid. *Nirāmisaṃ vā dukkhaṃ vedanaṃ vedayamāno" nirāmisaṃ dukkhaṃ vedanaṃ vedayāmī"ti pajānāti.*

115 Pavāraṇā is a ceremony at the end of the annual rains retreat wherein monks invite one another to make a kind remark concerning their moral conduct if they did something wrong during the annual rains retreat.

116 Ibid. *Sāmisaṃ vā adukkhamasukhaṃ vedanaṃ vedayamāno "sāmisaṃ adukkhamasukhaṃ vedanaṃ vedayāmī"ti pajānāti.*

117 Ibid. *Nirāmisaṃ vā adukkhamasukhaṃ vedanaṃ vedayamāno "nirāmisaṃ dukkhamasukhaṃ vedanaṃ vedayāmī"ti pajānāti.*

118 Ibid. *Samudayadhammānupassī vā . . . vayadhammānupassī vā vedanāsu viharati . . .*

119 Ibid. *"Atthi vedanā"ti vā panassa sati paccupaṭṭhitā hoti.*

120 Ibid. *Sarāgaṃ vā cittaṃ "sarāgaṃ cittan"ti pajānāti. Vītarāgaṃ vā cittaṃ "vītarāgaṃ cittan"ti pajānāti.*

121 Ibid. *Sadosaṃ vā cittaṃ sadosaṃ cittanti pajānāti. Vītadosaṃ vā cittaṃ vītadosaṃ cittanti pajānāti.*

122 Ibid. *Samohaṃ vā cittaṃ samohaṃ cittanti pajānāti, vītamohaṃ vā cittaṃ vītamohaṃ cittanti pajānāti.*

123 *Yasmiṃ yasmiṃ khaṇe yaṃ yaṃ cittaṃ pavattati, taṃ taṃ sallakkhento attano vā citte, parassa vā citte, kālena vā attano, kālena vā parassa citte cittānupassasī viharati.* (Sv; Ps)

124 *The Middle Length Discourses*, 151. *Samudayadhammānupassī vā . . . vayadhammānupassī vā cittasmiṃ viharati.* (MN 10.35)

125 Ibid. *"Atthi cittan"ti vā panassa sati paccupaṭṭhitā hoti.*

126 Ibid. *"Atthi me ajjhattaṃ kāmacchando"ti pajānāti.*

127 Ibid. *Santaṃ vā ajjhattaṃ byāpādaṃ . . . thīnamiddhaṃ . . . uddhaccakukkuccaṃ . . . pajānāti.*

128 For example, doubt about whether delusions result in formations and so on.

129 Ibid. *Santaṃ vā ajjhattaṃ vicikicchaṃ "atthi me ajjhattaṃ vicikicchā"ti pajānāti.*

130 Ibid. *Santaṃ vā ajjhattaṃ vicikicchaṃ "atthi me ajjhattaṃ vicikicchā"ti pajānāti.*

131 *Yoniso manasikāro nāma upāyamanasikāro pathamanasikāro. Anicce aiccanti vā, dukkhe dukkhanti vā, anattani anattāti vā asubhe asubhanti vā manasikāro.* (Ps; Sv)

132 *Yonisomanasikāro* [*nāma*[MS]][. . .[VRI]] *kusalādīnaṃ taṃtaṃsabhāvarasalakkhaṇaādikassa yāthāvato avabujjhanavasena uppanno ñāṇasampayuttacittuppādo. So hi aviparītamanasikāratāya "yonisomanasikāro"ti vutto, tadābhogatāya āvajjanāpi taggahikā eva.* (DN-ṭ)

133 *Ayonisomanasikāro nāma anupāyamanasikāro uppathamanasikāro. Anicce niccanti vā, dukkhe sukkhanti vā, anattani attāti vā, asubhe subhanti vā manasikāro.* (Ps; Sv)

134 See Appendix 2: Stream of Consciousness.

135 *The Middle Length Discourses*, 151. *Yathā ca anuppannassa kāmacchandassa uppādo hoti tañca pajānāti, yathā ca uppannassa kāmacchandassa pahānaṃ hoti tañca pajānāti, yathā ca pahīnassa kāmacchandassa āyatiṃ anuppādo hoti tañca pajānāti.* (MN 10; DN 22)

136 Ibid. *Iti rūpaṃ . . . ; iti vedanā . . . ; iti saññā . . . ; iti sankhārā . . . ; iti viññānaṃ . . .*

137 *Iti rūpanti idaṃ rūpaṃ, ettakaṃ rūpaṃ, na ito paraṃ rūpaṃ atthīti sabhāvato rūpaṃ pajānāti. Vedanādīsupi eseva nayo.* (Sv)

138 *The Middle Length Discourses*, 151. *Iti rūpassa samudayo, iti rūpassa atthaṅgamo.*

139 Ibid. *Iti vedanāya samudayo, iti vedanāya atthaṅgamo.*

140 Ibid. *Iti viññāṇassa samudayo, iti viññāṇassa atthaṅgamo.*

141 Referring to the four reflections above. These reveal that the four causes of disappearance are: there is no craving, no kamma, and no individual causes such as nourishment, object, contact, and so on without ignorance.

142 See Appendix 2: Stream of Consciousness, H2.

143 This etymology plays on the idea that the Pāḷi noun *nāma* has its origin in the verbal root √*nam*, which means "to bend or bow."

144 This etymology plays on the idea that the Pāḷi noun *rūpa* has its origin in the verbal root √*rup*, which means "to molest or violate."

145 *The Middle Length Discourses*, 153. *Yañca tadubhayaṃ paticca uppajjati saṃyojanaṃ tañca pajānāti, yathā ca anuppannassa saṃyojanassa uppādo hoti tañca pajānāti, yathā ca uppannassa saṃyojanassa pahānaṃ hoti tañca pajānāti . . .* (MN 10; DN 22)

146 Ibid. *Yathā ca pahīnassa saṃyojanassa āyatiṃ anuppādo hoti, tañca pajānāti . . .*

147 *The Dhammapada*, 91. *Sabbaratiṃ dhammarati jināti.* (Dhp 354)

148 *The Middle Length Discourses*, 153. *Santaṃ vā ajjhattaṃ satisambojjhaṅgaṃ "atthi me ajjhattaṃ satisambojjhango"ti pajānāti . . .* (MN 10; DN 22)

149 Ibid. *Asantaṃ vā ajjhattaṃ satisambojjhangaṃ "natthi me ajjhattaṃ satisambojjhango"ti pajānāti . . .*

150 Ibid. *Yathā ca anuppannassa satisambojjhaṅgassa uppādo hoti, tañca pajānāti.*

151 Ibid. *Yathā ca uppannassa satisambojaṅgassa bhāvanāya pāripūrī hoti, tañca pajānati.*

152 The word *dukkha* is generally translated as "suffering," "unsatisfactoriness," "distress," or "affliction." The Pāḷi word, however, also connotes impermanence, insubstantiality, emptiness, imperfection, and insecurity.

153 Ibid., 278. *Jātipi dukkhā, jarāpi dukkhā, maranaṃpi dukkhaṃ.* (MN 28, 141; DN 22; AN 6.63; etc.)

154 Attachment (*taṇhā*) is technically not considered suffering because it is regarded as the origin of suffering.

155 *The Connected Discourses*, 1271. *Taṃ kho panetaṃ bhikkhu mayā saṅkhārānaṃyeva aniccataṃ sandhāya bhāsitaṃ—"yaṃ kiñci vedayitaṃ, taṃ dukkhasmin" ti . . .* (SN 36.11)

156 *The Numerical Discourses*, 964. *Saṃkhittena pañcupādānakkhandhā dukkhā.* (AN 6.63)

157 See Appendix 2: Stream of Consciousness, at the death of an ordinary unenlightened being.

158 *The Middle Length Discourses*, 135. *Yāyaṃ tanhā ponobbhavikā nandīrāgasahagatā . . .* (MN 9, 44, 141)

159 *The Connected Discourses*, 1844. *Yo tassāyeva taṇhāya asesavirāganirodho . . .* (SN 56.11)

160 This passage is not a literal translation but includes explanations by Mahāsi Sayadaw.

161 *Tattha purimāni dve saccāni vaṭṭaṃ pacchimāni vivaṭṭaṃ. Tesu bhikkhuno vaṭṭe kammaṭṭhānābhiniveso hoti, vivaṭṭe natthi abhiniveso. Purimāni hi dve saccāni "pañcakkhandhā dukkhaṃ, tanhā samudayo"ti evaṃ saṅkhepena ca, "katame pañcakkhandhā, rūpakkhandho"ti-ādinā nayena vitthārena ca ācariyassa santike uggaṇhitvā vācāya punappunaṃ parivattento yogāvacaro kammaṃ karoti. Itaresu pana dvīsu saccesu—"nirodhasaccaṃ iṭṭhaṃ kantaṃ manāpaṃ, maggasaccaṃ iṭṭhaṃ kantaṃ manāpan"ti evaṃ savanena kammaṃ karoti. So evaṃ karonto cattāri saccāni ekapaṭivedhena paṭivijjhati ekābhisamayena abhisameti. Dukkhaṃpariññāpativedena pativijjhati, samudayaṃ pahānapaṭivedhena pativijjhati, nirodhaṃ achikiriyāpaṭivedhena, [pativijjhati*MS*], maggaṃ bhāvanāpaṭivedena pativijjhati. Dukkhaṃ pariññābhisamayena [abhisameti. Samudayaṃ phānābhisamayena. Nirodhaṃ sacchikiriyābhisamayena.*MS*] [. . . pe . . . *VRI*] Maggaṃ bhāvanābhisamayena abhisameti. Evamassa pubbabhāge dvīsu saccesu uggahaparipucchāsavanadhāraṇasammasanapaṭivedho hoti, dvīsu panasavannapaṭivedhoyeva. Aparabhāge tīsu kiccato paṭivedho hoti, nirodhe ārammanappaṭivedho.* (Sv)

162 *Addhā imāya paṭipadāya jarāmaraṇamhā parimuccissāmī.* (Dhs-a)

163 *Vaṭṭe kammaṭṭhānābhiniveso sarūpato pariggahasabbhāvato. Vivaṭṭe natthi avisayattā, visayatte ca payojanābhāvato* [. . . *MS*] *Iṭṭhaṃ kantanti nirodhamaggesu ninnabhāvaṃ dasseti, na abhinandanaṃ, tanninnabhāvoyeva ca tattha kammakaraṇaṃ daṭṭhabbaṃ.* (DN-ṭ)

164 *The Middle Length Discourses*, 154. *Idaṃ dukkhanti yathābhūtaṃ pajānāti.* (MN 10; DN 22)

165 The three worlds are the sense sphere (*kāma*), the fine material sphere (*rūpa*), and the immaterial sphere (*arūpa*).

166 *Thapetvā taṇhaṃ tebhūmakadhamme idaṃ dukkhan"ti yathāsabhāvato pajānāti.* (Ps; Sv)

167 *Yathāsabhāvatoti aviparītasabhāvato. Bādhanasakkhaṇato yo yo vā sabhāvo yathāsabhāvo, tato, ruppanādi kakkhaḷādisabhāvato.* (DN-ṭ)

168 *The Connected Discourses*, 158. *"Yattha [nu*AN*] kho āvuso na jāyati na jiyyati na mīyati na cavati na upapajjati, nā'haṃ taṃ gamanena lokassa antaṃ ñāteyyaṃ diṭṭheyyaṃ patteyyanti "vadāmi"ti . . . a kho panāhaṃ āvuso appatvā lokassa antaṃ dukkhassa antakiriyaṃ vadāmi. Api ca khvāhaṃ āvuso, imasmimyeva byāmamatte kalevare sasaññimhi samānake lokañca paññapemi, lokasamudayañca, lokanirodhañca, lokanirodhagāmininca patipadaṃ . . ."* (SN:2.26)

169 *Lokanti dukkhasaccaṃ. Lokasamudayanti samudayasaccaṃ. Lokanirodhanti nirodhasaccaṃ. Paṭipadanti maggasaccaṃ. Iti "nāhaṃ āvuso, imāni cattāri sac cāni tinakaṭṭhādīsu paññapemi, imasmiṃ pana cātumahābhūtike kāyasmiṃyeva paññapemī"ti dasseti.* (Spk)

170 *Sasantatipariyāpannānaṃ dukkhasamudayānaṃ appavattibhāvena pariggay-*

*hamāno nirodhopi sasantatipariyāpanno viya hotīti katvā vuttaṃ "attano vā cattāri saccānī"ti. Parassa vāti etthāpi eseva nayo.* (DN-ṭ)

171 *Tasseva kho pana dukkhassa janikaṃ samuṭṭhāpikaṃ purimataṇhaṃ "ayaṃ dukkhasamudayo"ti.* (Sv)

172 This includes experiences such as seeing, bending, and so on.

173 This shows that unpleasant feeling is the type of truth of suffering that is especially easy to understand.

174 *Dukkhasaccañhi uppattito pākaṭaṃ. Khānukaṇṭakapahārādīsu "aho dukkhan"ti vattabbatampi āpajjati. Samudaympi khāditukāmatābhuñjitu-kāmatādivasena uppattito pākataṃ. Lakkhanapaṭivedato pana ubhayampi [taṃ*[SNCom'y]*] gambhīraṃ. Iti tāni duddasattā gambhīrāni.* (Sv and Spk)

175 *"Duddasattā"ti attano pavattikkhaṇavasena pākaṭānipi pakatiñāṇena sabhāvarasato daṭṭhuṃ asakkuṇeyyattā. Gambhīreneva ca bhāvanāñāṇena, tathāpi matthakapattena ariyamaggañāṇeneva yāthāvato passitabbattā gambhīrāni.* (Sv)

176 See also *The Path of Discrimination*, 60. *"Uppādo bhayaṃ, anuppādo kheman" ti . . ."* (Paṭis 1.300)

177 See also *The Path of Purification*, 654–55. *Yañcassa udayabbayadassanaṃ, maggovāyaṃ lokikoti maggasaccaṃ pākaṭaṃ hoti . . .* (Vism 20.100)

178 *Ñāyo vuccati ariyo aṭṭhaṅgiko maggo, tassa adhigamāya, pattiyāti vuttaṃ hoti. Ayañhi pubbabhāge lokiyo satipaṭṭhānamaggo bhāvito lokuttaramaggassa adhigamāya samvattati.* (Ps and Sv)

179 *Pahānameva vuttanayena paṭivedhoti pahānappaṭivedho.* (MN-ṭ and DN-ṭ)

180 See also *The Path of Purification*, 696. *Tattha paṭhamamaggañāṇaṃ tāva sampādetukāmena aññaṃ kiñci kātabbaṃ nāma natthi. Yañhi anena kātabbaṃ siyā, taṃ anulomāvasānaṃ vipassanaṃ uppādentena katameva.* (Vism 12.3)

181 An Abhidhamma commentary.

182 *Esa lokuttaro ariyo atthaṅgiko maggo. Yo saha lokiyena maggena dukkhanirodhagāminīpatipadāti saṅkhyaṃ gato, . . .* (Vibh-a)

183 *Nānāntariyabhāvena panettha lokiyāpi gahitāva honti lokiyasamathavipassanāya vinā tadabhāvato.* (Vism-mhṭ)

184 *The Connected Discourses*, 180–81. *Idhānanda bhikkhu sammā-diṭṭhiṃ bhāveti vivekanissitaṃ virāganissitaṃ nirodhanissitaṃ vossaggapariṇāmiṃ, sammā-saṅkappaṃ bhāveti . . . pe . . . sammā-vācaṃ bhāveti . . . pe . . . sammā-kammantaṃ bhāveti . . . pe . . . sammā-ājīvam bhāveti . . . pe . . . sammā-vāyāmaṃ bhāveti . . . pe . . . sammā-satiṃ bhāveti . . . pe . . . sammā-samādhiṃ bhāveti vivekanissitaṃ virāganissitaṃ nirodhanissitaṃ vossaggaparināmiṃ. Evaṃ kho Ānanda bhikkhu kalyānamitto kalyānasahāyo kalyānasampavaṅko ariyaṃ atthaṅgikaṃ maggaṃ bhāveti, ariyaṃ atthangikaṃ maggaṃ bahulīkaroti.* (SN:3.18)

185 *Vivekanissitanti tadaṅgavivekanissitaṃ, samucchedavivekanissitaṃ, nissaranavivekanissitañca sammādiṭṭhiṃ bhāvetīti ayamattho veditabbo. Tathā hi ayaṃ ariyamaggabhāvanānuyutto yogī vipassanākkhaṇe kiccato tadangavivekanissitaṃ, ajjhāsayato nissaranavivekanissitaṃ, maggakāle pana kiccato samucchedavivekanissitaṃ, ārammaṇato nissaranavivekanissitaṃ, sammādiṭṭhiṃ bhāveti. Esa nayo virāganissitādīsu.*

*Vivekatthā eva hi virāgādayo. Kevalañhettha vosaggo duvidho pariccāgavossaggo ca pakkhandanavossaggo cāti. Tattha pariccāgavossaggoti vipassanakkhane ca tadaṅgavasena, maggakkhaṇe ca samucchedavasena kilesappahānaṃ. Pakkhandanavosaggoti vipassanakkhaṇe tanninnabhāvena, maggakkhane pana ārammaṇakaraṇena nibbānapakkhandanaṃ, tadubhayampi imasmiṃ lokiyalokuttaramissake atthasamvaṇṇanānaye vattati.*

*Tathā hi ayaṃ sammādiṭṭhi yathāvuttena pakārena kilese ca pariccajati, nibbānaca pakkhandati. Vossaggapariṇāmin'ti iminā pana sakala vacanena vossaggatthaṃ pariṇamantaṃ parinatañca, paripaccantaṃ paripakkañcāti idaṃ vuttaṃ hoti. Ayañhi ariyamaggabhāvanānuyutto bhikkhu yathā sammādiṭṭhi kilesapariccāgavossaggatthaṃ nibbānapakkhandanavosaggatthañca paripaccati, yathā ca paripakkā hoti. Tathā naṃ bhāvetīti. Esa nayo sesamaggaṅgesu.* (Spk)

186 *Esa nayo sesamaggaṅgesu . . .* (Vibh-a)

187 *Sammāvācādayo tayo [pubbabhāge*[ANCom'y, PSMCom'y]*] [musāvādāveramaṇītiādivibhāgā*[UdCom'y]*] [pubbabhāge nānākkhaṇā nānārammaṇā*[Abhi. Com'y]*] viratiyopi honti cetanādayopi maggakkhaṇe pana viratiyova.*

188 A commentary on the Abhidhamma.

189 *Sikkhāpadavibhaṅge: "Viraticetanā, sabbe sampayuttadhammā ca sikkhāpadānī"ti vuttāti tattha padhānānaṃ viraticetanānaṃ vasena "viratiyopi honti cetanāyopī"-ti āha. Musāvādādīhi viramanakāle vā viratiyo, subhāsitādivācābhāsanādikāle ca cetanāyo yojetabbā.* (DN-ṭ)

190 *Sammāvācādayo tayo [pubbabhāge*[ANCom'y, PSMCom'y]*] [musāvādāveramaṇītiādivibhāgā*[UdCom'y]*] [pubbabhāge nānākkhaṇā nānārammaṇā*[Abhi. Com'y]*] viratiyopi honti cetanādayopi maggakkhaṇe pana viratiyova.* (DN-ṭ)

191 *Tattha assāsapassāsapariggāhikā sati dukkhasaccaṃ, tassā samuṭṭhāpikā purimataṇhā samudayasaccaṃ ubhinnaṃ appavatti nirodhasaccaṃ, dukkhaparijānano, samudayappajahāno, nirodhārammaṇo ariyamaggo maggasaccaṃ. Evaṃ catusaccavasena ussakkitvā nibbutiṃ pāpunātīti idamekassa assāsapassāsavasena abhiniviṭṭhassa bhikkhuno yāva arahattā niyyānamukhanti.* (Sv)

192 *Sā pana sati yasmiṃ attabhāve, tassa samutthāpikā tanhā, tassāpi samutthāpikā nāma hoti tadabhāve abhāvatoti āha "tassā samutthāpikā purimataṇhā"ti, yathā "saṅkhārapaccayā [viññāṇan*[MS]*]"ti. Tamviññāṇavījataṃsantatisambhūto sabbopi lokiyo viññāṇappabandho "sankhārapaccayā viññāṇaṃ" teva vuccati suttantanayena.* (DN-ṭ)

193 See *The Path of Purification*, 176. *Addhā imāya paṭipadāya jarāmaraṇamhā parimuccissāmi . . .* (Vism 6.22)

194 *Ekayāna*. Ven. Bhikkhu Bodhi translates this word as "direct path," but it can also be read as Mahāsi Sayadaw has read it, "the only way" or "the only path."

195 *The Middle Length Discourses*, 155. Translation modified according to Mahāsi Sayadaw's reading. *Ekāyano ayaṃ bhikkhave maggo sattānaṃ visuddhiya, sokaparidevānaṃ samtikkamāya, dukkhadomanassānaṃ atthaṅgamāya, ñāyassa adhigamāya, nibbānassa sacchikiriyāya, yadidaṃ cattāro satipaṭṭhānā.* (MN 10; DN 22)

196 *Ekāyano ayaṃ bhikkhave maggoti ettha ekamaggo ayaṃ, bhikkhave, maggo na dvidhā pathabhūtoti evamattho daṭṭhabbo.* (Ps and Sv)

197 *Ekamaggoti eko eva maggo. Na hi nibbānagāmimaggo añño atthīti. Nanu sati-*

*paṭṭhānaṃ idha maggoti adhippetaṃ, tadaññe ca bahū maggadhammā atthīti? Saccaṃ atthi, te pana satipaṭṭhānaggahaneneva gahitā, uddese pana satiyā eva gahaṇaṃ veneyajjhāsayavasenāti daṭṭhabbaṃ. "Na dvidhāpathabhūto"ti iminā imassa maggassa anekamaggabhāvābhāvaṃ viya anibbānagāmibhāvābhavañca dasseti.* (DN-ṭ)

198 *The Middle Length Discourses*, 155. *Yo hi koci bhikkhave ime cattāro satipaṭṭhāne evaṃ bhāveyya sattāhaṃ, tassa dvinnaṃ phalānaṃ aññataraṃ phalaṃ pāti-kaṅkhaṃ diṭṭheva dhamme aññā; sati vā upādisese anāgāmitāti.* (MN 10; DN 22)

199 See *The Middle Length Discourses*, 704–9 (MN 85).

200 Ibid., 708. *Imehi pañcahi padhāniyaṅgehi samannāgato bhikkhu tathāgataṃ vināyakaṃ labhamāno sāyamanusiṭṭho pāto visesaṃ adhigamissati, pātama-nusiṭṭho sāyaṃ visesaṃ adhigamissati.* (MN 85)

201 *Advejjhavacanā buddhā, amoghavacanā jinā . . .* (Buddhavamsa)

202 See *The Connected Discourses*, 1646 (SN 47.16).

203 U Pe Thin and Myanaung U Tin have produced a fine translation of this chapter under the title *Practical Insight Meditation* (Kandy: Buddhist Publication Society, 1971). Readers familiar with that work will notice some differences in language and substance in our translation. We have tried as much as possible to retain Mahāsi Sayadaw's original wording and style and have corrected a number of translation errors or omissions that appear in the earlier translation.

204 See chapter 1, "Purification of Conduct," of *Manual of Insight*.

205 *The Connected Discourses*, 890. *Rūpaṃ bhikkhave, yoniso manasi karotha, rūpāniccatañca yathābhūtaṃ samanupassatha.* (SN 22.52)

206 Ibid., 889. *Aniccaññeva, bhikkhave bhikkhu Rūpaṃ aniccanti passati. Sāssa hoti sammādiṭṭhi.* (SN 22.51)

207 Ibid., 1218. *Phoṭṭhabbe, bhikkhave, bhikkhu yoniso manasikaronto. Phoṭṭhab-bāniccatañca yathābhūtaṃ samanupassanto.* (SN 35.159)

208 Ibid., 1217. *Anicceyeva, bhikkhave, bhikkhu phoṭṭhabbe aniccāti passati, sāssa hoti sammāditthi.* (SN 35.157)

209 Ibid., 1187. *Phoṭṭhabbe . . . abhijānaṃ parijānaṃ virājayaṃ pajahaṃ bhabbo duk-khakkhayāyā* (SN 35.112). Mahāsi Sayadaw's reading of this passage is as follows: "Directly knowing, realizing, disowning, and abandoning tangible objects leads to the end of suffering, *arahatta* fruition knowledge, and *nibbāna*."

210 Ibid., 1148. [*Photthabbe*[MS]] *aniccato jānato passato avijjā pahīyati, vijjā uppajjati.* (SN 35.53)

211 *The Middle Length Discourses*, 282. *Yā ceva kho pana ajjhattikā vāyodhātu, yā ca bāhirā vāyodhātu vāyodhāturevesā. Taṃ "netaṃ mama; nesohamasmi, na meso attā"tievametaṃ yathābhūtaṃ sammappaññāya datthabbaṃ.* (MN 28, 62, and 140)

212 *The Connected Discourses*, 1847. *Dukkhaṃ, bhikkhave, ariyasaccaṃ pariññeyyaṃ.* (SN 56.12)

213 *The Middle Length Discourses*, 146. *Yathā yathā vā panassa kāyo panihito hoti, tathā tathā naṃ pajānāti* (MN 10; DN 22). Mahāsi Sayadaw's reading of this passage: "Whatever posture the body is in, be aware of it as it really is."

214 This describes the outdoor bathing commonly done in Burma where cold

running water is piped into an interior shower stall. Use similar noting of all actions involved in bathing if using modern indoor plumbing.

215 This describes the traditional way of eating with one's fingers that is common in Burma, particularly in monasteries. When eating with utensils, the same meticulous noting of every moment of seeing, smelling, intention to lift a utensil of food, lifting, opening the mouth, placing food in the mouth, closing the mouth, withdrawing the utensil, lowering the utensil, beginning to chew, chewing, tasting, swallowing, and so on should be noted throughout the entire meal.

216 See also *The Path of Purification*, 609. *Yathā yathā hissa rūpaṃ suvikkhālitaṃ hoti nijjaṭaṃ suparisuddhaṃ, tathā tathā tadārammaṇā arūpadhammā sayameva pākaṭā honti.* (Vism 18.15)

217 *The Path of Purification*, 631 and 650. *Aniccaṃ khayaṭṭhena . . . hutvā abhāvato aniccā.* (Vism 20.14 and 20.84)

218 *Yadaniccaṃ taṃ dukkhaṃ . . . dukkhaṃ bhayaṭṭhena . . . udayabbayappīḷanato dukkha.* (Ps and Sv)

219 *The Numerical Discourses*, 507: . . . *dukkhavatthutāya . . . rogato . . . gaṇḍato . . . sallato . . .* (AN 4.124)

220 *Anattā*. Bhikkhu Bodhi translates this term as "non-self." We have altered it to maintain consistency with Mahāsi Sayadaw's usage of the term.

221 *The Connected Discourses*, 869. *Yaṃ dukkhaṃ tadanattā.* (SN 22.15)

222 *The Path of Purification*, 631: . . . *Anattā asārakaṭṭhena . . .* (Vism 20.16)

223 . . . *Avasavattanato anattā.* (Mp)

224 *Practical Insight Meditation* at this point says: "By and large, these are feelings hard to bear." However, the correct translation of Mahāsi Sayadaw's original Burmese is as written here.

225 The six kinds of conditioned mental and physical phenomena are, in order of frequency: touching, knowing, hearing, seeing, tasting, and smelling.

226 *A Comprehensive Manual of Abhidhamma*, 248 (translation modified): *appanājavanaṃ iriyāpathampi sannāmeti.* (Abhidh-s 6.11)

227 This is Mahāsi Sayadaw's own Pāḷi composition: *Bhāvetabbā satacevaṃ, satipaṭṭhānabhāvanā, vipassanā rasassādaṃ, patthentenīdha.*

228 *The Connected Discourses*, 620. *Yathābhūtam ñāṇāya satthā pariyesitabbo.* (SN 12.82)

229 Ibid., 717. *Nayidaṃ sithilamārabbha nayidam appena thāmasā; nibbānaṃ adhigantabbaṃ sabbadukkhappamocanaṃ.* (SN 21.4)

# Bibliography


Bodhi, Bhikkhu, trans. 2012. *The Numerical Discourses of the Buddha: A New Translation of the Aṅguttara Nikāya*. Boston: Wisdom Publications.

———, ed. 2005. *In the Buddha's Words: An Anthology of Discourses from the Pāḷi Canon*. Boston: Wisdom Publications.

———, ed. 1999. *A Comprehensive Manual of Abhidhamma: The Abhidhammattha Sangaha of Ācariya Anuruddha*. Onalaska: BPS Pariyatti Editions.

———, trans. 1999. *The Connected Discourses of the Buddha: A New Translation of the Saṃyutta Nikāya*. Boston: Wisdom Publications.

———, trans. 1995. *The Middle Length Discourses of the Buddha: A New Translation of the Majjhima Nikāya*. Boston: Wisdom Publications.

Fronsdal, Gil, trans. 2005. *The Dhammapada: A New Translation of the Buddhist Classic with Annotations*. Boston: Shambhala Publications.

Ireland, John D., trans. 1997. *The Udāna: Inspired Utterances of the Buddha, and The Itivutakka: The Buddha's Sayings*. Kandy: Buddhist Publication Society.

Mahāsi Sayadaw. 2016. *Manual of Insight: Mahāsi Sayadaw*. Translated and edited by the Vipassanā Mettā Foundation Translation Committee. Somerville, MA: Wisdom Publications.

———. 1971. *Practical Insight Meditation*. Kandy: Buddhist Publication Society.

Ñāṇamoli, Bhikkhu, trans. 2009. *The Path of Discrimination: Paṭisambhidāmagga*. Oxford: Pali Text Society.

———, trans. 1991. *The Path of Purification: Visuddhimagga*. Onalaska: BPS Pariyatti Editions.

Ñānarama, Mahāthera Matara Sri. 1998. *The Seven Contemplations of Insight: A Treatise on Insight Meditation*. Kandy: Buddhist Publication Society.

———. 1993. *The Seven Stages of Purification and the Insight Knowledges: A*

*Guide to the Progressive Stages of Buddhist Meditation*. Kandy: Buddhist Publication Society.

Walshe, Maurice, trans. 1995. *The Long Discourses of the Buddha: A New Translation of the Dīgha Nikāya*. Boston: Wisdom Publications.

# Index

**B**

## D

**F**

## U

# About Vipassanā Mettā Foundation

The Vipassanā Mettā Foundation was incorporated in 1995 with the mission of sharing the liberation teachings of the Buddha rooted in the Theravāda tradition with those who aspire to free themselves from suffering of heart and mind. We are fulfilling this mission by offering instruction in retreats around the world and by creating a sanctuary—a secluded environment for silence, solitude, and meditation—on the Hawaiian island of Maui. The Foundation teaches the practices of generosity, ethics, meditation/tranquility, love, and insight/wisdom to foster greater compassion and wisdom in the world through the personal lives of individuals. The Vipassanā Mettā Foundation is a federally recognized 501(c)3 Theravāda church in the lineage of Mahāsi Sayadaw.

The Vipassanā Mettā Foundation supports development of the following values in all mental, verbal, and physical actions.

- *Harmony*. We value sincere, honest communication and action carried out with integrity that do not cause harm in personal, organizational, economic, and communal interactions.
- *Generosity*. We value the generosity of heart that offers compassionate service to others for the relief of suffering through sharing material as well as human resources.
- *Simplicity*. We value moderation through responsible stewardship of financial, human, and environmental assets.
- *Awareness*. We value awareness for the benefits that it brings in the form of clarity, flexibility, stamina, stability, inclusivity, and for its role in understanding that liberation of heart is what brings the greatest happiness—peace.

- *Diversity*. We value living with the full diversity of life. We offer the Dhamma to all who wish to "come to see for themselves."

The Vipassanā Mettā Foundation was founded by Kamala Masters (formerly ordained as Ven. Vipulañānī) and Steve Armstrong (formerly ordained as Ven. Buddharakkhita), who are its guiding teachers. Both have practiced Dhamma in the Mahāsi Sayadaw tradition under the guidance of Anagarika Munindra and Sayadaw U Paṇḍita.

The Vipassanā Mettā Foundation has funded the translation, research, editing, and preparation of this book. All proceeds from the sale of this book will be used to freely distribute copies to monastics, libraries, Buddhist retreat centers and organizations, as well as to provide support for practice of the method outlined in this book.

For more information, please visit our website at vipassanametta.org.

# What to Read Next from Wisdom Publications

**In This Very Life**
*The Liberation Teachings of the Buddha*
Sayadaw U Pandita, Kate Wheeler, and U Aggacitta
Foreword by Joseph Goldstein

"Essential Buddhadhamma from one of the great meditation masters of our time."—Sharon Salzberg

**The State of Mind Called Beautiful**
Sayadaw U Pandita and Kate Wheeler

"One of the greatest living meditation masters."—Daniel Goleman, author of *Emotional Intelligence*

**The Four Foundations of Mindfulness**
Sayadaw U Silananda
Foreword by Larry Rosenberg

"*The Four Foundations of Mindfulness* is, like all of Wisdom's books, beautiful in all respects."—Jon Kabat-Zinn, author of *Wherever You Go, There You Are*

**Abhidhamma Studies**
*Buddhist Explorations of Consciousness and Time*
Nyanaponika Thera and Bhikku Bodhi

"One of the most profound and lucid interpreters of Buddhist psychology in our time."—Daniel Goleman, author of *Emotional Intelligence*

**A Heart Full of Peace**
Joseph Goldstein
Foreword by H. H. the Dalai Lama

"In this short but substantive volume, Joseph Goldstein, who lectures and leads retreats around the world, presents his thoughts on the practice of compassion, love, kindness, restraint, a skillful mind, and a peaceful heart as an antidote to the materialism of our age."—*Spirituality & Practice*

**In the Buddha's Words**
*An Anthology of Discourses from the Pali Canon*
Bhikkhu Bodhi
Foreword by H. H. the Dalai Lama

This landmark collection is the definitive introduction to the Buddha's teachings—in his own words.

# About Wisdom Publications

Wisdom Publications is the leading publisher of classic and contemporary Buddhist books and practical works on mindfulness. To learn more about us or to explore our other books, please visit our website at wisdompubs.org or contact us at the address below.


Wisdom Publications
199 Elm Street
Somerville, MA 02144 USA


We are a 501(c)(3) organization, and donations in support of our mission are tax deductible.

Wisdom Publications is affiliated with the Foundation for the Preservation of the Mahayana Tradition (FPMT).

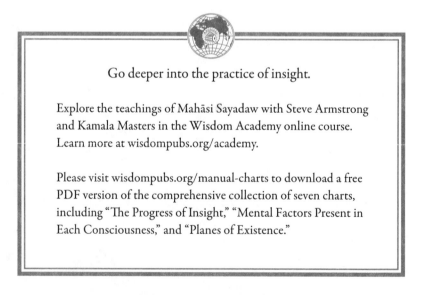